Previous books by Glen T. Martin:

From Nietzsche to Wittgenstein: The Problem of Truth and Nihilism in the Modern World. (1989)

Millennium Dawn: The Philosophy of Planetary Crisis and Human Liberation. (2005)

World Revolution through World Law: Basic Documents of the Emerging Earth Federation. (2006)

Ascent to Freedom: Practical and Philosophical Foundations of Democratic World Law. (2008)

Emerging World Law: Basic Documents and Decisions of the World Constituent Assemblies and the Provisional World Parliament, Volume One (co-edited with Eugenia Almand). (2009)

Triumph of Civilization: Democracy, Nonviolence, and the Piloting of Spaceship Earth. (2010)

Constitution for the Federation of Earth: With Historical Introduction, Commentary, and Conclusion (2010)

The Earth Federation Movement

Founding a Social Contract for the People of Earth

History, Documents, Philosophical Foundations

Glen T. Martin

Institute for Economic Democracy Press
IED
Pamplin, Virginia
2011

Published by: the Institute for Economic Democracy Publishers
Sun City, Arizona; Pamplin, Virginia, USA
888.533.1020 / www.ied.info / ied@ied.info

In Cooperation with the Institute on World Problems
www.worldproblems.net

Printing 1.0

Library of Congress Cataloging-in-Publication Data

Martin, Glen T., 1944-
The Earth Federation movement : founding a social contract for the
people of Earth / Glen T. Martin.
    p. cm.
Includes bibliographical references (p. 243) and index.

ISBN 978-1-933567-36-5 (trade paper : alk. paper) –
ISBN 978-1-933567-37-2 (trade cloth)

1. Earth Federation movement. 2. International cooperation.
3. International law. 4. Institute On World Problems.
5. World Constitution and Parliament Association.
6. Provisional World Parliament.   I. Title.

JZ1318.M37635 2011
341.2--dc22

                            2011012494

Book cover designed by Bill Kovarik.

Dedicated to
Dr. Mujibur Rahman

Bangladesh freedom fighter,
socialist,
Earth Federation leader,
and friend,

For these many years
Director of WCPA, Bangladesh,
and leader in the global struggle
for peace with justice.

Foreword

This volume was inspired by the many inquiries concerning the Earth Federation Movement that have flooded into our offices during the past year. It seemed that an inexpensive book was needed to explain the main features of the history, basic ideas, ethical vision, and philosophical foundations of this movement. The successful passage of several documents included here by the 12th session of the Provisional World Parliament in Kolkata, India, in December of 2010 made it clear that the writing of an Earth Federation book was now clearly possible.

The *Constitution for the Federation of Earth*, included here, is the most important document produced in the 20th century. It alone can transform the current omnicidal trajectory of the human project before it is too late. The *Constitution* establishes a *global social contract* for humanity, uniting all human beings under non-military democratically legislated, enforceable world law. This social contract brings civilization to the higher level necessary to deal with our lethal global crises and creates a decent future for our children and the Earth's other living creatures.

The creativity and vision of those first-generation pioneers of the Earth Federation Movement who created the *Earth Constitution*, however, has not abated. A new generation continues to engage the world's present international institutions, nations, and problems with a creativity and vision reflected in their multifaceted activist efforts to get the nations and people of Earth to ratify the *Earth Constitution* and thoughtfully implement the documents and decisions of the Provisional World Parliament, several of which are included in this volume.

I am deeply indebted to a number of people who have read and commented on the manuscript. These include Dr. Eugenia Almand, Mr. Mike DeVries, Mr. Kevin Edds, Dr. Roger Kotila, Dr. Patricia Murphy, Dr. Richard Perkins, Ms. Phyllis Turk, and Dr. Sid Smith, who was wonderfully helpful as Director of IED Press. My friend and colleague at Radford University, Dr. Bill Kovarik, generously helped with the book cover. I remain responsible, of course, for the final product.

As a philosopher engaged for many years in continual research, learning, and reflection concerning ethics, political philosophy, and human spiritual development, I have come to believe that the *Earth Constitution* represents, in many ways, a culmination and fulfillment of the historic human quest for freedom, justice, peace and prosperity for all. Part One of this book attempts to express, within a relatively brief space, the core of this understanding. Some of my other books, listed on the first page of this volume, develop these themes at greater length.

Table of Contents

Part One

Part Two

Part Three

Constitution for the Federation of Earth   148

Part Four

Part Five

Part One
History, Vision, and Legitimacy

A Global Movement for Establishing
The Rule of Law in Human Affairs

Disobedience to the law, civil and criminal, has become a mass phenomenon in recent years, not only in America, but also in a great many other parts of the world....The telling symptom of disintegration is a progressive erosion of governmental authority, and that this erosion is caused by the government's inability to function properly, from which spring the citizen's doubts about its legitimacy.

Hannah Arendt

*This leads directly to the conclusion that national sovereign states at the present time can no longer **ensure to their own peoples the security that they originally promised and that was the essential justification of their raison d'être**.... As the sole condition on which sovereign power can be legitimized is that it can maintain the conditions of the good life, strictly speaking the nation-state is no longer the legitimate bearer of sovereign authority.*

Errol E. Harris

The Earth Federation Movement is a worldwide movement to establish the democratic rule of law in human affairs, in other words, a *global social contract*. The lack of the rule of law in the international arena between nations is patently obvious and clearly poses a serious threat to the future of humanity. However, the Earth Federation Movement understands that the absurd violence and chaos of the international realm has serious consequences *within* nations as well: disintegrating their democratic freedoms, fostering fear and hate, and calling into question the very legitimacy of the democratic ideal.

1

The Earth Federation Movement is not about civil disobedience but about democratic *civil obedience, obedience to the legitimate rule of law*. Citizens everywhere long for a rule of law in the world that establishes peace, freedom, justice, and reasonable prosperity for all. People everywhere on Earth long for a decent world system in which they can live their lives with dignity and security. Under the present world disorder there is no prospect that this simple requirement of human decency can ever happen. Nor is there any prospect that we can protect the planetary ecosystem from imminent collapse.

No national government on the planet can any longer provide the rule of legitimate law that protects the common good of its citizens. Global crises and instability transcend the borders of every nation. The interdependence of all peoples – in terms of economics, in terms of the environment, in terms of security, in terms of resources – is patently clear. Through all four of these areas, disaster is descending upon the nations. This means that no national legal system is any longer fully legitimate, for no government, even the most powerful, can any longer secure the good of its citizens. We have crossed the Rubicon and there is no turning back. Our only hope is to establish democratic world law directed to the common good of all nations and peoples.

The Earth Federation Movement (EFM) is a living, growing social reality welcoming governments at all levels, non-governmental organizations, and individual persons from around the globe. It was founded in 1958 with the founding of the World Constitution and Parliament Association (WCPA) dedicated, in those early years, to writing a constitution for the Earth. It organized thousands of world citizens from dozens of countries through constant communication and many international meetings in a successful effort to create the *Earth Constitution*. The Fourth Constituent Assembly in Troia, Portugal, in 1991 voted to ratify the *Constitution for the Federation of Earth* in its present and final form. Since then, the Earth Federation Movement in coordination with the World Constitution and Parliament Association and the Institute on World Problems (IOWP) has promoted final ratification of the *Constitution* in a wide variety of venues throughout the world.

The Earth Federation Movement also includes the Provisional World Parliament and the other initiatives that have developed with respect to provisional world government for the Earth since 1982, the year in which both the Provisional World Parliament and the Graduate School of World Problems were begun. As we shall see, the Earth Federation Movement has developed many ways for integrating with existing global institutions like the U.N., the International Criminal Court, and other international organization or conventions. We work at the global level for global democracy: to unite humanity under a single democratic constitution. We understand that the only genuine hope for the future is a new social contract committing all human beings to live under the democratic rule of law in relation to one another.

At the deepest level, the commitment that we have to democracy, freedom, justice, peace, and environmental sustainability arises from love and compassion. If one loves the Earth, its beauty, its diversity, its people, its cultures, its astonishing plants and animals, and its magical fullness that make such a wonderful home for humanity and the world's other creatures, then one will act to protect, preserve, and restore the Earth. Only ratification of the *Earth Constitution* will really accomplish this. If one loves humanity, the wonderful diversity of the "worlds within worlds," of human identities, values, and ways of living and being, then one will act to create a decent world for human beings to live in, a world of freedom, justice, peace, and sustainability. At the deepest level, love is the central force behind the Earth Federation Movement.

The "defining documents" included in Part Two below, express the spirit and vision of the Earth Federation Movement as this has been examined and articulated by those world citizens from many countries and all continents who have participated in sessions of the Provisional World Parliament that have debated and ratified these documents. The perspectives on the "rights of people," the "rights of animals," "citizen and governmental responsibilities," etc., expressed in these documents represent the judgment of the many people who have voluntarily taken responsibility under the authority of the *Earth Constitution* to move the world forward toward the rule of democratic world law in human affairs.

In this respect, like the *Constitution* itself, these documents form the very core of this book, for they do not represent the views of any one person but the collective judgment of the Parliament attendant upon discussion, deliberation, and ratification through a democratic voting procedure. If the reader wishes to visualize as rapidly as possible the kind of world created by the *Earth Constitution,* he or she is urged to read Document Eleven, the "Conceptual Model of the Earth Federation under the *Constitution.*" This will perhaps give the clearest idea concerning the transformed world for which the Earth Federation Movement is working.

We do not take part (as a movement) in politics *within* nations. Our single goal is the establishment of non-military, democratic Earth Federation. For more than five decades, therefore, the Earth Federation Movement has worked – in many ways and venues – to get the *Earth Constitution* written and then ratified by the people and nations of Earth under the criteria specified in its Article 17. We have worked to educate the people of Earth to understand the need for democratic world law, to integrate the *Earth Constitution* with existing international institutions, and to develop vibrant and effective provisional world government as a model and precursor for establishing the democratic rule of law in human affairs. We want people to see that love of the Earth and other human beings is the key to establishing a decent world system that provides a dynamic framework for the fullness of life for all persons and the Earth's other living creatures.

1.1 Historical Overview

Our foremost visionary leader who led the effort to create a world constitution was Henry Philip Isely.[*] Isely had been confined to a U.S. Federal Prison during the Second World War as a war resister who believed that both world wars had been caused at the deepest level by the lawless rivalry of sovereign imperial nations, and not, as war propaganda would have it, simply from a struggle of freedom against fascism. After the war, Isely took over the magazine *Across Frontiers* from World Federalist Gerry Krause and proceeded to set in motion systematic, step by step plans for creating a world constitution. In 1950, he wrote a pamphlet entitled "The People Must Write the Peace" stating that the situation in the world was so dire that the people cannot wait for the moribund national governments to take the lead.

In the early 1950s, Isely and others joined the Campaign for World Government at its Chicago offices, at that time under the direction of Mary Georgia Lloyd. By 1958 the basic concept of WCPA was founded. Key activists understood that the foremost need was to create a quality constitution for the Earth. Along with Thane Read, Guy Marchand, Marie Philips Scot, Margaret Isely, and others, a "World Committee for a World Constitutional Convention" was formed which, by 1961, established its headquarters in Denver, Colorado. The public call for a World Constitutional Convention was issued by the committee that same year with committed delegates from 50 countries and endorsements from several Heads of State.

By 1966 the decision was made to change the name of the World Committee for a World Constitutional Convention to the World Constitution and Parliament Association (WCPA). Margaret and Philip Isely had been using the profits from their successful Denver-based business to travel widely, recruiting prominent persons to sponsor the development of a world constitution and prepare the call for a World Constitutional Convention. Among the recipients of Philip Isely's

---

[*] This subsection and the next are drawn from my introduction to *Constitution for the Federation of Earth: With Historical Introduction, Commentary, and Conclusion* (2010). The version presented here has been substantially updated and expanded.

immense correspondence were Dr. T. P. Amerasinghe of Sri Lanka and Dr. Reinhart Ruge of Mexico, both leading world federalists who had independently arrived at similar conclusions. These activists eventually became Co-Presidents of WCPA and worked together for more than 40 years in this capacity, with Philip Isely as Secretary-General and Margaret Isely as Treasurer.

Three preparatory congresses were held in the mid-1960s, systematically building support and ideas for a world constitutional convention. The Convention, which took place in 1968 in Interlaken, Switzerland, and nearby Wolfach, Germany, drew 200 delegates from 27 countries and five continents. The Convention (now calling itself the First Constituent Assembly) formulated the major elements to be included in this constitution and elected a drafting commission of twenty-five persons, chaired by Dr. Reinhart Ruge, to complete a draft and circulate it worldwide for comment and criticism, setting the date of 1977 for its next meeting and the completion of this process. In his autobiography, Ruge writes:

> Wolfach was the real beginning of the attempt to create a stable world, which would save future generations from war and misery. This was all basically due to the clear line of thought of Philip Isely, and his capacity to find and bring together so many likewise intentioned people from around the world. I am very proud that I could be present at this important and historic Constituent Assembly. (2004: 305)

In early 1972, five key members of this drafting commission met for two continuous months at world headquarters in Denver, Colorado, to create the first draft of *A Constitution for the Federation of Earth*. These primary authors of the initial draft of the *Constitution* were Henry Philip Isely from the U.S., Dr. T. P. Amerasinghe from Sri Lanka, Hon. S. M. Husain from the Supreme Court of Bangladesh, D. M. Spencer, professor of law from Mumbai, India, and, through regular telephone conversations, Dr. Max Habicht, prominent international lawyer from Switzerland.[†]

[†] Along with Philip Isely and Dr. Reinhart Ruge, Dr. Amerasinghe, Ph.D, Ed.D, J.D., (1917-2007) was clearly the leading figure in this effort. Originally from a prominent family in Sri Lanka, and long active in Sri Lankan politics and education, Amerasinghe later became the President of the English Speaking Union for Southeast Asia and the head of the Sri Lanka Chapter of the Universal Love and Brotherhood Association (ULBA). He was known throughout Southeast Asia for his work on behalf of world peace and world government.

He graduated with honors in History from the University of London in 1939, then studied at the School of Oriental and African Studies at the University of London where he obtained an M.A. and Ph.D. in Oriental History. He also studied at the Council of Legal Education, U.K., and obtained the degree of

The following year this draft was circulated worldwide for comments and criticisms. In 1975, all these comments were collected and again circulated worldwide. In 1976 a second draft of the *Constitution* was prepared by the commission. This new draft was then also circulated worldwide in preparation for the Second Constituent Assembly that met in Innsbruck, Austria in June 1977. At Innsbruck, this collectively revised draft for the *Constitution* was debated and amended paragraph by paragraph by the delegates. It was then adopted with 138 signatories from 25 nations and six continents.

A.B. Patel (General Secretary and Treasurer of World Union International Center, Sri Aurobindo Ashram, Pondicherry, India) presided over the signing of the *Constitution* and was himself the first signatory. He became Co-President of WCPA at that time along with Dr. Reinhart Ruge. After his death in the late 1980s, Dr. Terence Amerasinghe became the Co-President along with Dr. Ruge.

In the following two years, the *Constitution for the Federation of Earth* was translated into a number of languages, sent to all Heads of State, and circulated widely. In response to a common criticism that no national governments had participated at Innsbruck, a Third Constituent Assembly met at the Hotel Ranmuthu in Colombo, Sri Lanka, in 1979, hosted by Dr. Terence Amerasinghe. This body did not find it necessary to amend the *Constitution*. Rather, the Assembly issued an appeal to all national parliaments to ratify the *Earth Constitution* along with a sample draft resolution for these parliaments to use. The Assembly also issued a Declaration of the Rights of People to assemble, draft a constitution, and obtain ratification.

A key issue of world federalism (one important for the future of humankind) was thus delineated at this point. Does the future of the world lie entirely in the hands of illegitimate sovereign national entities

---

Barrister-at-Law (Gray's Inn). He was called to the English Bar in 1954, and practiced in the Privy Council, then the highest court of appeals from Asian countries that had been under British rule.

Dr. Amerasinghe spent the years 1952-1955 studying and teaching at foreign universities, entering the University of Wisconsin at Madison, and working as visiting Educator in the School of Education. While in the United States, he obtained the degree of Doctor of Education from Hamilton State University. He was Smith-Mundt Fulbright Scholar in 1954. From the 1960s on, he worked as a leader and later Co-President (with Dr. Reinhart Ruge) of the World Constitution and Parliament Association. At Dr. Ruge's retirement to the post of Honorary President for Life in 2001, Amerasinghe be became President of WCPA until his death in 2007. He was also President of the Graduate School of World Problems which he helped found in 1982 and the first President of the Institute on World Problems, founded in 2003.

militarizing the world and creating ever more weapons of death and destruction? Or do citizens of the Earth have the right and duty to take charge in creating a decent world order for themselves and future generations? The Earth Federation Movement understands that governments alone, especially at the nation-state level, will not and cannot create a decent future for humanity. It is the duty of world citizens everywhere to take the lead.

During the 1980s, the World Constitution and Parliament Association focused on organizing sessions of the Provisional World Parliament under the authority of Article 19 of the *Earth Constitution*. The Parliament met in Brighton, England, in 1982, Delhi, India, in 1985, and Miami Beach, Florida, in 1987. However, criticisms of small details in the wording of the *Constitution* kept surfacing to the point where it was deemed necessary to call one final World Constituent Assembly for 1991. This was held in Troia, Portugal, at which time the delegates adopted 59 (mostly small) changes in wording within the *Constitution* and renewed the worldwide campaign for its ratification, which was then called the Global Ratification and Elections Network (GREN) and later known as the Earth Federation Movement (EFM).

During the 1980s, the initial sessions of the Provisional World Parliament were quite successful. The first session in 1982, at the famous Royal Pavilion in Brighton, England, attracted delegates from 25 nations and six continents. The impressive inauguration of the Parliament was presided over by Sir Chaudry Mohammed Zafrullah Kahn of Pakistan, who was former President of the U.N. General Assembly and former foreign minister for his country. Officers of the Parliament included such notables as Dr. Lucile Green (later Co-founder and President of the World Citizens Assembly), Max Habicht (renowned international lawyer and legal advisor to WCPA), and A.B. Patel, then Secretary-General of the Sri Aurobindo Movement and World Union, who served as Speaker for the Parliament.

The Second Session in 1985 inaugurated before a packed house in the Vigyan Bhavan in Delhi, where it was opened by the then President of India, Zail Singh. The Parliament continued on successive days in the famous Constitution Club (where the Constitution of India had been signed) and was chaired by the then Speaker of the Lok Sabha (the lower house in India's Parliament), the Hon. Bal Ram Jakhar. The Third Session met at the huge Fontainebleau Hilton Hotel in Miami Beach, Florida, for eleven days of intense work during June 1987. Along with passing a number of important world legislative acts, it included an exposition for developing countries to show their products and wares and began the elaboration of the Ministries of Provisional World Government as sanctioned by Article 19 of the *Earth Constitution.*

Article 19 sanctions the development of all agencies or functions specified by the *Constitution* as aspects of provisional world government. Shortly after the initial sessions of Parliament in the early 1980s, the opportunity arose to organize the first Provisional District World Court in collaboration with Los Angeles lawyer Leon Vickman, who wished to prosecute the nuclear weapons researching and possessing nations for this criminal activity. Three eminent law professors sat on this court: Burns Weston of the University of Iowa, Francis Boyle of the University of Illinois, and Alfred Rubin of Tufts University.

All nuclear weapons nations (including some suspected of working to develop these) were arraigned and a few responded in writing to the court's summons. India, for example, wrote a letter denying that it ever intended to develop nuclear weapons. Most did not respond. A defense was appointed; all were tried in absentia and found guilty in 1987 (with some variation of opinion as to the degree of guilt). This court did not continue in its work beyond the 1980s, although it might have done so had resources been available. A similar initiative (to create a provisional World Court system) has recently been passed by the 12th session of the Provisional World Parliament in December 2010. It goes without saying that if there were a global social contract under which these prosecutions took place, the leaders of Russia, the USA, England, France, Israel, China, and other nations would be in prison where they properly belong.

The reader may know that something similar took place in the 1990s. Peace oriented NGOs from around the world brought the issue of nuclear weapons before the International Court of Justice in The Hague. The 1996 judgment of the court was similar: nuclear weapons are illegal and cannot legitimately be developed or possessed, let alone used, by any nation. And the result was also the same precisely because we live in a world without enforceable law: no one has gone to prison for possessing these weapons and no nation has begun to disarm because of this judgment.

During this decade of the 1980s, hundreds of organizations worldwide were committing support to the *Constitution for the Federation of Earth*. The heads of some of the poor nations were expressing interest and meeting with WCPA leaders. The campaign for ratification of the *Constitution* was in full swing with the signatures of personal ratifiers flooding into the Denver offices of WCPA, and a large network of WCPA chapters and organizational affiliations were developed throughout the world.

The WCPA claims that it has experiential evidence, going back to the early 1980s, of intentional subversion of its movement by behind the scenes superpower manipulation. But after the very successful first three sessions of the Provisional World Parliament in 1982, 1985, and 1987, this subversion became devastating. Heads of State of small countries who were very interested suddenly and inexplicably reversed themselves and would have nothing more to do with WCPA. Massive, last minute, unexplained denial of visas prevented successful meetings for which hundreds of delegates were registered to come. Nations that had offered to host a reception for Provisional World Parliament delegates suddenly turned hostile, without explanation.

For whatever reasons, the growing success of the movement to ratify the *Constitution for the Federation of Earth* momentarily slowed, although the organization to this day remains committed to the project. Philip Isely was personally quite devastated by the obvious behind the scenes subversion of the Fourth and Fifth sessions of the Parliament that took place in Barcelona, Spain, in 1996 and on the island of Malta in 2001 (both of which the present author attended). Margaret Isely had died in 1996, and Philip remarried in 2001. Now 85 years old, his activism and support for the movement soon began to wane. Alarmed members of the Executive Council reconstituted a "new WCPA" (described in section 1.2 below) that began with the Sixth Session of the Parliament in Bangkok, Thailand, in March 2003. Yet Isely's truly great contribution remains: for he was the central figure behind the worldwide movement to create the *Earth Constitution* that remains the greatest hope for humankind today.

The subversion directed at the rapidly expanding movement to ratify the *Earth Constitution* underlines the significance and essential nature of our work. To our knowledge no other world federalist organization has experienced this kind of intentional subversion. The dominant powers do not care if federalists try to reform the U.N., or hold their own NGO elections, etc., for none of these activities seriously threaten the current world order of superpower domination and corporate exploitation of poor nations worldwide. The fact that the Earth Federation Movement has been singled out for subversion is yet another indicator of the significance of our efforts to create a global social contract that embraces all nations and peoples. The fact that the dominators and exploiters of poor nations and peoples of the Earth do not want such a social contract to happen may indicate that we are doing precisely the right thing.

The central concept behind the Earth Federation Movement could be expressed by the words of Mortimer Adler: "All – when what is meant is *all without exception* – is the most radical and, perhaps, also the most revolutionary term in the lexicon of political thought" (1991: 90). This is what the imperial dominators fear most: a global social contract that embraces all of humanity and brings real peace, justice, and equality under law to the Earth. This is why the *Earth Constitution* is the most important document of the 20th century. Of all the documents of that century, it alone has the power to rapidly establish a decent world system under the rule of enforceable law.

Due to the intimidation that small countries have received after expressing interest in the *Earth Constitution*, the Earth Federation Movement presently deems it best not to urge individual small countries to ratify alone. There is a realistic fear that such action could lead to their overthrow or subversion, perhaps even to military invasion. The current campaign for ratification urges countries to talk to one another privately and then to ratify the *Constitution* simultaneously as a group, thus greatly reducing the possibility of subversion, overthrow, or invasion.

Over more than five decades of development, the Earth Federation Movement has had contact with thousands of NGOs worldwide, with millions of persons, and with many legislators and other officials in the governments of the world. It has evolved into a very large, informal network from these sources that are today centered on, and sponsored by, the World Constitution and Parliament Association and the Institute on World Problems.

Today, in the early 21st century, the threat of nuclear weapons and other weapons of mass destruction remains very high. The chaos of international criminal activity and the military violence of nation-states continues everywhere unabated. Essential resources like fresh water and arable land are disappearing at astonishing rates. International criminal syndicates flourish: trafficking in weapons, women and children, drugs, and terrorist activities. Global warming and possible climate collapse threaten the future of life on our planet. And the internal legitimacy of nation-states, like that of the U.N., is called into question because of their apparent impotence in the face of these calamities. The Earth Federation Movement, as the only effective solution to the present global chaos, is again growing by leaps and bounds. Everywhere, people are beginning to understand that our only viable option is to ratify a non-military, democratic *Constitution for the Federation of Earth.*

1.2 The Earth Federation Movement since 2003

The fundamental moral and existential principle of human life is the universal brotherhood and sisterhood of all human beings. This idea has been affirmed in all the great religions of the world and in every great culture since ancient times. A fundamental unity – our common humanity – underlies the immense diversity of cultures, nations, and persons everywhere on Earth. Article 1 of the U.N. Universal Declaration of Human Rights states that "all human beings are born free and equal in dignity and rights. They are endowed with reason and conscience and should act towards one another in a spirit of brotherhood." This statement sums up a fundamental principle of human civilization that has been recognized by thoughtful people since time immemorial.

Nevertheless, this truth remains a mere ideal unless it is translated into a legally binding social contract for humanity. One can only really affirm the wonderful diversity of humankind when that diversity is established in a more fundamental unity that surpasses an abstract moral ideal. The Preamble to the *Constitution for the Federation of Earth* affirms precisely this "unity in diversity" of "nations, races, creeds, ideologies, and cultures," and, of course, of individual persons whose diversity and freedom are protected adamantly by the document. Unlike the U.N. Universal Declaration, however, within the *Constitution* this principle of the unity of humanity is expressed in a binding social contract, in the principle of democratically legislated laws universally enforceable and equally protecting the unity in diversity of everyone on Earth.

The new WCPA that emerged out of the crisis of 2001-2003, grounds itself more firmly than ever in this paradigm shift that is at the heart of the *Earth Constitution*. In addition to the two basic initiatives of the older WCPA listed here, five newer initiatives have been added that strengthen and undergird the power of this new, holistic paradigm.

(1) *The first and most fundamental principle remains ratification of the Earth Constitution.* The work of WCPA members worldwide to actualize the demand inherent in our human situation for a world of justice, equality, and freedom did not end with the creation of the *Constitution for the Federation of Earth*. The great accomplishment of those thousands of world citizens led by Philip and Margaret Isely, Terence Amerasinghe, and Reinhart Ruge, was the creation of the most important document of the 20th and 21st centuries. However, with the retirement or death of these leaders, new leaders and many local activists have come to the fore, equally committed to the great task of civilizing human life on Earth under the equitable rule of justly legislated laws for everyone.

Ratification of the *Earth Constitution*, under Article 17, may involve one of several possible combinations of two criteria: grass roots support for, and ratification of, the *Constitution* and/or a group of leaders of nation-states coming together in a founding ratification convention. WCPA continues to work in both areas. Through our WCPA chapters, we promote community involvement and a growing mass movement toward ratification of the *Constitution*. We also continue to contact political leaders, justices, parliamentarians, and prominent citizens to promote the possibility of a founding ratification convention of national leaders.

(2) The second principle continued by the renewed Earth Federation Movement involves the p*romotion of provisional world government and sessions of the Provisional World Parliament.* Since 2003, the new WCPA, in collaboration with the IOWP and NGOs within the Earth

Federation Movement, has successfully organized the 6th session of the Provisional World Parliament in Bangkok, Thailand, the 7th session in Chennai, India, (both in 2003), the 8th session in Lucknow, India in 2004, the 9th session in Tripoli, Libya in 2006, the 10th session in Kara, Togo, in 2007, the 11th session in Nainital, India, in July 2009, and the 12th session in Kolkata, India, in December 2010. At the 11th session, the delegation from Bangladesh presented the Parliament with the *Constitution for the Federation of Earth* newly translated into its 23rd language: Bengali, also known as Bangla (the language of at least 160 million people). This work was spearheaded by Dr. Mujibur Rahman and Mr. Mabubul Islam, WCPA leaders also associated with the largest youth and environmental organizations in Bangladesh and members of the World Peace Council, a U.N. recognized international NGO.

These Parliaments have also created, to date, a body of very sophisticated and professional provisional world law that models for the world the possibility of a truly alternative world of peace with justice. The Parliament has also studied the *Constitution* for strengths and weaknesses and has undertaken legislation to implement and strengthen its democratic intent. For example, the Parliament created a Global People's Assembly to supplement the House of Peoples (see WLA 29 below). This body of law and its implications will be detailed in the three volume edition of *Emerging World Law*, edited by Eugenia Almand and Glen T. Martin. The first volume appeared in 2009. The provisional world laws passed to date can also be found at www.worldproblems.net.

These two broad initiatives remain at the heart of the WCPA mission. However, the new WCPA has expanded and developed implications found in these initiatives in four additional ways:

(3) *Loving service to humanity.* As detailed below, we are developing service projects in poor countries under the auspices of WCPA. We sponsor schools, environmental projects, permaculture development, and other projects that directly address the needs of people in poor countries.

(4) *Study and learning projects.* The WCPA had earlier created the Graduate School of World Problems under the leadership of Dr. Amerasinghe. The new WCPA sponsored creation of the non-profit Institute on World Problems (IOWP), as a successor to the Graduate School, to emphasize study of world problems and their means of solution under the *Earth Constitution.* To this effect, we have become an educational organization promoting worldwide thought and study concerning our endangered future.

(5) *Collaboration and dialogue with other world federalists and their organizations.* This is a truly new feature of the WCPA-IOWP mission. We have developed relationships and contacts around the world with world federalist movements and organizations, collaborating as far as

possible without compromising the vision of establishing a truly new, holistic paradigm under the *Earth Constitution*. Some of our supporters advocate a "two-track strategy." They simultaneously support, for example, U.N. reform and ratification of the *Earth Constitution*. WCPA does not deny that this kind of good work is legitimate, for a better world "has many kingdoms," many possibilities for dedicated work in the service of a decent world order.

(6) *The development of concrete strategies for integrating the world's existing international institutions in relation to the Earth Constitution.* The work of the Provisional World Parliament since 2003 has become highly professionalized in terms of its legislative work, vision, and mission, largely due to the leadership of Eugenia Almand, J.D. and legal advice and participation from renowned participants and sponsors of the Parliament such as former India Supreme Court Justice A.P. Mishra and Puan Sri Datin Seri N. Saraswathy Devi, Barrister at Law from Malaysia and prominent member of the International Federation of Women Lawyers.

In the 8th session of the Provisional World Parliament in 2004 and again in the 12th session in 2010, the Parliament issued directives and legislation detailing how a conversion of the U.N. into an effective world democracy under the *Earth Constitution* can and should take place. The Parliament has already worked out many of the details.

For example, the Education Act (WLA 26) allocates major funding to a number of U.N. agencies that promote education in the world as soon as these agencies ratify the *Earth Constitution.* It names the following agencies for allocations: U.N. Development Programme (UNDP), U.N. Children's Fund (UNICEF), U.N. University (UNU), International Research and Training Institute for the Advancement of Women (INSTRAW), U.N. Institute for Training and Research (UNITAR), and U.N. University for Peace (UPAZ). Unlike the U.N., the Earth Federation government will not be dependent on the voluntary donations of sovereign nation-states but will have entirely sufficient funds to serve all human needs, including massive worldwide educational development.

This principle of inclusion by the Earth Federation Movement is also true with regard to the Peoples' Congress that has, for many years, been holding elections of world citizens to its membership, and with the Assembly of States Parties that have signed the treaty behind the development of the International Criminal Court. The Elections Act (included among the documents below) calls on the People's Congress to use the progress it has already made in electing a body of world citizens by recognizing the *Earth Constitution* and constituting itself as the House of Peoples within the tricameral world parliament created by the *Constitution*.

The principle of inclusion is then extended to the nations supporting the ICC. The official national representatives of the governments comprising the Assembly of States Parties (currently assigned as delegates to the ICC) would be constituted as the House of Nations within the World Parliament. The present membership of the Provisional World Parliament (comprising all those who have been delegates going back to its first session in 1982) would serve as the House of Counselors (which in effect, the PWP is already doing). The final result would be that an effective initial World Parliament as mandated by the *Constitution* would be created through combining the People's Congress, the Assembly of States Parties, and the Provisional World Parliament.

Legislation enacted by the Provisional World Parliament has also often drawn from U.N. documents (e.g., WLA 27 on the Rights of Children), existing legal conventions (e.g., WLA 34 on Nuclear Weapons Dismantling), or from the excellent legal documents written for the ICC by lawyers representing the Assembly of States Parties (e.g., WLA 20 on a Court Bench for World Criminal Cases or WLA 37 on World Federal Privileges and Immunities). (See www.worldproblems.net.) In every case the PWP version is stronger because it has a constitutional base and gives real power, for example, to the World Court for Criminal Cases, a power lacking to the International Criminal Court as presently constituted as an agent empowered only by so-called sovereign nation-states and lacking a global social contract.

The convergence and correspondence of these international documents fosters integration of the various institutions producing these documents and speeds the recognition of the *Earth Constitution* as the most effective and comprehensive framework for fostering the rule of law in the world. For example, Earth Federation representatives to the General Review Conference of the ICC in Uganda during June 2010 distributed a memorandum to the ICC Secretariat (Document Five below) detailing how the ICC can be strengthened by referring its work to the *Earth Constitution* and raising the possibility that the Assembly of States Parties could begin to function as a House of Nations.

In another such initiative, the 12th session of the Provisional World Parliament enacted legislation creating a "Collegium of World Judges" made up of former Supreme Court justices from any of the nations around the world. A number of former Supreme Court justices from India have participated in various sessions of the Parliament held in India and may form the core of this newly created Collegium. The *Earth Constitution* calls for such a Collegium as the pool of qualified justices from which the various benches of the World Supreme Court will be chosen. By establishing this provisional Collegium, the Parliament is drawing on the existing institution of supreme courts within all nations and creating the groundwork for a Provisional World Court system that will have more effectiveness and authority than either the International Court of Justice or the ICC because, unlike these limited institutions, it will function under a global constitutional basis and will not be hamstrung by the system of sovereign nation-states.

In these ways and others, therefore, the Earth Federation Movement is promoting active integration and collaboration not only with other world federalist organizations but with established international institutions that have the potential to become the seeds of effective emerging world law. Much of present international law can be transformed into effective world law by persons (like Provisional World Parliament jurists) who understand the dynamics and possibilities of the legal institutions of the world. Our initiatives in this respect go far beyond what most world federalist organizations have accomplished.

(7) *Modeling and conceptual development of the world order deriving from the Earth Constitution.* The 52 world legislative acts of the Provisional World Parliament, and its many declarations and resolutions, have articulated a vision of an alternative world order derived from the *Constitution* that can be studied, modeled, concretely envisioned, and analyzed. This work has been spearheaded and systematized by Dr. Eugenia Almand, Secretary of the Provisional World Parliament.

These documents together concretize the world order implicit in the *Constitution* and show, for the entire world to see, how things can genuinely be different. We *can* establish a peace system, a debt-free economic system of reasonable prosperity for all, an environmentally sustainable system, and a system in which diversity is empowered and protected precisely because it is constitutionally affirmed and legally grounded within the unity of the Earth Federation.

The legislation of the first five sessions of the Provisional World Parliament did not consciously follow professional legislative drafting rules, nor was this legislation conceptualized as part of a coherent body of integrated world law. Delegates at these sessions, rather, addressed what they took to be the world's greatest needs, such as making all nuclear weapons illegal (World Legislative Act # 1. Since the 6th session of the Parliament in Bangkok in March of 2003, under the leadership of Dr. Almand, there has been a professionalization of the parliament, its procedures, and its legislation.

In pursuit of these goals, the new WCPA has continued to hold regular Executive Council meetings and recently appointed new and energetic leaders to the Council. With the death of Dr. Amerasinghe in 2007, WCPA headquarters for Asia was moved from Colombo, Sri Lanka, to the active WCPA offices in Chennai, India, under the direction of Professor Ramanujam Ananthanarayanan. Dr. Preeti Shankar of Lucknow has become Deputy Director for Asia.

Dr. Phichai Tovivich, President of the Office of the World Peace Envoy and of WCPA, Thailand, has become a Vice-President of worldwide WCPA, and Dr. Santi Nath Chattopadhyay, who is also Director of the International Society for International Study and Research (ISISAR) in Kolkata, India, has also become a WCPA Vice-President. Dr. Dauji Gupta, former Mayor of the City of Lucknow, India, and Sri Jagdish Gandhi, founder/manager of the City Montessori School system of Lucknow, remain important, long standing Vice-Presidents.

In Bangladesh, Mr. Mahbubul Islam has become WCPA World Youth Director. He has worked for years with Dr. Mujibur Rahman in developing WCPA for Bangladesh. Every session of the Provisional World Parliament since 2003 has been deeply indebted to WCPA activists in the host countries who have facilitated numerous local arrangements, including food, transportation, housing, publicity, etc. Justice A. P. Mishra, former Supreme Court Justice of India, and Saraswathy Devi, prominent international lawyer from Malaysia and head of the International Women Lawyers' Commission on Human Trafficking, are both recent Honorary Sponsors of the Provisional World Parliament.

In Costa Rica, we have established a vibrant WCPA chapter known as the "Rodrigo Carazo Odio Chapter," named after the great peace leader and former President of Costa Rica, Rodrigo Carazo. Lic. Celina Garcia, Director of the Costa Rica Center for the Study of Peace (Fundación CEPPA) and principle founder of this chapter, has become a Vice-President of WCPA worldwide with the goal of developing Costa Rica as a center for the Earth Federation Movement throughout Latin America.

The WCPA has also had an official presence at every one of the ten annual, international conferences of Chief Justices of the World and corresponding Global Symposiums that have taken place in Lucknow, India, for the past ten years. These impressive events on behalf of world peace through law are sponsored by the City Montessori School of Lucknow and its founder/manager, Dr. Jagdish Gandhi. At the 10th session in December 2009, the *Constitution for the Federation of Earth* was distributed to these Chief Justices from around the world in any one of five languages: English, French, Spanish, Hindi, and Esperanto. At the 11th Session, in 2010, the *Earth Constitution* was again distributed to all participants, both justices and representatives of NGOs. These international conferences of Chief Justices are particularly important because Justices understand the need for the rule of law and, within nations, are often above the political fray of party politics. Many justices at these conferences have affirmed the need to ratify the *Earth Constitution*.

Leaders of the Earth Federation Movement have established the Institute On World Problems (IOWP) as a 501c3 educational institution in the United States to work closely with WCPA in our worldwide educational efforts. Trustees of IOWP overlap with the membership of the Executive Council of WCPA (those listed on the WCPA letterhead) but the IOWP is a smaller organization focused on studying global problems and their interconnections, recommending integrated solutions, and educating the people of Earth with respect to the issues and choices we are all facing.

The IOWP helps sponsor the Provisional World Parliament, holds educational seminars around the world, and promotes study and learning regarding global issues and the *Earth Constitution*. While the WCPA has chapters in many countries around the world, the IOWP has established only one official branch in Zagreb, Croatia, under the direction of Dr. Slavko Kulic and Dr. Marija Pavkov. Since it was established in 2003, the IOWP has held international seminars for WCPA members and other interested people in Chennai, India (twice), Lucknow, India (three times, hosted by Dr. Gandhi), Erodes, Tamil Nadu, India, several cities in Ghana (three times), Kara, Togo (twice), Dhaka, Bangladesh (three times), Kalamata, Greece, Tepotzlan, Mexico, Kameoka, Japan, Bangkok, Thailand, Colombo, Sri Lanka, Zagreb, Croatia, Radford, Virginia, Raquette Lake, New York, Toronto, Canada, and San Jose, Costa Rica (twice).

Seminar participants are empowered and educated on the basic principles of the *Earth Constitution*, democratic world law, and the Earth Federation Movement. In 2004, IOWP also published the *Manifesto of the Earth Federation* which has been widely distributed in English and Spanish. (The Manifesto is included within my 2005 volume entitled *World Revolution through World* Law.) At present, WCPA-IOWP is also mounting a mailing campaign in the U.S. with brochures and information that will be going to thousands of organizations and individuals.

Thousands of copies of the *Earth Constitution* have also been distributed in French, English, Hindi, or Spanish in all of these places and WCPA leaders have met with key political officials, giving them copies of the *Constitution*. From WCPA offices in the USA, Togo, India, and Sri Lanka, we have corresponded by email and surface mail with WCPA members and chapters all over the world. The large chapter in the Tamil Nadu state of India has recently moved into new, larger offices and has had a late model automobile donated to facilitate its work. A number of prominent businessmen there support this work for world peace.

Supporters in Kolkata, India, have been raising funds for an independently constructed World Peace Center there, which will have separate offices for WCPA and IOWP, and new WCPA offices are opening up in Mexico City and San Jose, Costa Rica. A working relationship has been developed with the Sri Aurobindo Movement and with the World Prout Movement, both of which are worldwide movements that support the idea of democratic world government. For many years, we have also had a strong relationship with the Oomoto religion, based in Japan, and its Universal Love and Brotherhood Association (ULBA), which also support democratic world government.

The office of the World Peace Envoy in Thailand (that has operated there for 40 years under the direction of his holiness, the late Ariyawanso Bhikku) has been re-empowered and reorganized under the direction of Dr. Phichai Tovivich to lead a movement for a WCPA-sponsored World Peace Envoy designated for every country. Supporters in Togo, under the leadership of WCPA Coordinator for Africa, Dr. Dominique Simfei Balouki, have acquired donated land in two cities for WCPA permaculture projects and have begun farming these projects as models for a future sustainable world. They are also working on developing a "World University" there that will house WCPA and IOWP and be organized around truly universal principles of democratic world government. In Bangladesh, the Earth Federation Movement is developing two ecovillage projects, which will serve as centers for educating people concerning sustainable living as well as concerning the need for ratifying the *Earth Constitution*.

In Liberia, a substantial WCPA chapter has been flourishing for nearly 30 years. They are currently involved in establishing a new chapter in neighboring Sierra Leone. Officials from the Liberia Chapter have served as independent observers in national elections in Liberia (as have WCPA officials in Togo for Togo elections). WCPA officials have often been asked to perform such non-partisan functions, since we represent a world organization dedicated to free and fair democracy that does not take partisan sides within the politics of any nation-state.

In Ghana, the WCPA chapter near the capitol city of Accra, led by Reverend and Mrs. Tawiah and Bishop Isaac Taylor, has renovated a building that has become an international school, following in the tradition of WCPA chapters worldwide doing beneficial social projects in the service of ordinary people. A second chapter in Ghana has been founded by Bishop Emmanuel Mensah in the city of Kumasi. Bishop Mensah has used the non-partisan and international peace status of WCPA to foster reconciliation among groups in Northern Ghana that are threatening violence against one another. WCPA South Africa, under the leadership of Bernardo van Heerden-Baez and Ms. Nomhle Mahlawe, is presently distributing and promoting the study of the *Earth Constitution* in that country and organizing a large international meeting in southern Africa for June 2011. In Nepal, the long standing WCPA chapter is in the process of expanding and revitalizing itself.

During this period WCPA leaders have met with two African Heads of State, many members of various parliaments, many supreme court justices and world peace leaders, as well as the Vice-President of the European Union, promoting the uniting of the Earth under its only viable, practical *Constitution*. They have been working to meet with South American leaders such as President Hugo Chávez, and have been making efforts through contacts to get personal meetings directly devoted to Earth Federation work. The *Earth Constitution* in Spanish is currently being sent to all Latin American Heads of State.

WCPA and IOWP, under the leadership of Dr. Almand, have also designed and developed a model Earth Currency in several denominations that has been mailed to many Heads of State, heads of national banks, etc., by IOWP sociologist, Dr. Bob Blain. On behalf of IOWP and the *Earth Constitution*, Dr. Blain continues to send samples of currency and descriptions of truly empowering economic principles to Heads of State and key people around the world, along with graphs and charts showing them the way out of the world's current economic imperialism and slavery. A transformed, debt-free economic system is already explicit in the *Earth Constitution*, and this new world currency has been integrated into the emerging Earth Federation under the *Constitution* through carefully designed acts of the Provisional World Parliament.

During this period WCPA and IOWP have come to a permanent agreement with the Institute for Economic Democracy (IED) Press, an established progressive publishing house in the U.S., to serve as an Earth Federation publishing house. The Press has published *World Revolution through World Law*. It has published my *Ascent to Freedom: Practical and Philosophical Foundations of Democratic World Law*, and, in spring 2009, came out with the first of the three volume publication *Emerging World Law: Key Documents and Decisions of the World Constituent Assemblies and the Provisional World Parliament*, edited by myself and Dr. Almand. Most recently it has published my *Triumph of Civilization: Democracy, Nonviolence and the Piloting of Spaceship Earth* and my *Constitution for the Federation of Earth: With Historical Introduction, Commentary, and Conclusion*.

The Press has also published *Earth Federation Now!* (2005) and *21st Century Democratic Renaissance* (2008) by renowned British philosopher Errol E. Harris (a Vice-President of WCPA until his recent death). Both books argue for the necessity of world democracy under the *Earth Constitution*. The Press has had a great productivity in the past six years

19

of first class publications devoted to the conceptual and practical foundations of the *Earth Constitution* as the only viable option for humanity, as well as to genuine economic democracy.

There are a number of websites that represent our work, such as www.wcpa.biz, www.worldproblems.net, www.radford.edu/gmartin, www.protectourplanet.org (developed my Mr. Kevin Edds, a Trustee of IOWP) and www.earthfederation.info (developed by Dr. Roger Kotila, a WCPA Vice-President and IOWP Senior Fellow from California). Dr. Kotila, one of the original signatories of the *Earth Constitution,* has been active in helping carry on the large correspondence required of WCPA and IOWP. These websites continue to be under development even though they already contain an immense amount of information. There are also several other WCPA-related websites that were established by the old WCPA under Philip Isely, and a number of independent sites that host the *Earth Constitution.* Since 2003 our world headquarters has been in Radford, Virginia, USA.

As should be clear from the above account, WCPA and IOWP do not simply exist as electronic mirages (web sites or email lists), which is the case for some international NGOs advocating world federal government. WCPA chapters and members around the world are working concretely as part of the Earth Federation Movement to establish the foundations and infrastructure of the coming Earth Federation. The moral and existential principle that all human beings are brothers and sisters animates our dedication to ratifying the *Earth Constitution* and creating a decent world order for all of the Earth's creatures as well as future generations.

1.3 Ethical Holism

Since the thought of the ancient Stoics, many philosophers and thinkers have recognized that all human beings are morally related to one another simply in virtue of being human. Every normal adult human being is a free, rational moral agent, capable of making choices in relation to others. This makes every person responsible for his or her actions and gives every person, in the language of Immanuel Kant, an intrinsic dignity requiring that he or she be treated as "an end in themselves, never merely as a means." This ethical view can be called "cosmopolitanism" and is sometimes opposed to an alternative ethical view often known as "communitarianism" (Loriaux 2010, 187). The Earth Federation Movement affirms the universal dignity and equality of all human beings with respect to both of these ethical orientations.

Communitarianism argues that persons are inseparable from the communities from which they emerged and that their primary moral responsibilities are to these communities rather than to all other human beings understood as individuals. The insight that people necessarily emerge from communities and do not exist as individuals possessing natural rights prior to these communities (as John Locke, for example, argued) is an important one. It shows that human beings are essentially social creatures and responsible to one another in a positive sense. Their governmental and societal forms, therefore, must go beyond systems that protect the private rights of isolated individuals from government interference (negative freedom) to forms of "positive freedom" in which people cooperatively and democratically empower one another to fulfill their life potentials as well as their citizenship obligations to the common good of the whole community.

Cosmopolitanism (holding that all humans have the same dignity) and communitarianism (holding that all humans are rooted in communities), however, are not necessarily opposed to one another, since the concept of the communities from which we emerge can be understood on various levels and does not exclude the concept of universal dignity. A compelling argument can be made that we all ultimately emerge from the human community, especially since the 20th century. During the past century, the concept of *one world* has begun to predominate: a world populated by one species (*homo sapiens*) having global economic, scientific, political, and informational intercourse. The dominant institutions of this globalized human community, however (World Bank, International Monetary Fund (IMF), World Trade Organization, U.N., multinational corporations, etc.), are neither governments nor democratic and therefore often *actively interfere* with the actualization of a world community with its attendant moral obligations among the citizens of the Earth.

One of the most fundamental ways that communities establish, systematize, and protect the moral relationship of citizens with one another is through government. Democratic and republican forms of government can be said to legally constitute such communities (often formalizing elements found in "natural" communities) and protect a concept of legal personhood that allows freedom to flourish in both its negative and positive forms. It is here that cosmopolitanism may come into conflict with communitarianism. For our cosmopolitan moral duties to every other person on Earth cannot be fulfilled or actualized in the absence of an additional dimension of the global community that might be legally and formally established by global government.

As with today's dominant global institutions mentioned above, the present structure of sovereign nation-states actually prevents (to a significant extent) free and open relationships (including travel) as well as face to face interaction with persons around the world not of one's own country. The system of sovereign states therefore conflicts with our moral obligation to all other persons. More than this, because it rests on a conception of national sovereignty that recognizes no binding authority beyond the national level, it structurally prevents the people of Earth from creating a democratic world government that would actualize, empower, and legally establish our planetary human community.

This system (sometimes arbitrarily created, sometimes formally constituting communities that evolved "naturally") has conceived of these nation-state communities as *incommensurable* with one another (national sovereignty implies this), and, hence, this world system is fundamentally *fragmented*. Our moral relation with all others, and the human community, is therefore in contradiction with the system of sovereign nations. Indeed, all forms of assumed incommensurability violate this holism: religious, ethnic, racial, cultural, gender-based, ideological, etc. Holism embraces the reality of commensurability. Nation-state incommensurability is particularly grievous because it has governmental power and is armed and dangerous.

Ultimately, since it is inherently a war system, the nation-state system makes us either "murderers or accomplices of murderers," to quote Albert Camus' famous 1946 essay. The only possible solution, Camus asserts, is a "new social contract" that he calls "international democracy": "The only way of extricating ourselves is to create a world parliament through elections in which all peoples will participate, which will enact legislation which will exercise authority over all national governments" (1980 edition: 49). Only such a world government could make every human being a legal world citizen with rights, duties, and moral responsibilities articulated in a world constitution and formulated in the form of world laws by a democratic world parliament and enforced by world courts in cooperation with civilian world police. It would immediately transform our relations with one another from being "murderers or accomplices of murderers" to those of legally recognized moral responsibility and reciprocity.

This institutionalized war system structurally prevents the deeper dimension of positive freedom from emerging in human affairs. Between autonomous nation-states, there is no genuine freedom, only license to do whatever they can do and get away with. Genuine freedom (both negative and positive) only arises from a democratic social contract in which government both protects our personal rights and privacy (negative freedom) and empowers our life-prospects through a system of cooperation with others (positive freedom). Without democratic government to bind our moral relations through universal laws protecting all equally, our intrinsic moral relation with one another is corrupted by the might or deviousness of the stronger or more unscrupulous. If government itself is constituted so as to be incommensurable with other governments, as it is today, this corruption is only reproduced at the global level.

The communitarian tradition in Western thought was articulated in the form of political theory by such thinkers as G.W.F. Hegel, T.H. Green, Ernest Barker, Benjamin Barber, Errol E. Harris, and Jürgen Habermas. The crux of their political theory is that properly constituted democratic or republican government establishes and enhances human communities to the point where the dimension of *positive freedom* emerges in which citizens support a common good enhancing the life prospects of all citizens. For Barker, positive freedom can only find its "perfection" under democratic world government: "We can imagine a high measure of general liberty under a system of national societies and national states. We can imagine a perfect liberty only in a world society and a world State" (1967:28)

The function of good government, therefore, is to establish a positive freedom well beyond what might be possible for government that merely protects private rights of individuals who do not conceive of themselves as moral participants in the larger community constituted by government. As Habermas expresses this idea:

> Freedom, even personal freedom, freedom of choice in the last instance, can only be thought in internal connection with a network of interpersonal relationships, and this means in the context of the communicative structures of a community, which ensures that the freedom of some is not achieved at the cost of the freedom of others. Interestingly, abstract right is not sufficient for this purpose. One must make the effort to analyze the conditions of collective freedom, which remove the dangers of individual freedom, its potential for social-Darwinist menace.
>
> The individual cannot be free unless all are free, and all cannot be free unless all are free in community. (1992: 146)

The Earth Federation Movement sees many of today's sovereign nation-states (among those that have some claim to being democratic) as supporting only a negative freedom, reducing government to a kind of umpire that merely regulates the private competition among individuals, corporations, and groups. However, even within the so-called democracies, a primary function of government is also to promote the welfare of the plutocratic class that controls the lion's share of political power and to pursue a foreign policy of lawless, naked self-interest. Hence, the negative freedom that governments support has strict limits since most governments also support the accumulation of power in the hands of the wealthy at the expense of everyone's freedom.

This conception of negative freedom, along with each government's promotion of the global economic interests of its plutocracy, is projected by the sovereign nation-states onto the world stage with respect to the relation between nations, economics, cultural competition, etc. All these competing elements are supposed to have the "freedom" of global trade rules prohibiting interference from the internal regulations of governments (such as tariffs or sectors of the economy that are off limits to private investment). At the same time, the more powerful governments promote the foreign economic interests of their investor classes. The result is the destructive anarchy that we see all around us in today's world.

Freedom, as a consequence, becomes more and more truncated, since this system always results in absolute winners and losers, in endless wars, in the accumulation of wealth and power in only a few hands, and in planetary economic disasters. The common good of the whole community (which today can only be conceived as the human community) is left to atrophy along with the positive freedom that it might engender. The result is a dangerous world system of militarized sovereign nation-states who see their national "freedom" in terms of a negative struggle with the freedom of all other nations. As a consequence, freedom *within* nations is sacrificed to national security concerns while the struggle for negative freedom *between* nations inevitably results in war, deception, manipulation, economic conflict, and terrorism.

The more freedom is eroded within nations, and the more global public freedom is blocked between nations (a freedom which would require democratic world government), the more the ethical foundation of human life is diminished. Our dignity as moral persons arises from our ability to make free choices in our relation with others, within a community that makes these relations possible, and ultimately, within the human community. The truncating of freedom within nations, between nations, and in our relations with all other persons, therefore, constitutes an attack on our very dignity and personhood. It is morally unacceptable on many levels, and the Earth Federation Movement understands that it is our duty to reverse this situation and enlarge freedom both within nations and at the planetary level. The former can only be enlarged if we establish the latter.

There are those who would separate the ethical dimension from politics. They often argue that our ethical obligations to others do not extend into politics. We may have moral obligations to our neighbors or immediate community, but we are not obliged to ensure justice or ethical relationships throughout society through the medium of politics. Henry David Thoreau, for example, argued that one should disobey any law that "requires you to be an agent of injustice to another." However, this is a personal moral decision made when laws directly impinge on the moral integrity of one's life. On the other hand, Thoreau attempted to steer clear of politics on the grounds that he was "not responsible for the successful working of the machinery of society" (N.D.: 304, 310).

Moral principles here appear to be purely negative. Following one's conscience appears as not doing harm to others. Like all principles, this view of morality as a purely negative private affair often links up with a certain set of views concerning the self, society, and government. Thoreau was a proponent of so-called "liberal democracy" who believed, like his 19th century counterpart John Stuart Mill (1956), that the sole purpose of government was negative. The purpose of government was to maximize personal freedom and the only activities that could be legitimately governed by law were those that impinged on the freedom of others.

Thoreau and Mill, however, were still operating under the early modern assumption (disproven today by every 20th century social science) that the individual was prior to society and that society was merely a collection of individuals who created government to maximize their personal freedoms by providing an umpire for their activities and an impartial judge to adjudicate their conflicts and indiscretions. The social contract theory of John Locke, who was very much in the intellectual background of the founders of the U.S. Constitution, assumes this false atomism of the early modern social paradigm, an atomism that continued through the 19th century by thinkers such as Thoreau and Mill.

We understand today that this image of the rugged individual prior to society possessing inherent natural rights that are the sole duty of society to protect was in error. It was an ideological product of the Newtonian scientific paradigm that looked at the world (and society) on the model of a machine constructed of separate, autonomous parts, the final result (the whole) being merely a mechanism for adjusting the workings of the parts. The reader will recall Thoreau's metaphor quoted above concerning the workings of "the machinery of society."

The dominant metaphors for the world revealed by 20th century science are holistic and organic, not mechanical. It has been revealed by every science, from biology to physics, that the world at every level is composed of dynamic unities that organize and enliven the diversities flourishing within them. The parts are not prior to the holistic systems within which they flourish. The principle of unity in diversity, a unity necessary to the diversity and vice versa, operates throughout the universe, including within human life. As Jürgen Habermas has demonstrated at length regarding human beings as language-using beings, our individuality emerges from community and cannot be conceived prior to our linguistic communities (2003: 34-35). Ethical holism understands that every human being lives under moral obligation to every other, and that these relations are not merely individual but arise as functions of our planetary human community (2003: 40 & 63).

1.4 Democratic Holism

Those envisioning a more holistic concept of human life and democracy go back at least to Baruch Spinoza and Gottfried Leibniz in the 17th century. Their ideas developed through the thought of Jean-Jacques Rousseau and Immanuel Kant in the 18th century. These thinkers proved to have a philosophical understanding that has been corroborated by the 20th century scientific discoveries of the pervasive holism of nature and human life. Habermas (1998a) discovered that the very possibility of language requires other persons in a *communicative relationship* with the speaker presupposing equality, freedom, and mutual recognition. Manipulative or strategic uses of language are secondary and parasitical upon its primary communicative function.

Hence, language itself, in its very possibility, presupposes the rudiments of a democratic relationship among persons who have a right to challenge claims of "truth, truthfulness, or normative rightness" implicit in every utterance. For this reason, communicative uses of language directed toward mutual understanding form the core of human relationships and point to the development of legitimate, morally grounded, "political will formation" through horizontal processes of dialogue and debate (Habermas 1998b: 450).

A properly structured democratic society provides the "public space" for such dialogue and debate that results not in an atomistic struggle for power but in a transformation of all the parties to the dialogue through their formation of a "general will" (Harris 2008) or a societal mutual understanding that then allows citizen participants to see the laws of society as products of their own communicative actions. The "vertical" relation of government to citizens, Habermas affirms, rests upon the "horizontal" relation of citizens in dialogue with one another within the public spaces making such dialogue possible (Habermas 2003: 76-77).

Ernest Barker describes democratic holism in which the development and communicative function of the human self is inseparable from democratic society. This positive freedom, we have seen him assert, could only find its perfection in "a world society":

> So far as society exists by dynamic process, it exists for and by the mutual interchange of conceptions and convictions about the good to be attained in human life and the methods of its attainment. It thus exists for and by a system of social discussion, under which each is free to give and receive, and all can freely join in determining the content or substance of social thought – the good to be sought, and the way of life in which it issues. Now such discussion is also, as we have seen, the essence of democracy.... A regime of political or constitutional liberty is a necessary part of the

development of human personality in and through a society of selves. (1967: 19)

However, even while the foundations of democracy and positive freedom in the human community were being articulated during the 20th century, the structural problems of democracies, predicated on negative freedom and economic competition among the plutocracies of various nations, continued to multiply. As a result, a number of critiques of democracy developed in the 20th century have had considerable influence.

Authors such as Carl Schmitt, Joseph Schumpeter, Friedrich von Hayek, and Leo Strauss presented a variety of reasons why the historic attempts at popular democracy, beginning with the 18th century American and French Revolutions that led to the 19th and 20th century spread of democracies around the world, had largely failed. Behind all of these critiques lay empirical observations of the immense problems and difficulties facing democracies in the 20th century in conjunction with the suspicion that ordinary people *en masse* were not capable of governing themselves. Carl Schmitt, the Nazi legal theorist who supported Hitler, asserted that the spirit of the people needed to be embodied in a strong leader whose policies the people were only capable of ratifying in a "yes" or "no" plebiscite (Harris 2008: 96-97).

Strauss asserted that modern democratic equality ignored the crucial role of elite leaders of exceptional excellence and virtue that are essential to good governance. He emphasized the role of such people of exceptional excellence in the ancient thought of Plato and Aristotle. In terms of modern democracy, Strauss suggested that elite leaders need to lead the masses using forms of deception akin to Plato's "noble lie" that was designed to secure the loyalty of the masses while their guardians ruled for the common good in ways that the masses could not comprehend.

One assumption behind many of these views critical of liberal democracy was the assumption that political parties, advocacy groups, and individuals within modern democracy were most fundamentally engaged in a struggle for political (and economic) power within the state. In this respect, these critics of democracy retained the Newtonian model that saw the world as made of individuals and corporate entities for which government was simply a mechanism for controlling and regulating their competitive affairs. Like the international system of power politics, internally democratic polity was also basically a form of power politics. These views were also developed in the light of the social-Darwinism that arose after 1859 when Darwin published his *Origin of Species*, for now society and politics could be understood under a model of natural selection and survival of the fittest.

We have seen, however, in what ways these critics missed the ethical and holistic foundations of both genuine democracy and freedom. For they continued to operate under the outmoded Newtonian and social-Darwinian model of atomistic negative freedom in which a multiplicity of parts (whether nations, persons, parties, or corporations) struggle in competition with one another. They critiqued the so-called liberal democracies as incapable of successful working by using the very same false premises that prevented these democracies from successfully working in the first place.

Kant (1957) had already argued in the 18th century that the first and foremost moral obligation of persons is to live under republican government that protects their freedom, equality, and independence. Republican government, for Kant, created a legal and moral framework for persons to be and act as ethical beings. For this reason, government itself is mandated by the ethical principle of the "categorical imperative" which states that the will of every rational being should submit itself to universal laws equally applicable to all. A free rational ethical being is as much a politically responsible being as a personally responsible one. For Kant (1974), the whole of society and the individual are inseparably tied together within a holistic relation of unity in diversity. Republican government is simply the moral framework of our relations with other persons writ large.

Kant's insight into the holism of human life underlines both the cosmopolitanism emphasizing our moral obligations to all other persons and that form of communitarianism requiring democratic government to bind persons into a legal, holistic moral community. As pointed out above, Kant's insights were confirmed by 20th century science. MIT professor of linguistics, Steven Pinker, for example, writes that "Just as there is a universal design to the computations of grammar, there is a universal design to the rest of the human mind – an assumption that is not just a hopeful wish for human unity and brotherhood, but an actual discovery about the human species that is well motivated by evolutionary biology and genetics" (1994: 425-426).

Kant deeply understood the implications of his own holistic thought. The world was divided, then as now, into a collection of "sovereign" nation-states recognizing no enforceable law above themselves. This situation, Kant understood, places them in an *immoral relation to one another*, a relation that he called "war." Any relation in which individuals or nations stand apart from one another outside the framework of the enforceable laws of republican government is one in which the stronger can dominate or manipulate the weaker.

This situation is an immoral one of "war" since the only possible moral relationship of nations or persons is one in which the freedom, equality, and independence of each is protected by republican government providing a universal legal-moral framework for their diversity. Kant stated unequivocally that the system of sovereign nation-states is immoral (he called it "savage" and "barbaric") and that nations were under an absolute moral command to join together in an Earth Federation under one republican government over all the nations (1957, originally published 1795).

On the global level today, for example, we confront a situation of immense, cruel poverty crushing the life prospects of some 20% of the world's population, or nearly two billion people. A person embracing cosmopolitan moral principles would want to find ways to alleviate this suffering through some form of distributive justice (Loriaux 2010). However, there is currently no effective or meaningful way to address global poverty. There are no planetary institutions that even come close to an adequate attempt at global distributive justice.

Ethics and politics are inseparable for Kant. The moral imperative demands that we establish a "kingdom of ends" in human society in which everyone treats everyone else as an "end in themselves." This is demanded because "morality consists in the relation of all action to the making of laws whereby alone a kingdom of ends is possible" (1964: 100-101). Morality, whether on the personal level or the governmental level, consists in the making of universal laws directed toward establishing moral relations among all human beings. Clearly, only democratic world law could make this effectively possible.

Kant understands that good laws promoting civilized human freedom will help develop the moral level of citizens, making us capable of dealing with ever-larger moral issues. As contemporary thinker Terry Eagleton expresses this: "What really alters our view of the world is not so much ideas, as ideas which are embedded in routine social practice. If we change that practice, which may be formidably difficult to do, we are likely in the end to alter our way of seeing" (2011: 94). Our moral level can be elevated through decent political and economic institutions, which, in turn, allow us to address global moral problems.

The same dynamic applies to our moral obligation to deal with global poverty. There is no effective way that we can discharge this obligation without creating a democratic world government with the authority and resources to address this moral requirement of distributive justice. Just as government is necessary to provide freedom, equality, and independence (and hence a moral framework) for all, so, too, government is necessary to address the massive injustice of global poverty. Ethical and political obligations are fashioned from the same holistic cloth.

Similar conclusions follow if we turn to the great statements that have been made concerning human rights in the modern world. We have seen that the U.N. Universal Declaration of Human Rights is a holistic (unity in diversity) document. Its very first article expresses the foundation of cosmopolitan global ethics: "All human beings are born free and equal in dignity and rights. They are endowed with reason and conscience and should act towards one another in a spirit of brotherhood." Ethical principles are universal because they follow from the dignity of each as a moral being who can freely choose the principles by which he or she will operate in daily life.

The 30 articles of the U.N. declaration articulate in great detail the rights of individuals to freedom from political interference from government, the rights to be left alone, for freedom of religion, thought, and conscience. However, the document also includes "communitarian" ethical principles in the sense of social and economic rights that can only be protected through the common efforts of governmental communities. For example, Article 25 states that "everyone has the right to a standard of living adequate for the health and well-being of himself and of his family, including food, clothing, housing and medical care and necessary social services...."

Under the current world system such rights are not (and cannot be) recognized by the prevailing institutions (such as the World Bank or the World Trade Organization) since they would immediately deny the ability of globalized "free trade" to exploit poor people by paying sub-living standard wages within poorer countries for the benefit of foreign corporations located in richer countries. Universal economic and social rights (to a living wage, health care, sanitation and clean water, or education) require a global social contract – democratic world government – to actualize and enforce them.

Article 28 as much as admits this: "Everyone is entitled to a social and international order in which the rights and freedoms set forth in this Declaration can be fully realized." And this is why the entire set of human rights in this declaration is considered by most governments of the world, the U.N., and international institutions as "merely symbolic." The declaration serves as an ideal, a goal, but does not have the force of international law. Clearly, an international order that protected the rights specified in the Universal Declaration would have to be democratic world government, which the U.N. Charter abjures in favor of nation-state sovereignty. Compare the political, economic, and social rights given in Articles 12 and 13 of the *Earth Constitution*. These articles are not merely symbolic. They become enforceable world law upon ratification of the *Constitution*, thereby fulfilling for the first time Article 28 of the U.N. Declaration of Human Rights.

Some commentators on human rights speak of first generation rights (e.g., traditional political freedoms), second generation rights (social and economic guarantees), and, finally, third generation rights, such as the right to peace and to a healthy environment (Wacks 2006: 58). This evolution of the concept of rights indicates a growing, historically developing understanding of the concept of rights and what it entails. All three generations of rights require the moral framework of democratic world government to make their actualization possible.

Social and economic rights, like political rights, may be possible to a limited extent within sovereign nation-states but the fact that economics is globalized and the fact that most nations are militarized (creating an unstable and dangerous world system) militates against success in this respect. With regard to third generation rights, however (such as peace and a protected planetary environment), actualization is clearly impossible within the system of sovereign nations precisely because they violate the holism of humanity which is required for both peace and sustainability. We have the right, therefore, to democratic world government (as Article 28 of the U.N. Declaration implies), as the only possible form of world order that can holistically implement and protect the entire range of our human rights.

The language of "rights," however important and necessary it may be, can be misleading, because all so-called rights are correlative to responsibilities and to a relational community that forms the supporting matrix of both rights and responsibilities. The false atomistic assumptions behind the negative conception of freedom as competition among autonomous individuals, groups, or nations is often couched in the language of rights, as if rights inhered in individuals or groups apart from the community that necessarily forms the matrix and context for rights, responsibilities, and freedoms. (See Document Eight below: Declaration of Citizen and Government Responsibilities under the *Earth Constitution*.)

With the development of second generation social and economic rights and third generation peace and environmental rights, the language of rights has moved from atomism to the holism of community, since the latter two generations of rights necessarily require a social community for their actualization. And, with the development of the third generation of rights (to peace and environmental protection), we have moved to the level of the global community since neither of these can be realized at the level of sovereign nations. These rights can only be actualized if we legally and intentionally found a world community, a global social contract. (See Documents Three and Four below that legislate on behalf of our global environmental rights.)

This is the primary function behind the ratification of the *Earth Constitution*. Ratification will formally and legally establish the world community that already exists in the form of our universal humanity and our universal moral relationship with one another. The *Constitution* embodies the *global social contract* necessary to institutionalize our ethical relationship with all other persons. This ethical relationship requires that we engage in dialogue with one another at the planetary level within a public space that makes this dialogue possible and within an institutional framework that makes consequent genuinely ethical political action possible.

Democratic holism understands that we are morally obligated (in the several ways described above) to leave our present immoral, *defacto* state of war (that is a consequence of our false conception of negative freedom). This condition of *de facto* war is a product of the fragmentation (of nations, peoples, classes, religions, races, etc.) brought on by the outmoded Newtonian and social-Darwinian paradigm to which we continue to cling (cf. Harris 2000). We must join together within a republican governmental framework that actualizes our moral relation to one another in the holistic form of universal liberty, equality, justice, peace, and sustainability. Democratic global government actualizes the moral-political obligation that we all have to one another.

1.5 Political Holism

Philosophical history contains a wealth of insightful documents that reflectively consider the basis of a viable and legitimate political and social order. These go back to ancient Greek and Roman thinkers such as Plato (who reflected on the nature of justice), Aristotle, and Cicero. They continue through medieval thinkers such as Thomas Aquinas, and emerge with great vigor in the Renaissance reflections of such thinkers as Athanasius, Duplessis Mornay, and Machiavelli.

Reflections systematically laying the groundwork for contemporary democratic theory especially emerged in the 17th century thought of writers like Gottfried Leibniz, Baruch Spinoza, and John Locke. During the 18th century, thinkers such as Baron de Montesquieu, Jean-Jacques Rousseau, and Immanuel Kant brought reflection on the social contract through which society defines legitimate government into a powerful focus, helping to define the democratic societies that emerged out of the French and American revolutions toward the end of that century.

In the 19th century, thinkers such as G.W. F. Hegel, Jeremy Bentham, John Stuart Mill, Alexis de Tocqueville, and Karl Marx helped refine and critically analyze democratic theory, defining many of the issues and difficulties faced in the functioning democracies. Marx, for example, saw political democracy (with equal political rights such as voting) as a great step forward, but not sufficient for "substantive democracy": "Political emancipation certainly represents a great progress. It is not, indeed, the final form of human emancipation" (1978: 35). For "people cannot be liberated as long as they are unable to obtain food and drink, housing and clothing in adequate quantity and quality" (1978: 169). Political freedom must be accompanied by substantial economic freedom from want and deprivation. Democracy is impossible without actualizing that moral dimension of equality under the law that necessarily includes reasonable economic equality. Marx's critique was a great step forward in the philosophical understanding of democracy.

The 20th century saw new and deeper understandings emerge concerning the nature of the social contract, the nature of humans in relation to language, the relation between individuals and society, and the role of technology and mass society. Our understanding of the nature, extent, and meaning of the social contract deepened even while serious threats to democracy arose in the form of totalitarian societies like Nazi Germany, the USSR under Stalin, or Maoism in Communist China.

A wealth of studies and political theories emerged, too numerous to mention here (some of which are listed in the bibliography). Outstanding thinkers such as T.H. Green, Herbert Spencer, Bernard Bosanquet, Ernest Barker, Hannah Arendt, John Rawls, David Held, Benjamin Barber, Errol E. Harris, and Jürgen Habermas created substantial theoretical underpinnings for democracy in the light of a more sophisticated contemporary understanding of the human condition. At the heart of their understanding, as we will see in greater detail, is the insight that democracy requires a genuinely "public space" where persons can transcend their partisanship, special interests, and individual particularities and engage in communicative discussions that, on some level, transform the participants and allows a higher perspective ever more closely representing the common good of the whole to emerge.

Ironically, as suggested above, at the same time that this profound insight into the fundamental requirement of democracy developed during the 20th century, rapidly changing global conditions and technologies began undermining functioning democracies worldwide. This fostered regimes premised on fear and national security that severely curtailed civil liberties and modified the democratic "spirit of the laws" that Montesquieu had identified as a fundamental feature of a social contract predicated on "consent of the governed."

The idea of a social contract between people to create government over themselves as an impartial authority, representing the common good and responsible to the people who remain sovereign, was articulated by John Locke, Montesquieu, and the other 18th century theorists. Montesquieu insists on a clear separation of the branches of government, creating a diversity of power centers and the checks and balances necessary to keep government responsible to the people as a whole whom it serves, rather than to special interests, a ruling elite, or an absolute monarch. Locke distinguished clearly between "tacit consent" by the people and "overt consent." Overt consent is what is given at the founding of the social contract, when, for example, a constitution is signed by the founders and then is ratified in a free and fair referendum by the people whose law of the land it will become.

The idea of tacit consent presents greater conceptual difficulties. Can people born and raised within a society be said to have given tacit consent to its laws? In Plato's *Crito*, Socrates argues that the coherence and order of the society within which he lived, the fact that he was free to leave and never left, and the fact that he was free to "persuade" his government to change its laws, together indicate that he has consented to obey its laws. However, most people are more embedded within their social situations than Socrates appears to have been when he claims he was free to leave at any time. Many people have family, friends, recognition in their local communities, a job, and other forms of significant investment in the societies within which they were born and grew up. The fact that they do not immigrate hardly indicates an active consent to obey laws that they may consider unjust or an active consent to some non-democratic government that happens to reign in their societies.

Does the right to vote indicate consent of the governed? There are, of course, many variations on this right, and many ways governments can allow people this right without compromising their undemocratic or even dictatorial character. In his study of the United States entitled *Democracy in America* that appeared in two volumes in 1835 and 1840, Alexis de Tocqueville speaks of a kind of universal tacit consent that characterized the society in the United States. He characterized it as a general feeling among the people of a *"consensus universalis."* This feeling was perhaps generated by the right to participate in government and the freedom of speech and association that prevailed (in addition to voting), a freedom that allowed even many minorities to form associations and become active political advocates.

In her 1972 discussion of Tocqueville's observations, Hannah Arendt asserts that this *consensus universalis*, if it ever existed, has been lost in the United States, having been replaced by lobbying for special interests and party politics directed toward winning power for certain interests rather than political debate based on alternative conceptions of how best to realize the common good of the whole society (1972: 85-102). This loss of a sense of the legitimacy of today's democratic societies is clearly a worldwide phenomenon. The idea of a common good, developed and pursued through citizen participants who feel they can effectively participate in the generation of the laws under which they are governed, is disappearing from many so-called democratic societies worldwide.

The reasons for this are, doubtless, many and complex. The present writer has had the opportunity to gain some familiarity with the governing of both Bangladesh and Libya, for example. In the former the "Freedom Fighters Movement" and in the latter the "Revolutionary Committees Movement" claim to be struggling against odds to keep alive what each perceives as the original democratic spirit of their society. Threats to this struggle come from a number of sources, including fundamentalist religious forces within each of these societies. However one evaluates these claims, perhaps the intent of these movements are not that different from movements in the United States like "People for the American Way" that struggle against the destruction of democracy within the U.S. by fundamentalist religious forces and other right wing threats to a free society.

However, the reasons for the threat to democracy within many nations today have much to do with a globalized world that has generated immense forces transcending the boundaries of nation-states. The development of ever-faster and ever-more-lethal weapons in a militarized world threatens civil liberty within nations and forces their governments into a national security state mode. Gigantic global economic forces, stripping economic independence and internal economic control from nations, means that governments can no longer protect their citizens in the interest of a common economic good. The consequent separation of extreme wealth for a few within every nation and serious poverty for the majority further erodes the social contract.

The disappearance of basic resources such as fresh water and arable land worldwide (and the power for foreign interests to control the internal resources of sovereign nations) has forced governments to take measures that appear to violate the social contract. Global climate activity has created major droughts, storms, flooding, and other severe weather patterns that, again, force governments to interrupt the coherence, consistency, and regularity of the social processes of free association, dialogue, and citizen participation that appear fundamental to generating a *consensus universalis* among the population.

These globalized historical forces will necessarily worsen over time, making it clear that there is no possibility of reversing the historical process and returning to the kind of "democracy in America" described by Tocqueville in the 19th century. If democracy is to be protected and defended, this can only be through *a new social contract* that is now globalized to the point where an Earth Federation government can deal with the international forces (military, economic, resource depletion, and climate destruction) that now destroy legitimate political processes everywhere on our planet. Consent of the governed within a free society cannot function when government exists in a perpetual state of emergency, which is exactly what our globalized world order has imposed on all nation-state governments.

The idea of an active consent of the governed within a sustainable society that protects peace, freedom, and justice to the point where the citizens recognize that government represents their will and their sovereignty can no longer happen at the nation-state level. Even the most powerful nation-states have lost the ability to sustain functioning democracy within their borders. We return to the inseparability (described above) of the moral dimension from the dimension of political responsibility. Our moral and political responsibility requires that we establish a genuine community among human beings living on the Earth, a community that necessarily requires a protected *planetary public space* where genuine dialogue and communication can take place.

How are human beings to come together in a forum capable of action to reach, through honest dialogue and debate, a mutual understanding concerning the realities of our human situation (its totality) and how are we to move into the future on the basis of this understanding? How are we to reach collective decisions on the coordinated actions that must be taken to create and protect a future for humanity and our common home, the Earth? It is clear that there is little public space for genuine discussion *within* nations, since their false assumptions about negative freedom have led to an internal space dominated by slogans, ideologies, accusations, public relations, and other forms of strategic language. The wealthy plutocracy, on the one hand, and government with its militaristic propaganda, on the other, colonize the internal informational spaces within nations. However, at the planetary level, there is no significant space at all for open dialogue. There are no global institutions at present that might even make this a genuine possibility.

The U.N. General Assembly, as is widely admitted, is merely a forum for representatives of sovereign nations to represent the negative sovereign "rights" and the fragmented interests of their nations *vis-à-vis* one another. Some agencies of the U.N. (such as UNESCO) attempt to create a framework for genuine dialogue among cultures and peoples of the world, but the militarized, political framework of sovereign nation-states everywhere defeats these feeble attempts. A global public space framed by a global community making possible dialogue concerning our endangered future does not exist at the international level of nation-states. Hannah Arendt writes:

> Only in the freedom of our speaking with one another does the world, as that about which we speak, emerge in objectivity and visibility from all sides.... The freedom to interact in speech with many others and experience the diversity that the world always is in its totality....is rather the substance and meaning of all things political. In this sense politics and freedom are identical, and wherever this kind of freedom does not exist, there is no political space in the true sense. (2005: 128-129)

"The world," as an objective set of qualities, processes, and characteristics, only emerges in its fullness through the intersubjective encounter of different human viewpoints with one another. In today's globalized situation, such a dialogue requires a global social contract. Only such a contract could create a public political space for humans to intersubjectively articulate an objective "world" in terms of which we might take action to forge a decent future for ourselves. Where this democratic public space for authentic politics does not exist, as on the global level, then neither does freedom exist. Human beings on planet Earth are pulled toward a calamitous future, as if by a raging river, yet lack any meaningful freedom to determine their common destiny.

The more this dialogic encounter of differing perspectives is lacking, the more our ideas about the "world" become illusory ideological fantasies. Without genuine dialogue among the diversity of human beings, the more we get institutions like the Pentagon, employing the immense violence at the disposal of its ideological fantasies (ideas about "the world"), and wondering why its policies always lead to unmitigated disaster both at home and abroad. Such illusions (products of a lack of genuine dialogue) are the stock in trade of most of the nations in the U.N. General Assembly.

Freedom and the public space for communicative interaction (politics in its highest, ethical sense) are substantially identical, and neither exists at the global level where concerted action on the part of nations, corporations, groups, and citizens is so fundamental to human survival and the creation of a decent future for ourselves as well as future generations. The "objectivity and visibility" of the world emerge when people dialogue from different points of view and come together in mutual understanding or, at the very least, mutual toleration and respect, which allows them to collectively act to create a future for the community.

Freedom requires not only public space but human beings who have entered that public space as full human beings, not as distorted mouthpieces of some ideology, interest group, or social pathology. The ratification of a global social contract and the creation of the public space of the World Parliament will likely attract the best among us who see the opportunity to express their deeper and common humanity in service to the planet and its citizens. The Earth Federation government will function *above* the vast concentrations of wealth in banking and multinational corporations and *above* the fanatical religious or other interest groups that today colonize governments worldwide.

The *Constitution* is designed to prevent such colonization. Mature human leaders, capable of intelligence and compassion and internally free of compulsion, fear, and hate, will likely staff both the World Parliament and the agencies of the Earth Federation. Humanity will be in the process of taking its next step from fragmentation to wholeness. Psychologist Erich Fromm expresses something of the kind of freedom to which I am referring:

> This discussion of "humane experiences" culminates in the statement that freedom is a quality of being fully humane. Inasmuch as we transcend the realm of physical survival and inasmuch as we are not driven by fear, impotence, narcissism, dependency, etc., we transcend compulsion. Love, tenderness, reason, interest, integrity, and identity – they all are children of freedom. Political freedom is a condition of human freedom only inasmuch as it furthers the development of what is specifically human. Political freedom in an alienated society, which contributes to the dehumanization of man, becomes un-freedom. (1968: 89-90)

The creators of the *Earth Constitution* deeply understood the urgent need for an institutionalized public space, a viable global social contract, where peoples and nations could together participate within the protected public space of a tricameral world parliament to make those laws and decisions that open up a viable future for humanity. In deeply alienated societies like the U.S. today, what remains of "public freedom" in the national security state has become the "unfreedom" of hate speech, political hypocrisy, partisan dogma, and vicious self-interest at the expense of the common good.

The *Constitution* provides humankind with a carefully worked out structure for democratic world government centered on public freedom. It articulates a process of discussion, decision-making, and action that completes and embraces the historical human project of temporalized freedom that all along (going back to the ancient Stoics) included the entire human community as its most basic presupposition. Its Preamble expresses the dynamics of a mature, compassionate response to the human condition. Its detailed structure as a global social contract invites fully humane and mature human beings to step into that hallowed public space and create the conditions of freedom for all of humankind.

Article One of the *Constitution* states six *"broad functions"* of the Earth Federation – revealing that the sphere of action of the world government shall be all those global problems beyond the scope of individual nation-states. The ability to deal with these global problems constitutes grounds for ratification of the *Constitution* by the people and nations of Earth. But the ability of the Earth Federation government to act effectively with regard to these global problems depends on the public space created for decision-making by the World Parliament and within the ministries responsible to the Parliament. The history of political philosophy with its reflection on the grounds of human freedom culminates in human beings taking practical steps to create public space and mature public freedom at the planetary level.

The sixth "broad function" of the *Constitution* captures something of this dimension: "to devise and implement solutions to all problems which are beyond the capacity of national governments, or which are now or may become of global or international concern or consequence." Drawing on the collective knowledge of the world (especially represented in the House of Counselors within the World Parliament) and the entire World Parliament representing the people of Earth (in the House of Peoples) and the nations of Earth (in the House of Nations), the Earth Federation government makes it possible for humanity to address global problems that are beyond the capacity of the nation-states.

Having understood the communitarian foundations of our individual personal freedoms, political philosophy has articulated the theoretical and practical foundations for democratic and republican forms of government. However, with the ascent to the philosophy of democratic world government, political philosophy now fulfills its historical quest to understand and properly institutionalize the relation between individual and public freedom in its only fully coherent and logical possible form – public freedom for the entire human community that can only be affected through a global social contract (Harris 2008, Ch. 8). The maturity of this planetary political form will enhance the process of transformation toward personal maturity of all the citizens, religions, and associations comprising the Earth Federation.

The social contract within nations can no longer function properly. The democratic agreement between people and government assigning rights and duties to both disintegrates as global forces influence nation-state contracts from without and make functioning democracy focusing on the common good of the nation impossible. Freedom, national self-determination, and self-governance arising from the limited communities of nation-states is no longer possible in the face of a multiplicity of economic, political, environmental, and military decision-making forces beyond the scope of national sovereignty. The social contract, democratic governance, and corresponding human freedom can now only authentically exist at the planetary level.

We have seen that the Preamble to the *Constitution for the Federation of Earth* provides the most basic philosophical framework for the *Constitution* through making clear that the "principle of unity in diversity" is the only possible coherent basis for planetary peace, justice, and freedom. Unity in diversity is the principle of human maturity and holism that transcends puerile compulsion and fragmentation. And the *Constitution* itself provides a framework for global public space within the World Parliament encompassing all the peoples and nations of Earth along with the set of institutions, from judiciary to civilian police, necessary to maintain and protect that global public space. Here lies the real significance of the *Constitution* for world citizens and global thinkers. It culminates the human quest for freedom and draws humanity together into the global community that is *already presupposed* by every individual life-project and every community of decision-making on Earth.

The practical effects of this planetary political holism will likely result in binding humans together within a framework of common dialogue and decision-making regarding our common human fate. For institutions are established that make all persons equally responsible as legal world citizens before one, universal common law that allows for democratic diversity at every level within the world federal system. It brings the theoretically understood structure of human freedom (that the human community is presupposed in every individual freedom) into the practical public realm by institutionalizing a public freedom for the human community (where that public freedom ultimately belongs) to deal with issues unsolvable at the local and regional levels.

This public freedom is not only a fulfillment of the philosophical quest of political thought over the centuries and a major actualization of our human quest for mature freedom. It is also the foundation stone for human survival and flourishing upon planet Earth – for that survival and flourishing can only take place in freedom – through the establishment of a holistic planetary public freedom embracing and protecting the individual personal freedom (and hence the future) of every citizen of our precious planet Earth.

A new social contract is necessary, a newly-founded global society, in which the participants understand that their freedom, security, and survival depend on their universal affirmation of a *consensus universalis*. Political holism understands that positive freedom ultimately arises from a planetary human community that has consented to create that global public space necessary for human beings to envision their world and take action to actualize a peaceful, just, and sustainable future for the Earth and all its creatures. The ratification of the *Earth Constitution* constitutes by far our best bet for affecting this planetary social contract before it is too late.

1.6 Practical, Common Sense Democracy: Built-in Guarantees against Abuse

Some of the world federalist initiatives for transformation of our world order, such as reform of the U.N. or initiatives for creation of a world parliament independent of a constitutional framework appear to derive from an inadequate conception of democracy. The assumption often involves the idea that democracy consists in direct popular participation and, hence, the idea that popular votes are somehow sufficient to secure both the legitimacy of their efforts (e.g. to create a global people's assembly) and the democratic form of the outcomes. We have discussed some of the weaknesses and illegitimacy of these assumptions above. The Earth Federation Movement, on the other hand, has developed a much deeper and more coherent conception of democracy.

A number of the official documents of the EFM included in this volume bear on the democratic nature of the Earth Federation. Together these documents show the great efforts being made by the Provisional World Parliament and the citizens of the Earth Federation Movement to include popular, grass roots participation in the Earth Federation government. Such participation is indeed an essential aspect of effective democracy. The declaration of World Federal Distinction, for example, significantly increases the representation in the World Parliament from the vast areas encompassed by the U.S., India, and China, thereby further democratizing the World Parliament as defined in the *Constitution*.

The Declaration of Citizen and Governmental Responsibilities shows in detail how effective democracy is expected to function under the *Earth Constitution*. Mere voting is not nearly enough. Citizens must be encouraged to take mature responsibility for good government and the common good of the people of Earth in the multiplicity of ways detailed in this declaration, including the creation and maintenance of the public space necessary for genuine communication to take place. Yet the declaration does not reduce democracy under the Earth Federation to a simplistic "will of the people" but instead identifies the complex variety of factors at the heart of a truly democratic society.

World Legislative Act 29 develops further institutionalized structures to help make this possible. By creating the global people's assembly at the grass roots level across the world, it stimulates popular discussion of issues and communicative interaction between the people of Earth to the World Parliament. It makes clear that the global public space within which the World Parliament operates derives from, and is responsible to, the communities of local public spaces representing the sovereignty of the people the world over.

World Legislative Act 44, the Nonviolent Civil Disobedience Act, maximizes the possibility of citizen participation even to the point of civil disobedience, requiring the courts not to exclude the reasons for the civil disobedience and to take the morally inspired motivations of the protesters into consideration in prosecutions for their violation of the law. There is no naïve assumption within the Earth Federation Movement that human beings will suddenly become angels who will no longer need to struggle with one another because of perceived conflicts or injustices. The

Earth Federation government, however, is designed to transform inevitable human conflict into nonviolent forms and make possible the dialogue that can ultimately mitigate and eliminate much conflict based on misunderstanding or prejudice. WLA 44 requires courts and juries to *listen to the reasons* why dissidents engaged in civil disobedience. In doing this, it increases the scope of that public space necessary for freedom in human life.

Finally, the Conceptual Model of the Earth Federation (Document Eleven) shows how democracy works as a "freedom system" in which all the integrated elements under the *Earth Constitution* contribute to the collective result of "positive freedom." Democracy is not reducible to voting or the democratic will of some majority. It requires a complete, constitutionally defined, *system* of integrated elements for its existence. This Conceptual Model shows that a freedom system is *holistically inseparable* from a justice system, a peace system, a reasonable prosperity system, and a sustainability system. It makes clear that the fullness of freedom is impossible within sovereign nation-states, since they are incapable of creating peace, prosperity, justice, or sustainability within today's globalized world disorder.

The seven principles of authentic democracy, listed in the Declaration on Citizen and Governmental Responsibilities, therefore, spell out in what way democracy requires *an integrated system* to protect freedom within community. These include: (1) the dignity of all persons as human beings, (2) the idea that all persons have human rights that are inalienable, (3) universal political equality within a context of reasonable economic equality, (4) the existence of a public space necessary for genuine communication, (5) the idea that government only functions legitimately with the consent and active participation of the governed in formulating the laws under which they live, (6) a constitutional-legal framework and community spirit that reduces, as much as possible, the use of force in human affairs, and (7) representation of the common good of the whole. And with all of these principles, it is presumed that the rule of law applies equally to all, *including all persons within the government.* The government itself is limited by the rule of law.

Traditional theorists of democracy from John Stuart Mill to Henry David Thoreau to Alexis de Tocqueville argued that the efforts of democracy to free itself from the tyrannies of the few should not result in a similarly noxious "tyranny of the majority." Majority opinion can be just as tyrannical, bigoted, or stupid as the dictates of an absolute monarch. For example, it was an overwhelming popular mandate among the German people that brought Hitler to power in 1933.

Other theorists such as Rousseau and Kant distinguished between the legitimate common good or "general will" and the collective "will of all," the latter of which might be anything but democratic. Drawing on these seven principles listed above, I wish to point out ten ways in which the Earth Federation under the *Earth Constitution* builds in protections against both the tyranny of the few and the tyranny of the majority. These protections are built-in precisely because the *Constitution* does not confuse democracy with popular participation alone. The documents included in Part Two of this volume also illustrate each of these ten principles.

First, democracy requires reasonable holism in a community with a concomitant reasonable economic, social and political equality. The holistic dynamic of unity in diversity not only permeates the structure of the *Earth Constitution* but characterizes the global community established by its ratification. Today's immense democracy-destroying inequality of persons, nations, and corporations is immediately ameliorated with the ratification of the *Earth Constitution* which takes big money out of the election and selection processes that staff the agencies and houses of the Earth Federation. In addition, the Provisional World Parliament has passed the "Equity Act" further creating reasonable economic equality for the people of Earth.

Second, the holistic community characterizing genuine democracy will be and must be federal in structure. This means that relative governmental autonomy, and citizen participation in government, will exist in a multiplicity of levels from the local to the regional to the national to the world. Such a federal structure creates an important protection against both tyrannies of the minority and of the majority. There is no one component of a federal system that can easily dominate the rest. Majority prejudice or bigotry developing in one component of the system will be, in all likelihood, ultimately overcome by the rationality and toleration pervading the Federation as a whole.

Third, such a federal structure, along with other explicit constitutional protections, constitutes the protection and encouragement of mature diversity within the community. If diversity is consciously protected, people will come to understand diversity (of races, religions, nations, cultures, voices, traditions, etc.) as a good thing and find joy and value in its protection and preservation. This spirit is cultivated with the provision of genuinely public space for dialogue and debate at all levels within the Earth Federation.

Fourth, this feature of the Earth Federation simultaneously encourages affirmation of diversity and reduces the danger of tyranny of a majority. Majoritarian tyrannies result from mass produced emotions or ideologies that colonize the thought of large groups of people (Fromm 1941, Arendt 1958). They are often products of mass media oversimplifications, mistaken or misleading information, economic crisis, or unscrupulous leadership inculcating fear and insecurity on a large scale.

True space for genuine dialogue within government at all levels, within the media, and within civic organizations fosters genuine thoughtfulness, mutual respect, and a transformation of the understandings of all participants. People no longer operate out of simplistic generalizations and thoughtless slogans. They begin to see the legitimacy of opposing points of view and their own views are modified in the process.

Fifth, democracy requires a multiplicity of news organizations gathering and disseminating information from multiple points of view. It is the responsibility of government to encourage the multiplicity of voices with special concern that the dialogue not be colonized by wealthier or more powerful elements within society. None of these elements of authentic democracy identified so far reduce democracy to the will of some majority. If 90% of the people preferred some slanted and bigoted news source, it would be the responsibility of government to all the more encourage alternative sources of news and dialogue.

With regard to the Earth Federation government created by the *Constitution*, one can observe other essential features designed to protect democracy from tyrannies of both majorities and minorities. *Sixth*, the *Constitution* creates many structural checks and balances and diverse sources of power and authority under its umbrella. The Executive Presidium does not consist of just one person but a group of five, one from each of the Earth's continents. The Executive cannot declare a state of emergency and suspend the *Constitution*, nor can it refuse to execute the budget given to it by the World Parliament. The World Police form an independent branch of government not under the Executive. The World Ombudsmus, whose responsibility is to protect human rights worldwide even with respect to the conduct of the Executive or the World Police, is also an independent branch of government directly responsible to the World Parliament.

The *seventh* factor preserving genuine democracy is precisely this role of the World Ombudsmus that is tasked as a watchdog with investigative powers to ensure the world government remains democratic. The *eighth* factor consists in the fact that the World Police are *civilian police with civilian oversight*, with the explicit requirement to use a minimum of force in apprehending suspects. They are also tasked by the *Constitution* to set up systems of conflict resolution and to reduce the sources of violent conflict through cultivating mutual understanding worldwide.

Ninth, the *Constitution* creates multiple systems of overlapping agencies governed by independent criteria for quality results and independently responsible in various ways to the World Parliament. In this respect these agencies will function like the federal structure of government under the Earth Federation. Corruption or malfeasance in one will not likely infect the others, which will serve as a corrective counterforce within the whole of the government.

Tenth, the *Constitution* sets up similar methods and effective criteria for selecting qualified persons and for rewarding excellence and leadership within the Earth Federation. Again, Aristotle's concern (in his *Politics*) that good government find ways to reward excellence and leadership without compromising the common good of the whole is here fulfilled. The important point, Aristotle says, is that equal rewards follow equal accomplishments. So it is with the *Earth Constitution.*

The *Earth Constitution* creates government as a dynamic and balanced whole that protects against both minority and majority tyrannies. Authentic democracy is not reducible to grass roots public participation alone. This is a necessary but not a sufficient aspect of good government. The idea that a constitution for the Earth must somehow still be created from the "grass roots" of humanity (now current among some activists) is nonsense. The wheel has already been invented and does not have to be reinvented. The *Earth Constitution* must be ratified democratically (as specified under Article 17) by a vote of the majority of citizens in every nation or region that joins the Earth Federation. This is overwhelmingly sufficient to establish its legitimacy. Once established, good democracy is not run from the grass roots only, but includes the complex holism just described, ensuring freedom from both sorts of tyrannies.

1.7 Legitimacy and the Global Social Contract

Among various world federalist organizations and activists, there is a frequent misunderstanding about the relation between the *means* by which we attempt to transform the world into a global democracy and the *end*: the general characteristics of what is often thought of as our common goal. Many hold only a vague ideological conception of this *what*, the final end or goal sought by the federalist movement. They believe we need democracy, freedom, sustainability, etc., but they believe that the specific arrangements by which we are to realize these vague ideals belong to some future working out of the details by the democratic bodies that these activists are attempting to create in the present.

They may work, therefore, to create global elections supporting the idea of world government, or elect a citizen's parliament outside of any constitutional framework, or they may work to develop and empower the International Criminal Court, or to promote a U.N. sponsored environmental treaty. The ultimate goal remains the general ideal of a world of democracy, freedom, and sustainability. Sometimes the end is characterized by the relatively meaningless phrase "building global civil society," while the means become this particular effort to engender an election process, attend an international meeting, or this particular effort to lobby nations to pass an arms control treaty. Very often such activists believe they are doing what is most practical and possible within the present world situation.

Many within the Earth Federation Movement believe that this orientation involves a fundamental misunderstanding. First, it is very difficult to accomplish effective means when the ends are vague and abstract. Psychologist Stanley Milgram (1974) studied the thought patterns of U.S. veterans who had committed atrocities in Vietnam. Milgram found that in nearly every case the horrific means used were justified by some vague abstract ideal such as "fighting totalitarian Communism" or "defending democracy and freedom." Vague and noble sounding ends can be used to justify nearly any means.

If one insists, as Mahatma Gandhi did, that ends and means must be absolutely consistent with one another, in the absence of a specific set of ends to which the means can be compared, this consistency becomes problematic. If the ends remain a vague ideal like "global democracy," then what sort of means must be used to achieve that end? How about attending global conferences concerning these issues (which many activists do)? These means seem harmless and useful enough, but how are we to compare them with some vague, ideological end?

How about participating in the General Review Conference of the ICC that took place in Uganda in June 2010 (which many activists did)? The general review conference cost a lot of activists a great deal of time and money but accomplished very little. How about lobbying for ratification by the U.S. of the Kyoto environmental treaty? It may well be that such lobbying will never succeed and will end up as a waste of time and money. What about attending the World Social Forum, the gigantic gathering of "global civil society" that has been meeting annually since 2001? Thousands of activists walk away momentarily "empowered" every year, but these meetings do not appear to have made any specific positive changes in the world system. There is a general sense that the world needs global citizens expressing concern in a variety of forums but the specific ends and concrete changes needed to transform the world system remain elusive.

In every case it is difficult to know if what one is doing is the most effective (and consistent) means to the vague end of global democracy or primarily just a waste of time. If the goal is that abstract, almost any action can be claimed as an effective means consistent with the presumed end. The Supreme Court of the United States recently ruled that wealthy corporations could participate in U.S. elections through donations to candidates under the rationale that democracy was promoted by a "multiplicity of voices." The abstract end (democracy in the U.S.) appears to justify a very flawed means (big money participating in elections).

It takes no great knowledge of politics to understand that such a blank slate given to corporations is destructive of democracy at every level. If the goal is vague enough, the means can be almost anything. And there is no way to evaluate either the moral worth or the effectiveness of the means. After we have systematically lobbied for ratification of the Kyoto treaty, or after we have attended the General Review Conference of the ICC, how do we know we are any closer to global democracy?

Within a nation, in the view of political liberals, we might be able to estimate success concretely. For example, if we have managed to abolish segregation through the Civil Rights Movement in the U.S., then we may conclude that we have concretely helped democracy flourish in the U.S. So called "radicals," however, even challenge this notion. For example, Howard Zinn, in his 1994 memoir *You Can't be Neutral on a Moving Train,* writes:

> From that moment on, I was no longer a liberal, a believer in the self-correcting character of American democracy. I was a radical, believing that something fundamental was wrong in this country - not just the existence of poverty amidst great wealth, not just the horrible treatment of black people, but something rotten at the root. The situation required not just a new president or new laws, but an uprooting of the old order, the introduction of a new kind of society - cooperative, peaceful, egalitarian. (1994: 173)

Zinn was correct that the liberal ideology stating that the laws of the nation-state can be improved to the point of creating a decent democracy and society is false, but his vague ideal of a "cooperative, peaceful, egalitarian" society independent of government (which is one form of the anarchist ideal) is so vague and illusive as to border on meaninglessness.

Zinn appears to mean something of what Marx declared when he wrote: "To be radical is to grasp things by the root. But for man the root is man himself" (1978: 60). Zinn understands that we have to activate our "species-being," as Marx argued, living from our common humanity to the point where we establish human societies that are free, peaceful, and just. Both thinkers appear to be speaking of the freedom and communicative spirit of open, compassionate, mature persons in society.

Yet without a concrete vision of how such a society can come about, all Zinn can offer us is *ad hoc* and blindly hopeful resistance to this or that outrage against peace, justice, civil liberties, or human dignity. What is missing here, as with many world federalists, is any specific vision of a *global social contract* that can tell us how it can concretely work and how our fractured human condition can be transformed through institutional forms that can raise humanity to a more mature level. The root of the problem of "man himself" lies in our refusal to take the next concrete step to actualize the higher level of existence embodied in a global social contract, in "civil obedience" at the global level.

The root of the problem, therefore, is intimately connected with the lack of legitimate universal law in the world, protecting the unity in diversity of everyone equally. If the root of the problem is "man," then both level of maturity and our institutions must simultaneously be transformed. The solution to the problem, at least insofar as the next absolutely necessary step is concerned, requires non-military, democratically legislated enforceable world law. There is no possibility of creating a "cooperative, peaceful, egalitarian" order either within nations or between nations without this global social contract.

As many world federalists are aware, it is for these very reasons that we must work for global democracy. *Unless the social contract is planetary, it will not work.* If some retain their WMDs while others try to create cooperative and peaceful societies, it will not work. If the global population continues to explode, it will not work. If climate collapse continues unabated, it will not work. If resources continue to diminish so that there is wide-spread scarcity, it will not work. If global poverty continues to spread ever-more deeply worldwide, it will not work. If global hate, fear, and terror continue, it will not work.

The specific, stated functions of the *Earth Constitution* (Articles 1-4) address all these problems directly. History has forced us into the position that, in the words of Erich Fromm, "for the first time in history, the physical survival of the human race depends on a radical change in the human heart. However, a change of the human heart is possible only to the extent that drastic economic and social changes occur that give the human heart the chance for change and the courage and vision to achieve it" (1996: 9-10).

The first step toward going to the root of the problem, the first step toward affecting a radical change in the human heart, requires entering into the global social contract that is ready and waiting in the form of the *Earth Constitution.* We do not have time to reinvent some other contract because we object to this or that detail of the *Constitution* or because we think of ourselves as "the pioneers" and resent the fact that there were pioneers who came before us who have already marked out the path to a global social contract. The *Constitution* specifies those economic and social changes that Fromm indentifies as a necessary prerequisite for a radical change in the human heart. Structural and psychic transformation must go together from the very beginning.

The effort to create the rule of democratically legislated enforceable law in the world, however, does not fit well into the political categories recognized *within* nations. If the "liberal" solution is not viable, as Zinn asserts, what is needed is not the attempt to undercut the dominant system of any nation (Zinn's "radical" solution) but rather to create, strengthen, and foster the genuine rule of law in the world. In this sense, our work should resonate strongly with the predilection of political conservatives. As Hannah Arendt writes:

> No civilization – the man-made artifact to house successive generations – would ever have been possible without a framework of stability, to provide the wherein for the flux of change. Foremost among the stabilizing factors, more enduring than customs, manners, and traditions, are the legal systems that regulate our life in the world and our daily affairs with each other. This is the reason it is inevitable that law in a time of rapid change will appear as "a restraining force, thus a negative influence in a world which admires positive action." (1972: 79)

Our work for democratic world government is as much "conservative" as it is "progressive." It is a work that seeks what is most fundamental and stabilizing about civilization – the enforceable, democratically legislated law in human affairs. It transcends these political categories in ways that should appeal to both progressives and conservatives. We offer humanity both a progressive ideal of dealing with the problem of global injustice and the conservative ideal of bringing stability and the rule of law into a chaotic world.

We have seen in section 1.2 above the extensive work done by the Provisional World Parliament to foster integration of existing international institutions such as the U.N., the ICC, and the Assembly of States Parties into a growing political cooperation and consensus concerning recognizing an effective constitution for the Earth and the development of enforceable world law. The Earth Federation Movement is drawing on the means and instruments already created by international conventions of governments as well as the accomplishments of millions of world citizens working around the globe by promoting the integration of this valuable work into a global social contract under the *Earth Constitution.*

With respect to means and ends on the global level, however, the difficulties of creating global democracy multiply. For there is no constitutional framework (like the U.S. Constitution) lending legitimacy to citizen efforts (whether conservative or progressive). There is no constitution for which amendments, etc., can be passed. There are no effective laws that can be modified and enforced, (only unenforceable treaties, empty international agreements, etc.). Most accurately described, the change we seek is not "revolutionary" (since we are not attempting to overthrow any existing governments) but rather "civilizing." We want to bring civilization forward to establish the true rule of law in human affairs for the first time.

On the global level there exists by and large only the power politics of multinational corporations, giant banking cartels, imperial governments, unenforceable international treaties, and vast criminal associations trafficking in weapons, human beings, drugs, etc. There are no institutions in place that can be used to legitimize our activist efforts to create global democracy. At this point, in spite of the fact that we are attempting to bring civilization forward to the genuine rule of law in human affairs, we run into the question of legitimacy. Under what recognized system of law or recognized mandate do our efforts fall? There is no established precedent for our endeavors. In this respect, we may be somewhat like the "pilgrim citizens" named by Richard Falk (1992): responsible political persons on a journey for which there is no recognized path and no clear final destination.

So how are we going to organize elections or make our efforts the democratic means that we want them to be? There are no recognized institutional forms that legitimize our efforts to do this. Those who would elect representatives who would then become a world parliament, or those who would elect a world parliament, are electing persons under an *ad hoc* system of elections (devised by the organizers whomever they may be) that would not in itself create a legitimacy for the resulting assembly.

If one million people from around the world vote on the internet to create world government, we can ask under what legitimacy this *ad hoc* vote was organized and what is the significance of such a tiny minority of the world's population making this statement? If these one million people manage to elect some "representatives" to have non-governmental meetings to represent them, how is this legitimate since there are no governmental forms and no constitutional framework for these actions? If these representatives say they are going to sit together and write a constitution for the Earth, this is well and good, but it has no more special legitimacy than if one person sat down and wrote such a constitution.

If this assembly is created under the rationale that the people themselves are sovereign, then the problem arises regarding how to legitimately represent the sovereignty of the people of Earth. An *ad hoc* assembly devised by an association of well-meaning private individuals will not do it. It is very unlikely that such an assembly could be devised to enfranchise all the people of Earth. Rather, it would likely represent just an elite portion of those with access to computers, resources, etc. But even then, since there is no constitution to legitimize it, such an assembly would carry only a possible moral, never actual legal authority.

If such an assembly were formed and it designated itself (arbitrarily) as the "World Parliament," then what? Any *ad hoc* assembly elected for the purposes of moving closer to world law would face immense difficulties, since the assembly would have no pre-existing rules by which it could make decisions, no mechanisms for enforcing its determinations, no rules for how it would relate to sovereign nations, no judiciary for deciding cases according to its laws, and no institutions to support the Parliament with information and the necessary bureaucratic infrastructure.

It is often claimed by world federalists that the only way we will change the world for the better, and the only fully legitimate means for doing this, is through "grass roots organizing." The Earth Federation Movement already does a great deal of this through our WCPA chapters throughout the world, but there is little reason why this should be the only mode of organizing and promoting ratification of the *Earth Constitution* or any other document. We have seen above some of the problems that arise from the oversimplification of equating democracy and grass roots participation.

It is sometimes said (with Howard Zinn) that progress within nations only comes about through the organized efforts of many ordinary people, as in the protests, strikes, boycotts, and other actions taken by the people of the U.S. in past two centuries. Yet it is manifestly more difficult to do grass roots organizing *between* countries, not to mention the fact that successes achieved *within* countries are not always democratic. Sometimes votes are not followed; sometimes leaders decide what the votes mean. Sometimes the leaders are fighting between themselves, and many times decisions among protesting groups are made in undemocratic ways through group emotion or leaders anxious to take action under a spurious claim of "consensus."

Grass roots organizing is important but not in itself sufficient. As Hannah Arendt remarks, "If you look at the history of revolutions, you will see that it was never the oppressed and degraded themselves who led the way, but those who were not oppressed and not degraded but who could not bear it that others were" (1972: 204). Most world federalists that I have met fall into the latter category. They are from the privileged classes at the same time that many insist that the only real change must come from the "grass roots."

They imply that only the appeal to the grass roots can really make their efforts legitimate. However, this appeal does not surmount the above mentioned difficulties of creating legitimacy for one's activities on behalf of world democracy. Without a specific document to be ratified, these activities become questionable means aiming toward an undetermined end. Why must everything be "grass roots"? Why not talk to leaders and important, influential people? Why not talk with representatives of governments? Why not hold seminars for especially thoughtful or active people? Why not use the Internet (already an elitist mode of communication)? Why not write books that can only be read by literate people? Why not seek donations from wealthy persons or organizations?

Why not combine a multiplicity of morally legitimate means in the service of humanity and civilization? And why not direct all these efforts to the ratification of a specific document that addresses the very heart of our problems and our needs?

If a U.N. General Review conference were to take place, the decisions of such a conference would have no greater legitimacy than the U.N. itself, which is a mere confederation of sovereign nation-states, is not democratic, and which has proven itself to be ineffective in establishing peace, protecting the environment, protecting human rights, or protecting freedom. The means of trying to reform the U.N. toward greater democracy may have little more legitimacy (given the substantial illegitimacy of the U.N.) than the attempt to independently elect an *ad hoc* world parliament, unless such a general review conference were to affirm the replacement of the U.N. Charter with the *Earth Constitution*. In that case alone genuine legitimacy would be imminent because the people of Earth would then have to ratify the document under the democratic criteria specified in Article 17 of that *Constitution*.

All these problems, therefore, are significantly reduced or eliminated as soon as one chooses ratification of the *Constitution for the Federation of Earth* as the end and the creation of specific steps to that goal under Article 17 as the means. The ends are no longer vague, noble-sounding ideals but a specific constitutional framework open for everyone to see, study, discuss, and ratify if they choose. The *Constitution* itself creates a World Parliament along with a judiciary, world police, world executive, and all the organs of government necessary to establish world democracy.

With ratification of the *Constitution*, the creation of all these organs in a holistic system guaranteeing democracy is immediately fully legitimate. We do not want some ersatz substitute or patchwork temporary solution. What humanity absolutely needs – to address the root of the problem – is a binding democratic *social contract* for all. Only such a binding social contract can *unite* humanity in such a way that we can address our common, lethal problems.

In this way, the specific and concrete end that is open for everyone to see and evaluate is linked with specific concrete means that can be evaluated in terms of both their consistency with the end as well as their effectiveness. The goal is not some vague idea of "one world democracy" but the rule of law under a specific constitutional document. The system created by the *Constitution* can be modeled and studied as a whole as is done in Document Eleven below. This "Model of the Earth Federation under the *Earth Constitution*" was approved at the 12th session of the Provisional World Parliament as an official document of the Parliament. Means and ends are here able to match up perfectly. The means are these specific criteria for ratification and the steps required to make them operational, and the end is this specific social contract with these concrete results that can be studied and envisioned.

Those world federalists who believe they are being "practical" and concrete by trying to reform the U.N. or choosing limited goals like supporting the ICC are, in reality, not being that practical at all, since there is no way of evaluating the success of their actions in the light of their vague ideals about world democracy. Those world federalists who believe they are being more "democratic" by trying to create *ad hoc* elections in the world that will eventually elect a body who will elect a parliament who may write a constitution for the Earth are likewise being neither democratic or practical.

Legitimate democracy *begins* with the ratification of a constitution that provides what philosopher of law, H.L.A. Hart (1994), calls the "rules of recognition" by which a society recognizes what is legitimate enforceable law from the dictates of arbitrary power, whether these be world banks, big corporations, organized crime syndicates, militarized sovereign nation-states, or terrorist threats. Without preexisting rules of recognition, legitimated by the majority of a population as part of its *consensus universalis,* no social body can claim very much political legitimacy and the right to represent the sovereignty of all the people. That is why the most practical and democratic efforts that can be made today involve efforts to ratify the *Earth Constitution,* which contains everything within it that humankind needs to establish global democracy and which becomes immediately legitimated through ratification under the democratic criteria specified in Article 17.

Professor Errol E. Harris, in his 2005 book *Earth Federation Now!,* writes concerning the creation of the *Earth Constitution* through the efforts of hundreds, and ultimately thousands, of world citizens:

> None of this spectacular, professional and devoted work, conducted over the past forty-six years, is official, in the sense that it has any legal force, but it is obviously representative of a considerable body of opinion derived from a large number of different nations the world over.
>
> I have recounted all these various occasions in order to make plain the care, industry and effort that has gone into the drafting of the *Constitution for the Federation of Earth,* the international character and the extent of the representation among the delegates who took part in its production, and the effort and length of time spend on getting it right.
>
> The Association [WCPA] is genuinely international, and the persons who have been active in drafting the *Constitution* include the most eminent international lawyers and professors of law and politics, drawn from many countries.
>
> Moreover, it could all become official if ratified by a sufficient number of organizations and governments, a ratification that need commit nobody to anything more than the principle of world government, leaving

the details to be finally decided by a World Parliament properly elected as the Constitution provides.

Some world federalists have criticized the *Constitution* as undemocratic because it was not drafted by a popularly elected constituent assembly – but this criticism is misguided. What makes a Constitution democratic is not who drafted it but that it should be accepted by the peoples who are to live under its provisions.

The *Constitution* is an admirable document on which it would be difficult to improve and it provides (in Article 18) for its own amendment as soon as it becomes operative, either by petition or by a democratically elected world parliament, and for periodical special sessions thereafter to reconsider its details. So nobody who objects to its details need be reluctant to ratify it provisionally. (102-103)

Later in the same book Harris writes:

It should now be unquestionably apparent that World Government [under the *Earth Constitution*] offers no threats to liberty or repression of national identity and tradition, that it can be organized in a manner that is unlikely to be unduly unwieldy, bureaucratic or cumbersome, that it provides sufficient safeguards against all these dangers as well as against authoritarianism and abuse of power, while it offers the one and only hope of salvation from the predicaments that currently envelop mankind and the threats of impending disasters. (119)

Harris asserts that efforts to ratify the *Earth Constitution* are the most effective, practical, and legitimate of all activities directed toward global democracy. In spite of the immense pedigree behind the careful, professionally organized, multi-decade long creation of the *Constitution*, Harris correctly states that this is not what legitimates it. What legitimates it is ratification by the people of Earth under the criteria given in Article 17. Establishing a global social contract can be as simple as that.

This is not to deny that an Article 109 Review Conference of the U.N. Charter might be an effective method of ratifying the *Earth Constitution*. Such a review conference might well choose to replace the U.N. charter with the *Earth Constitution*, forming the U.N. General Assembly into a House of Nations and otherwise adapting U.N. institutions to the framework of the *Constitution*. The ultimate legitimacy for this action would still require the ratification of the *Constitution* by a general referendum of the people of each country joining the Earth Federation. However, the adapting of the U.N.'s extensive institutional structure to the *Earth Constitution* could considerably speed the conversion of the world to effective global democracy.

Governmental legitimacy at the global or local levels includes at least five aspects: (1) common recognition by people (consent of the governed), (2) established recognized mechanisms for assessing this common recognition by people (for example, elections), (3) intrinsically understood rational criteria for laws, actions, and ideas, traditionally called "natural law" or rationally "self-evident" propositions (often specified in constitutions as "inalienable rights"), (4) a unified, convincing set of institutions that show the viability and workability of the legitimate rule of law in human affairs (e.g. judiciary and civilian police), and (5) a mechanism for founding, establishing, and legislating (rather than evolving) a decent system under the rule of law (usually the criteria for ratification found in one article within a constitution).

This is why the legitimacy of a genuine social contract gives government the authority of *coercion over a well-defined body politic.* Democratic processes within voluntary associations may be well and good, and democratic forms used by world federalists in their efforts to create global democracy may be well and good, but they should not be confused with governmental legitimacy. Those who dislike decisions made by a majority within a voluntary association may withdraw from the association to avoid obeying the decision. But governmental authority requires that *everyone be equally subject to the law* whether they like its decisions or not. Equality before law enforceable over everyone is essential to legitimacy.

Legitimacy in the quest for global democracy requires a founding ratification process and a founding document. Evolution is a very poor method of generating legitimacy, even if it uses democratic forms in voluntary associations. Hannah Arendt speaks of the mistake of those who "substitute ideological commitments, political or other, for actual goals" (1972: 98). Those well-meaning world federalists who try to create *ad hoc* elections in voluntary associations, not legitimized by binding institutional forms, or those who work for world peace under global democracy without defining the final result, or those who try to reform the U.N. with no clear idea of what the final result might look like, have substituted vague ideological dreams for actual goals.

What distinguishes the Earth Federation Movement is the clarity and coherency of its specific goals: first and foremost, ratification of the *Constitution for the Federation of Earth.* Here everything is spelled out: what the goal is, how it would work, specific institutional arrangements, rights and duties, checks and balances, and criteria for ratification. Here, what one's ideology may be (concerning democracy, justice, sustainability, etc. – whether conservative or progressive) takes second place to the specific goal that stands forth clearly for everyone to see. The goal is creation of binding governmental legitimacy under effective world democracy as embodied in a specific, concrete document.

These ideas are elaborated in the Fundamental Principles of the Earth Federation Movement in Document One below. The process of perpetual compromise that is necessary when competing ideologies clash with one another is not required when the goal is ratification of this *specific document defining a new social contract for humanity.* Our "fundamental principles" state that the Earth Federation Movement avoids having to compromise with undemocratic forces. It makes clear what the world system would and should be like from the beginning, not opening the people of Earth to an unknown future in the hands of some *ad hoc* citizen World Parliament but rather to a specific document specifying the democratic structure of the government that would govern: its limits, checks and balances, and multiple functions.

The commitment to this specific goal, therefore, is so much more powerful than the commitment to some vague ideology no matter how noble or inspiring it may appear (as given, for example, in the popular Earth Charter document: http://www.earthcharterinaction.org). The Earth Federation Movement, for all its theoretical and ethical justifications detailed above, takes its most fundamental stand on a concrete, specific goal. In this lives its greatest power, its legitimacy, and its concrete practicality.

Those conservatives who (for religious or other reasons) fear the development of what they call a "new world order" that will create a militarized totalitarian regime over all the Earth also have their answer in this specific document. Most other world federalist initiatives cannot effectively address their concerns. In the *Earth Constitution* we can see the limits, conditions, and mechanisms for restraint of power and guarantee of freedom, peace, and democracy. Without this ability to show them specifically how it will work, their resistance will only continue to obstruct world federalist efforts to bring the rule of law to the Earth.

Zinn was indeed correct that the liberal ideology is false in its belief that the laws of the nation-state can be improved to the point of creating a decent democracy. The word "radical" that he uses comes from the Latin "radix" meaning to go to the "root" of the problem. But Zinn has not gone to the root. His assumption that a cooperative, peaceful, and egalitarian society can be built within any particular nation-state flies in the face of logic and reality.

For what prevents any society from achieving these goals of democracy is global. At every turn, nations, as well as the imperative for human cooperative maturity, are thwarted by global economics, global poverty and misery, global militarism, global environmental collapse, global resource depletion, global corporations, global criminal syndicates, and global terrorism. The root of the problem ("man") is inseparable from the lack of legitimate, enforceable law in the world, and its solution requires non-military, democratically legislated world law within a global social contract. Ratification of the *Earth Constitution* is the key to establishing worldwide democracy before it is too late.

1.8 Ethical and Metaphysical Possibilities

Some who envision the unity of humankind believe that human beings must evolve over a period of many years toward the kind of universalism of spirit and consciousness that will allow us to create democratic world government. Some believe that human beings will need to grow to maturity *before* they are capable of achieving a truly transformed world system. Peace educator Betty Reardon, for example, states that "it has long been my belief that authentic transformation of the global order is as much a matter of emotional maturity as of structural change.... Structural, even revolutionary, changes in the public order without significant inner psychic changes in human beings will be ineffective." (2000: 252). Professor Reardon correctly, however, promotes *both* emotional growth and structural change.

People who argue that the human race must mature *first* often miss the key point discussed above that our maturity is so thoroughly influenced by the structural and governmental features of our societies that these often precondition our developmental capabilities. If we change these flawed structures by ratifying a global social contract under the *Earth Constitution*, this will have an immense effect on the way people think, feel, and mature. The structural and psychological dimensions of our lives cannot be separated so neatly. An Earth Federation treating all as equal under the law, legally recognizing rights and responsibilities for every adult on Earth, and educating a new generation of children with these ideas, will have a tremendous impact on people's emotional maturity.

Still others who believe that a global social contract is impossible at this time often reflect assumptions about historical and causal determinism that today appear untenable. Such people argue that the existing economic and political institutions of the world (from global capitalism to militarized sovereign nation-states to religious or political institutions) will take a long time to overcome because these are so deeply rooted in the past. It took 2500 years, they say, to move from Greek city-state democracy to national democracies. Hence, it will take hundreds more years to move to global democracy. If these critics are world federalists, they often devote themselves to making small, incremental changes in the structures of things, quite sure that the process will be a long, slow, and laborious process of evolution.

Many people within the Earth Federation Movement think otherwise. Many within the Earth Federation Movement are so alive to the incomprehensible mysteries of time, existence, selfhood, and infinity that they are no longer trapped in the "myth of the origin" or in tired assumptions about universal causal determinism binding the present in terms of the past. Such assumptions have been challenged in many areas of 20th century thought, including the areas of cosmology and physics. Just as an awakened individual can be free of his or her personal past to take genuinely creative action, so humanity can break free of the dead hand of the past and rise to a higher level of existence within a very short time.

We are not locked within a closed "totality" in which the dominant sectors of humanity define the role and possibility for the 80% of humanity who possess little or nothing. Within the present world disorder, these 80% do not even possess the human rights or dignity that might allow them to create their own identity rather than being defined as "developmentally lost or retarded" by the dominant system. These 80% can and must take the creative action to ratify the *Earth Constitution* and transform the world system from one of dominating center and exploited periphery to one of universal unity in diversity. The ability to break free of this assumed totality is ever-present precisely because there is an "exterior" to existence that makes "miracles" possible.

Contemporary physicist, Henry Stapp, for example, applies the 20th century paradigm shift in physics to human mental acts. The early-modern idea of determinism no longer applies. The possibilities opened up by this understanding are immense:

> This classical view of man and nature is still promulgated in the name of science. Thus, science is seen as demanding a perception of man as nothing more than a local cog in a mechanical universe, unconnected to any creative aspect of nature. For, according to the classical picture, every creative aspect of nature exhausted itself during the first instant....
>
> In the Heisenberg ontology, the real world of classical physics is transformed into a world of potentialities, which condition, but do not control, the world of actual events. These events or acts create the actual form of the evolving universe by deciding between the possibilities created by the evolving potentialities. These creative acts stand outside space-time and presumably create all space-time relationships. Human mental acts belong to this world of creative acts, but do not exhaust it. (1988, pp. 56-57)

For Stapp, human mental acts, understood by contemporary physics, connect us to the creative foundations of the universe itself. In this section, I will quote directly from a number of other important 20th century thinkers in an effort to show the reader the intellectual legitimacy of the Earth Federation Movement's drive for rapid transformation of our human situation through ratification of the

Constitution for the Federation of Earth. Thinkers like Henry Stapp see the immense possibilities of human mental creativity that can actively influence the flow of space-time relationships. According to these thinkers and many others, the transformative potentialities that we encounter are very real, very concrete, and very practical.

There is an immense pressure on us to take the next step. As Errol E. Harris puts it, the "enormity" of the dangers faced by humanity is so great that "immediate ratification" of the *Earth Constitution* is indispensible if we wish to survive much longer (2005: 128). We need to think outside the box. We need to see both the possibility and the moral necessity of creating something genuinely new for humanity that will immediately raise humanity to a higher level of existence.

Betty Reardon may be right that human liberation will require a greater level of emotional, intellectual, and psychic maturity in human beings than what appears today, but she appears to minimize the fact that the potential for a breakthrough or conversion to this maturity is *already present within us.* Change can and has occurred in the form of rapid transformations. A deeper vision or "faith" in the immense potentialities of our human situation becomes a key to success.

Erich Fromm describes this dimension of our ever-present potential for transformation in terms of "hope" and "faith":

> When hope has gone life has ended, actually or potentially. Hope is an intrinsic element in the structure of life, of the dynamic of man's spirit. It is closely linked with another element in the structure of life: faith. Faith is not a weak form of belief or knowledge; it is not faith in this or that; faith is the conviction about the not yet proven, the knowledge of the real possibility, the awareness of pregnancy....Faith is based on our experience of living, of transforming ourselves. Faith that others can change is the outcome of the experience that I can change. (1968: 14)

I mentioned earlier that the Earth Federation Movement is based on love. This great love for the Earth, humanity, and life, is closely linked with the hope and faith that Fromm describes here. We have immense possibilities within all of us for "transforming ourselves," for a breakthrough to the life-affirming energies within each of us that are now repressed by our distorted technological, violent, and life-hating civilization. Such breakthroughs in maturity, indeed, throw us into conflict with our civilization, but not in terms of a violence that would force changes within the same distorted framework. Rather, our struggle now arises in terms of a love that can see the possibility of deep transformation emerging from the fundamental humanity that we all share.

Contemporary psychology by and large has moved from the reductionist and behaviorist models of being human popular in the early

20th century to an emphasis on *human potentialities* (cf. Martin 2008, Chap. 2). Drawing on this understanding of our immense human possibilities, thinkers like Ken Wilber (1996) and Robert Ornstein have argued that human beings are now in a position to begin consciously influencing the course of their own evolution. If we recognize this immense potential to transform ourselves and our present world disorder, the first step must necessarily be ratification of the *Earth Constitution*, which, we have seen, provides that necessary unity and public space through which human beings can begin to shape a decent future for our planet and our descendents. Ornstein writes:

> To echo the evolutionists Darwin and Rumi, there is a grandeur in this view of the mind, with an endless supply of possible capabilities, waiting to be called in response to the new necessities of the new world we've created. Undertaking conscious evolution, with an understanding of the complexity of our myriad minds within, may be easier, closer at hand, and more liberating than we might normally think (1991: 279).

Not only have we discovered the immense potentialities of the human mind, contemporary thinkers have also understood that transformative possibilities are built into the very structure of our universe. Perhaps the first inkling for this liberation and the framework for a development of the power of creatively actualizing what is genuinely new (through love and life-affirming energy) lies in this experience described by Karl Jaspers in his book *Truth and Symbol*:

> The world and everything that occurs in it is a mystery. The crudeness of finding everything to be self-evident through force of habit and the mania for mystery to the point of the sensational and the superstitious must disappear where genuine astonishment begins. Philosophy illuminates the mystery and brings it completely into consciousness. It begins with astonishment and increases the astonishment.... Then the world as a whole and in every individual feature shows infinite depth. This mystery is quiet; in flaring up it becomes revealed in an unfoldment. And this mystery is essential; in it Being Itself speaks. (1959:37)

In his book *Man in the Modern Age*, Jaspers adds to the above thought a reflection on our present situation:

> Even those who lack clear knowledge of the subject are becoming decisively aware that they are living in an epoch when the world is undergoing a change so vast as to be hardly comparable to any of the great changes of past millenniums. The mental situation of our day is pregnant with immense dangers and immense possibilities; and it is one which, if we are inadequate to the tasks which await us, will herald the failure of mankind.

> Is it an end that draws near, or a beginning? Is it perhaps a beginning as significant as that when man first become man, but now enriched by newly acquired means, and the capacity for experience upon a new and higher level? (1957: 22-23)

The framers of the *Earth Constitution* (people such as Philip Isely and Terence Amerasinghe) were among the great visionaries and creative benefactors of humankind. They were alive with the immense possibilities contained in our present planetary situation. They understood that human experience itself can be moved to "a new and higher level." They acted to bring this to light in the form of the *Earth Constitution* that itself proclaims in its preamble that "the principle of unity in diversity is the basis for a new age when war shall be outlawed and peace prevail."

The Earth Federation Movement continues to be enlivened by visionaries who understand the possibilities for rapid and immense transformation of our present world disorder into a world system premised on peace, freedom, justice, and sustainability. Document Eleven below presents a model of this transformed world system, making clear its systematic and integrated character. We may be very near, very close, to actualizing this transformative possibility. Hannah Arendt writes:

> Every act seen from the perspective not of the agent but of the process in whose framework it occurs and whose automatism it interrupts, is a "miracle" – that is something which could not be expected. If it is true that action and beginning are essentially the same, it follows that a capacity for performing miracles must likewise be within the range of human faculties. This sounds stranger than it actually is. It is in the very nature of every new beginning that it breaks into the world as an "infinite improbability," and yet it is precisely this infinite improbability which actually constitutes the very texture of everything we call real....
>
> The decisive difference between the "infinite improbabilities" on which the reality of our earthly life rests and the miraculous character in those events which establish historical reality is that, in the realm of human affairs, we know the author of the "miracles." It is men who perform them – men who because they have received the twofold gift of freedom and action can establish a reality of their own. (1968: 169-171)

Only in the past 2500 years since the famous "Axis Period" in human history (about 800-200 BCE) have human beings emerged out of a mysterious world process on planet Earth that has resulted in our ability to self-consciously evaluate and model our situation (Jaspers 1953). On the evolutionary scale of biological life on this planet (perhaps 3.8 billion years), or even the scale of human life on planet earth (about two million years), this event is just yesterday. Amazing and rapid changes took place during the Axis Period, and we have seen Karl Jaspers reflect above that current changes we are now facing may be even more momentous. We face the possibility of "miraculous" and rapid changes in human consciousness and human existence. Philosopher Ernst Bloch writes:

> The world-substance, mundane matter itself, is not yet finished and complete, but persists in a utopian-open state, i.e. a state in which its self identity is not yet manifest.... Consequently not only the specific existent, but all given existence and being itself, has utopian margins which surround actuality with *real and objective possibility*. (1970: 96)

Those persons awake to the astonishing and miraculous character of all existence and the possibility of "miracles" as the result of free human actions enliven and animate the leadership of the Earth Federation Movement. Such people may or may not be followers of one of the world's great religions: Islam, Christianity, Hinduism, Buddhism, Oomoto, Baha'i, Unitarianism, or Judaism (all these religions and others are represented in the Earth Federation Movement). They may or may not be followers of any religion at all. But this does not prevent them from sharing the profound sensibility into the miraculous possibilities and depths of existence.

The ethical demand alone, an awareness in awake people regardless of their religious orientation, suffices to illuminate our capacity for transformation. Protestant philosopher and theologian Paul Tillich describes these possibilities in the following way:

> For the demand calls for something that does not yet exist but should exist, should come to fulfillment. A being that experiences a demand is no longer simply bound to the origin. Human life involves more than a mere development of what already is. Through the demand, humanity is directed to what ought to be. And what ought to be does not emerge with the unfolding of what is; if it did, it would be something that is, rather than something that ought to be. This means, however, that the demand that confronts humanity is an unconditional demand. The question "Whither?" is not contained within the question "Whence?" It is something unconditionally new that transcends what is new and what is old within the sphere of mere development.... The breaking of the myth of the origin by the unconditional demand is the root of liberal, democratic, and socialist thought in politics.... The demand that separates from the ambiguous origin is the demand of justice. (1987: 143-144)

We have seen above that our moral obligation includes not only personal responsibility for the welfare of every human being but the moral obligation to create democratic world government that can effectively actualize and institutionalize that moral obligation. Tillich makes clear that there is a force that breaks the hold of the past and frees us for actualizing a transformed future. It is the unconditional demand for justice, equality, freedom, and sustainability on Earth, a demand that indeed makes "miracles" possible. The 80% of humanity now marginalized and dehumanized can immediately have their dignity restored with the ratification of the *Earth Constitution*. The fundamental prayer taught to humanity by Jesus, after all, asserts "Thy kingdom come, Thy will be done, on earth as it is in heaven" (Matt. 6:10).

Contemporary Jewish philosopher Immanuel Levinas names this demand "eschatology":

> Eschatology institutes a relation with being *beyond the totality* or beyond history, and not with being beyond the past and the present.... It is a relationship with a *surplus always exterior to the totality,* as though the objective totality did not fill the true measure of being, as though another concept, the concept of *infinity*, were needed to express this transcendence with regard to totality, non encompassable within a totality and as totality.... The eschatological, as the "beyond" of history, draws beings out of the jurisdiction of history and the future; it arouses them in and calls them forth to their full responsibility. (1961: 22-23)

The power of all these great thinkers lies in their transcendence of the mundane, the tired metaphors through which we resign ourselves to history, inevitability, or the drudgery of evolutionary incremental changes. For Levinas, what is "beyond the totality" of the world is the infinite God, which means that human life is not entirely determined by the past, by history, but lives in the possibility that the world can be transformed and that human beings can begin to assume their full ethical responsibility for one another.

Some of this excitement of genuine possibility informs the first document presented below called the "Foundational Principles of the Earth Federation Movement." What that document calls "integrity" is not blind loyalty to dogmatic principles but faithfulness to the highest insights that illuminate the immense possibilities before us for transformation of the world disorder into a place of peace, justice, freedom, and sustainability. Eschatological religions, which include both Judaism and Christianity, express and envision this transformation.

Of all the factors currently influencing the course of human history on the Earth, one of the most profound is the growing awareness of the possibility of extinction through either ecological collapse or nuclear war. We saw Karl Jaspers allude to this above as "immense dangers" that may "herald the failure of mankind." Roman Catholic thinker Jürgen Moltmann discerns in these dangers utopian or eschatological implications:

If the political form of liberty is democracy, the economic form of equality is socialism or communitarianism. If all human beings are created free *and* equal, then the task of modern societies is to harmonize between the right to individual freedom and the right to social equality. Without equal conditions and equal opportunities for living no democracy can function. Without the development of individual freedom no system of social justice can function. The universalism of these declarations can be put into practice only in a world-wide community of states which make these human rights the fundamental rights of their citizens. Of course this was, and is, largely a utopia but it will increasingly become a historical necessity if humanity is to survive. What began as a utopia of messianic humanism is becoming an ecological necessity: the unity of the human race is inexorably required by the unity of the Earth as an organism. (1996: 190-191)

The impending disaster, along with the awareness of the immense possibilities for transformation that inform the human situation, may conspire to effect the ratification of the *Earth Constitution* and the actualization of the Federation of Earth before we know it. It is impossible to predict the future, but many within the Earth Federation Movement have a very clear awareness of what is absolutely necessary for human survival and flourishing as well as the astonishing possibilities that confront humanity at any given historical point.

We are confronted not only with the breakdown of the planetary environment but with a breakdown of the global social system (capitalism and sovereign nation-states) as this developed since the Renaissance. This breakdown has fostered vast ideologies of irrationalism claiming a final conflagration in history such as apocalyptic Christian fundamentalism and Islamic exclusivism claiming an absolute incommensurability between Islam and Western civilization. The Earth Federation Movement is not an ideology claiming to possess the key to history or some "final solution" to human problems. The EFM repudiates all such idolatrous constructions arising from hatred, fear, and resentment. Love does not envision the destruction of some imagined enemy.

The Earth Federation movement understands that only through democratic dialogue with one another can we establish the possibility of a decent future for humanity and that this dialogue can only be effectively established through a binding global social contract. It is also based on a deep understanding of the dangers we face that only increase with each day that we postpone taking effective action. The Earth Federation Movement is the only movement that appears cognizant of both the urgency of our task to construct a non-military democratic Earth Federation and the deep possibilities of its actualization. Perhaps a practical utopia and practical necessity are merging within history as Moltmann argues, and this convergence will result in a rapid general awakening to the imperative of holding a founding ratification convention for the *Earth Constitution*.

The future appears pregnant with immense possibilities, and life in the present attempting to actualize these possibilities is exciting to say the least. We invite serious persons everywhere to sign the *Earth Constitution* and join the Earth Federation Movement, to commit themselves to this act of "civil obedience." To commit to living here and now under the *Earth Constitution* is an act that can be done precisely here and how. As Zinn puts it, "The future is an infinite succession of presents, and to live now as we think human beings should live, in defiance of all that is bad around us, is itself a marvelous victory" (1994: 208). We *should be* living in obedience to the *Earth Constitution*.

The Earth Federation Movement is the worldwide movement most connected to the future, most fundamentally on target as to what can and must be done. We live from what is highest in ourselves it terms of our astonishing human capacity for reason, dialogue, openness, compassion, and love. We are actualizing a global social contract for the people of Earth by living it in the here and now. I believe the official documents collected below, like the *Earth Constitution* itself, demonstrate the truth of this.

PART TWO

DEFINING DOCUMENTS

Document One

Note: Unlike most of other documents below, this one did not come before the Provisional World Parliament. These principles were formulated through discussion among a majority of members of the Board of Trustees of the Institute on World Problems (IOWP) during the fall of 2010 in order to clarify the exceptional character of the Earth Federation Movement in comparison with other international or world federalist organizations.

Earth Federation Movement
Fundamental Principles

Prologue. The Earth Federation Movement (EFM) is an interactive network of world citizens, non-governmental organizations, concerned governments, and peace thinkers dedicated to promoting planetary awareness of the *Constitution for the Federation of Earth.* Together, we also work tirelessly to secure ratification the *Constitution* by the people and nations of Earth. The seven principles expressed here comprise the creed by which we live and the goal to which we give our lives, energy, and resources. These principles are summed up in the following concepts: (1) a *free republic*, (2) *universality* applying to all human beings, (3) a regime *founded* on the highest principles, (4) creation of *living systems,* (5) an *in-depth principle of peace*, (6) deep *sustainability*, and (7) *integrity of the whole.* These principles form the conceptual foundation of the new paradigm of universal civilization embodied in the *Earth Constitution.* Together, they guide us toward a transformed future of human beings and our precious planet Earth.

1) The concept of a universal *free republic*. The very first principle of our movement involves the culmination of the history of political thought in the concept of a free republic embracing all the peoples and citizens of Earth. The idea of freedom, emerging from the deepest levels of the human spirit and the farthest reaches of recorded history, has culminated in the concept of a free, universal planetary republic under the *Constitution for the Federation of Earth.* Our present world of fragmentation and divisiveness defeats human freedom at every turn, replacing our deepest aspirations with violence, hatred, surveillance, systems of domination, and war.

A universal free republic places the emerging Earth Federation at a higher level than a planetary order that merely protects civil liberties for all persons. There exists a vast difference between political and economic thought predicated on the satisfaction of private desires through civil liberties and the political foundations of human freedom centered in a universal republic of free citizens. An authentic republic constitutes a regime of genuine public space for dialogue and debate among all persons and provides for the participation of citizens in all aspects of government.

It provides, therefore, a "public freedom," far transcending mere "private freedom," that brings the historical human quest for freedom to fulfillment within carefully designed planetary institutions. While civil liberties are necessary to a free republic, they are not sufficient – a level of "public freedom" must emerge in which citizens themselves engage directly in governing. The thousands of world citizens involved in the development of the *Earth Constitution* over the space of 33 years from 1958 to 1991 designed a brilliant framework for planetary public freedom, providing for the citizens of Earth to participate in self-government in the multiplicity of ways detailed within the *Constitution.*

2) The principle of universality. The concept of a free republic for the Earth necessarily includes the concept of "all." From the ancient Stoic affirmation of all human beings as creatures of rationality with common moral principles deriving from that rationality to the ringing words of the U.S. Declaration of Independence that "all men are created equal," philosophers and sages have used the word "all" throughout history. But only with the Earth Federation Movement, and some related contemporary global movements, have we begun to really mean "all" when this word is used.

The Stoics excluded "barbarians" from their "all," and the Declaration of Independence excluded women and slaves. However, unlike other contemporary movements that use the word "all," with the intent of true universality, the *Constitution for the Federation of Earth* is not only premised on the concept of "all," it embodies that concept in a set of institutions that brings a mere ideal down into the concrete world of legal, political, and economic arrangements that make this universality a living reality. Like the concept of a "free republic," universality remains a mere ideal until it us embodied in concrete institutions and institutional protections that make it a living reality. The Earth Federation Movement has pledged itself to actualizing this living reality for "all."

3) The principle of a *founded* public regime. The concept of a truly new beginning, of an origin that at the same time raises human life to a higher level of existence, is a principle of utmost importance for the Earth Federation Movement. For the founding principles in such a regime are public and there for all to see, shining through the concrete institutions and arrangements of the emergent Earth Federation. Those organizations of world citizens who are attempting to *evolve* the U.N., to affect small, incremental changes in the unjust and violent disorder of things, fail to understand that the compromises inherent in the evolutionary model of human affairs will forever prostitute the ideals one wishes to achieve. Perpetual compromises with immense systems of economic exploitation and imperial sovereign nation-states have led to disaster after disaster for the people of Earth.

In the ratification of the *Earth Constitution* as an integral, completed, and foundational document lies the assent of humanity to true freedom and dignity. An integral legal system, founded on explicit principles of freedom, justice, prosperity, and peace from the very beginning, avoids the prostitution of deeply held ideals involved in all merely evolutionary models by the forces of unfreedom, injustice, poverty, and war. The *Constitution* embodies its highest ideals within an integrated, holistic, legal system that can substantially actualize these ideals in the daily lives of the people of Earth.

The campaign for ratification of an already completed *Constitution* since 1991 indicates, therefore, a disciplined refusal to offer the *Constitution* as a mere draft that can be forever tinkered with by querulous academic pedants and duplicitous forces that would subvert human progress. The campaign for ratification understands that only a *founded* system, only ratification of a completed document of surpassing brilliance (whatever minor flaws might remain), can establish human freedom upon the Earth. The flourishing (and indeed survival) of human life on our planet can only be accomplished through a founding ratification convention bringing the peoples and nations of the world to a truly higher level of human and political existence.

4) The principle of *living systems* for human economic and political life. A logical implication of the principle of a *founded* free republic involves the principle that *living systems* establish freedom, peace, justice, and prosperity. A widely held assumption today looks at these ideals as reflections of the subjective attitude of people, nations, or economic managers. If the people in government or business are moral, peaceful, and just, it is believed, then this may lead to a world of peace with justice.

This attitude fails to examine the fragmented and distorted institutionalized systems that block morality, peace, and justice no matter who makes-up their institutional participants. If economic institutions are flawed and inherently destructive of people and the environment, it matters little whether the captains of banking and industry are moral or immoral. If the system of sovereign nation-states is inherently a war system and a system of power politics, it matters little who is president or prime minister of various countries.

The Earth Federation Movement understands that freedom, peace, justice, and prosperity primarily arise from properly designed institutions.

If we live under such institutions, democratically and transparently governed, then the flawed human beings who staff these institutions are much more likely to embrace freedom, peace, justice, and universal prosperity. People who staff today's dysfunctional and unjust economic and nation-state institutions are, for that very reason, more likely to embrace unfreedom, war, injustice, and vast poverty in a world of obscene power and riches for the few. The *Earth Constitution* establishes these ideals in an integrated and universal world legal system. It constitutes a freedom system, a peace system, a justice system, and a prosperity system for the people of Earth.

5) Multiple elements within the in-depth principle of *peace.* All seven principles expressed in this document imply one another, including the concept of peace. The condition of peace has remained an illusory ideal throughout recorded human history. The tragic history of war and violence has created a nightmare for a large portion of the Earth's citizens over the centuries, including today. Pursuit of the ideal of world peace in today's world has resulted in a number significant movements. Among the most prominent of these are movements for peace education and groups devoted to the quest for inner peace.

Both inner peace and peace education are important elements in the quest for a peaceful world order (which would necessarily also be a free, just, and prosperous world order). But inner peace and peace education can never be sufficient, for the most fundamental dimension of peace is yet missing: the institutionalization of a *peace system* for the Earth. The *Constitution for the Federation of Earth,* along with its principles developed by the Provisional World Parliament under the authority of Article 19, establishes a dynamic peace system for the Earth.

Among the *Constitution's* institutionalized elements of an in-depth peace system include (1) universal, transparent democracy for all nations and peoples, (2) enforceable, democratically legislated laws ensuring that no one is above the law, (3) systematic and carefully designed demilitarization for all the nations and organizations of the Earth, (4) mechanisms preventing remilitarization or reestablishing of institutions or organizations predicated upon violence, (5) prohibition of all military for the Earth Federation government itself, (6) judicial institutions for the peaceful settlement of disputes among all people and nations, (7) institutionalized protections of human rights and freedoms for all people on Earth, along with their right to participate in governing themselves on multiple levels from local to planetary, (8) the substantial elimination of poverty, misery, and disease from the Earth and creation of an infrastructure for keeping the people of Earth healthy and economically secure, (9) the development of worldwide institutions for mediation and conflict resolution designed to promote peace and mutual understanding among people, obviating in most cases the need to call upon the judicial system, and (10) worldwide peace education for all children in Earth Federation supported schools, and, through public radio, TV, and Internet, for all adults within the Earth Federation.

The principle of *living systems* is here briefly illustrated in the principle of an in-depth peace system for the Earth. All successful living systems must include a free republic, must be universal, must be founded, and must embody multiple, integrated elements, under the rule of enforceable law, as illustrated in this example of an in-depth peace system. The *Constitution for the Federation of Earth* is the only living document today that includes all of these elements necessary for moving the human project to the next higher level of planetary existence.

6) The principle of universal *sustainability*. The concept of sustainability developed from the ecological sciences has become a fundamental principle for understanding the relationship between human economic, political, and social activity and the carrying capacity and ecological integrity of the ecosystem of our planet. We live today, as in the past, in an unsustainable manner that destroys the ecological integrity of our planet's life-support system.

Today's unsustainable world disorder includes far more than a life-style carrying an "ecological footprint" greater than the planet will bear. It also includes vast poverty in the world's population forcing desperate people to deforest the world, to produce very large families, and to over-cultivate land and over-exploit resources. It includes the vast military apparatus of the world that is deadly for the environment not only in the production of horrid bombs and chemicals but even more deadly when these technologies of death and destruction are used around the world. It includes an economic system predicated on private profit without regard to any human values, including sustainability, that systematically externalizes the costs of production into the environment and onto society in a process that amounts to eating our planetary biosphere alive.

Sustainability, therefore, like peace, is a comprehensive principle requiring transformation of our entire planetary system as envisaged by the *Earth Constitution*. Sustainability applies not only to the ecological footprint of consumers. Rather, it is universal, as it applies to all the central institutions that structure our lives at every level. The present global economic system is unsustainable. The present system of sovereign nation-states is unsustainable. The present cultural patterns of consumption and personal gratification are unsustainable. Global poverty signifies unsustainability for our entire planet as does global militarism.

The *Earth Constitution* provides the foundation for political, social, ecological, and economic sustainability for our endangered planet Earth. Sustainability can only be achieved through democratic world law within a transparent, institutionally sound, democratic world system. Sustainability is a comprehensive financial, social and ecological concept that cannot be achieved without ratification of the *Constitution for the Federation of Earth.*

7) The principle of *integrity of the whole.* The integrity of the whole arises from the systemic and integrated wholeness of the system articulated in the *Constitution* and the understanding that *wholeness itself* is the most fundamental principle discovered by virtually every science of the 20th and 21st centuries.

Human life on Earth is a whole. Our personal individuality in relation to our "species-nature" as language using creatures is a whole. The biosphere of our planet is a whole; our solar system is a whole – our galaxy and, ultimately, our universe are integral wholes. In religious language, God is the principle of integrity and wholeness in all things, "through whom all things were made."

The *Earth Constitution* embodies this principle in human economic, political, and social life at the planetary level. It is wholeness that carries natural, spiritual, and moral integrity, not division, violence, or fragmentation. The integrity of the *Earth Constitution* lives in its wholeness, and in the wholeness of the Earth Federation that it establishes for the Earth. That is why freedom, peace, justice, and prosperity are the substantial consequences of its ratification and implication. It is the whole that has integrity, and the *Constitution* institutionalizes that integrity for human society for the first time in history.

This wholeness and its integrity can only be protected and concretely established through ratification of the *Earth Constitution*. The whole of our world system, a system of freedom, peace, justice, and prosperity, will then ascend to an inviolable integrity. These are the principles to which we pledge ourselves, and which we pledge to one another – to all humanity, and to future generations living upon the Earth. It is the institutionalized integrity of the whole that will lead future human beings to live lives of dignity, reverence, and honor upon our precious planet Earth.

Epilogue. The principles at the heart of the Earth Federation Movement are the most fundamental principles of ethical and political thought. Our thought and action are directed toward the primacy of human freedom for every person and community on Earth. The conceptual foundations of the *Earth Constitution*, upon which our work is based, involve only the most fundamental and universal of principles,

principles necessary for coherent, integrated, and consistent thought regarding the human condition at the dawn of the 21st century.

Our movement refuses to adulterate its conceptual foundations with the cynicism, skepticism, relativism, and superficiality that today dominate thought within both nation-states and the United Nations. We have not watered down our work with ideas of limited and secondary value, ideas that clandestinely import fragmentation, division, and violence into human affairs. Such limited and secondary ideas include the sovereignty of nation-states as well as false notions of unbridgeable divisions among religions, races, cultures, ethnicities, or creeds. Such adulterating ideas also include the necessity of compromise with the corrupt regimes and prostituted principles that we find everywhere prevalent within our current world of fragmentation, chaos, and disorder.

Our personal integrity resides in the rigorous honesty with which we critique the present world of injustice, violence, and unsustainability. It resides in our unfailing commitment to remain loyal to the highest principles arising from the human mind and human history, and from our determination to institute these principles within a transformed world order predicated on freedom, justice, prosperity, and peace for all human beings everywhere. Our integrity lies in our word, in the sanctity and faithfulness of our word in relation to the principles to which we have pledged ourselves. It also lies in the quality of thought and action arising from our principles, thought and action vigilant against a pragmatism that forever compromises with a corrupt status quo.

This rigorous honesty and sanctity of our words and pledges themselves arise from a yet deeper level of insight. We pledge not only to the highest principles of human thought that constitute the foundations of our movement, but we pledge to one another to engage the future and our commitments through mutual dialogue, respect, understanding, and shared vision. Our pledges, therefore, maintain an unfailing commitment while avoiding dogmatism and closed-mindedness. For we commit to the highest principles of dialogue, discussion, and communication with all willing persons. This communicative foundation constitutes the living, phenomenological dynamic from which our highest principles and concepts emerge. Our integrity flows from this communicative foundation and from our commitment to these highest principles of human and planetary life.

Document Two

Note: A version of this document was originally adopted at the Second Constituent Assembly in Colombo, Sri Lanka in 1979. It asserts the rights of people to create world government even without the cooperation of the nation-states. The expanded version below was deliberated and adopted by the 8th session of the Provisional World Parliament, meeting in August 2004, at City Montessori School, Lucknow, Uttar Pradesh, India.

Declaration of the Rights
of the People of Earth to create and ratify a World Constitution and hold sessions of the Provisional World Parliament

We, the citizens of the Earth, have the right and duty to establish a viable world government capable of maintaining the Rule of Law among all nations in place of the disastrous anarchy now prevailing among sovereign states, to abolish massively destructive armaments and end all wars, to protect the global environment for future generations, and to create economic justice and prosperity for all the citizens of our planet.

1. These are the times the world will not soon forget. Future historians will wonder how a few of us maintained our sanity and dignity in the face of the global breakdown of world order. Never in history have so many people been starving to death on Earth. Never have so many people lacked clean water or sanitation. Never has there been so much poverty and misery.

Never in history have so many people possessed so many weapons and engaged in continuous mutual slaughter of one another, in Columbia, Afghanistan, Sudan, Uganda, Chechnya, Iraq and elsewhere. Never have human beings everywhere on Earth been so insecure. Never has the average person anywhere on Earth felt so afraid and the future seemed so hopeless. Fifteen years after the collapse of the USSR, the threat of a global nuclear holocaust remains in place, while the superpower continues to develop space-based and tactical nuclear weapons.

Nowhere in previous history has the world faced a possible breakdown of its planetary ecosystem. Never has the ozone layer that protects the Earth from the sun's deadly radiation been threatened. Never have the ocean fisheries been collapsing from over-fishing, never before has grazing land been turning to desert on a global scale from overgrazing, never has agricultural land disappeared at the astonishing rates that we see today. Never before has the world's fresh water supply been endangered.

2. Some people in every age of historical crisis have been the visionaries, the civilizers, the advanced thinkers, who see the way forward beyond the narrow assumptions and petty issues of their day. Some people in every age have spoken for universal principles, for justice and human dignity, for equality and freedom among nations, peoples, and individuals of the Earth. These are the civilizers; these are the voices of legitimate creativity. These are the ones who establish new institutions and give renewed hope for the future.

The legitimacy of an action is not always whether it is approved by some majority. Very often in history the majority have represented reaction, intolerance, and injustice. The legitimacy of an action is whether it moves history forward toward greater universality. The innovators within history, like the writers of the French Declaration of the Rights of Man or the U.N. Universal Declaration of Human Rights, have always been a tiny minority.

The legitimacy of their work derives from its universality. The movement of history, the extension of rights, is from the tribe to the clan to the territory to the nation to the entire planet. The ultimate universality is the sovereignty of the people of Earth. New eras of legitimacy in history have been initiated by those who extended human rights and freedom to ever greater numbers of people and to those who promoted the just rule of law in human affairs.

The criterion of legitimacy in human affairs is moral universality. The core of democracy is not majority rule but the protection of minorities from both majorities and tyrants. It is equal rights for all under just laws. Nor is legitimacy derived from either power or existing institutions by themselves. Gigantic systems of power have existed historically from the Roman Empire to the many European Empires, to the present American Empire. The fact of military, bureaucratic, or institutional power does not lend legitimacy.

The only criterion is whether human rights, dignity, freedom, and justice prevail because of these institutions. This is why democracy is the ultimate criterion of legitimacy, democracy defined as any system that promotes rights, dignity, freedom, and justice in human affairs. Only global democracy represents the sovereignty of the people of Earth.

3. The present institutions of the world are failed institutions. The global economic system has not led to prosperity for most of the Earth's citizens, but to starvation, poverty, disease, and misery for the majority. The present global political systems of the world, called territorial nation-states, have not led to a just or peaceful world order, but to endless wars, destruction of peoples and cultures, imperial domination and conquest, and global systems of exploitation of the weaker by the stronger.

The United Nations has not led to a world where the many rights listed in its Universal Declaration of Human Rights have been extended to the Earth's citizens, but to denial of those rights for the majority and continuous increase in war, poverty, social chaos, and environmental destruction. By the criterion of legitimacy set forth in this document, these institutions have made themselves illegitimate. Citizens of Earth have the right and duty to create new institutions that represent the people of Earth.

4. The sovereignty of the people of Earth is represented in those who seek universal human political, social, and economic rights. The sovereignty of the people of Earth is represented in those who seek universal economic justice and the common good of all who live on Earth. The sovereignty of the people of Earth is represented by those who promote the rule of law on Earth and an end to the barbaric rule of militarized force and violence. The sovereignty of the people of Earth is represented by those who seek global democracy in the form of federal world government.

It is irrelevant whether the people of Earth elected representatives to write the *Constitution for the Federation of Earth*. What matters is that the people of Earth have the opportunity to ratify the *Constitution* and begin the rule of just law in the world. It is irrelevant whether delegates to the Provisional World Parliament were elected by their countries as representatives to the Parliament. What matters is that the delegates promote universal human rights, justice, freedom, and prosperity.

Those who represent the people of Earth in this quest are not self-appointed partisans of special interests. Such self-appointed demagogues are easily identifiable by their programs that always deny rights and dignity to those they oppose. Delegates to the Provisional World Parliament are appointed, under Article 19 of the *Constitution*, by the universal principle of morality on which the *Constitution* is based that is the criterion of legitimacy in human political and economic affairs. Their work includes all persons on Earth, and excludes none.

5. At this juncture of world history, no nation can have a fully legitimate democracy. For the very existence of "sovereign" nations means that the rights of those outside its borders are ignored or betrayed. At this junction of world history, no nation can protect the environment for future generations. The destruction of the planetary ecosystem is beyond the scope and effectiveness of any nation-state.

At this juncture of world history, no nation can create economic justice. For in today's globalized economy, prosperity for individual nations always involves exploitation and poverty for other nations. The nation-state system is dead. Only those representing global democracy through federal world government can possibly represent legitimacy in human affairs.

The present world system not only embodies failed institutions but it is also built on morally illegitimate institutions. Every human being is morally required to live under democratically legislated universal laws. Without the rule of enforceable world law, human affairs are always in a *de facto* state of war in which the stronger or more clever will be able to take advantage of the weaker.

Genuine law legislates equality, freedom, and the principle of justice for all. Yet in the world system today there is no genuine law, for nations are all victims to the social, military, and economic chaos that characterizes international affairs and afflicts all persons living within particular nation-states. The unenforceable pronouncements of the treaty system that constitutes the United Nations is a travesty of genuine "international law." We are morally required to live under universal democracy and federal world government representing all persons on Earth equally and creating the just rule of enforceable law on Earth.

6. In the face of our world condition in the past five decades, world citizens had every right to create the *Constitution for the Federation of Earth*. In the face of the global chaos resulting from monopoly capitalism and the system of sovereign nation-states, these world citizens also had a duty to write a *Constitution for the Federation of Earth*. We do not characterize these acts as the noble actions of do-gooders contributing to the human project. We describe here the universal duty of every citizen on Earth to live under the rule of enforceable world law.

Our work is not only more legitimate than that of politicians within nations who pass legislation excluding the majority of humanity from the laws they write. Our work is absolutely obligated by the demand for universality in human affairs and by the need to protect future generations from the lethal consequences of present institutions. It is with this understanding that we affirm our right and duty to hold future sessions of the Provisional World Parliament, to work unceasingly to activate the fledgling institutions of democratic world government, and to communicate to every citizen on Earth the absolute need to ratify the *Constitution for the Federation of Earth.*

Document Three

Note: This document was adopted 6th September, 1982, at the first session of the Provisional World Parliament meeting at the Royal Pavilion in Brighton, England. The first draft was written by John Stockwell. The work was introduced by Sally Curry, delegate Member of the Parliament from Canada. It clearly demonstrates the concern and compassion for animals and nature that have characterized the Earth Federation Movement and world legislation from the very beginning.

Declaration of the Rights of Animals and Nature in the Federation of Earth

Recognizing that, in the words of Sir Muhammad Zafrulla Khan, the human being must be a source of bliss for every being; recognizing also that the human being is not the only source of bliss;

Recognizing that, in the words of Sri Krishna, all are one–and that, in the words of Albert Schweitzer, the way back to civilization lies through the reverence for life;

Aware, as stated in the Preamble to the *Constitution for the Federation of Earth*, of the interdependence of people, nations and all life–and aware that man's abuse of science and technology has brought humanity also to the brink of ecological catastrophe;

Recognizing that, as described in the Global 2000 Report to the President of the United States, the destruction of the natural world has progressed to an advanced stage, to a stage where, many authorities agree, within 30 to 50 years perhaps 50% or more of the world's animal species will have become extinct– unless the prevalent attitude of humanity toward the status of animals changes radically;

Recognizing that, at least since the time of Darwin, it has been scientifically established that humankind shares in significant degree a common origin with the rest of the natural world and especially with its animal species;

Recognizing that, with few exceptions, under present law the inhumane treatment of animals is common practice in scientific laboratories, factory farms, and at the hands of hunters and trappers–and that present national basic laws do little to implement an ethic of the protection of nature;

Recognizing that we need to be concerned not only with the future of humanity, but also, under the *Constitution for the Federation of Earth*, with the fate of the planet;

Recognizing, finally, that under the Call to the Provisional World Parliament, the business of the Parliament includes a concern with global environmental protection;

And as an expression of love;

THEREFORE, be it enacted by this provisional World Parliament in first session, 1982:

1. From the date of adoption of this resolution by the provisional World Parliament, in all considerations and decisions bearing upon the present conditions and future of humanity, the Earth Federation shall consider the interests of other species.

2. From the date of adoption of this resolution by the provisional World Parliament, the following activities are strongly discouraged or prohibited:

2.1. All practices of factory farming involving animals;

2.2. Research using animals as experimental subjects, of the trapping and hunting of animals except by peoples for their own subsistence use, and not including for cash sales or trade;

2.3. Employment of animals in cruel sport;

2.4. Removal of species from native habitat, in disregard of protective standards for removals;

2.5. Production of so-called animal "products" for profit.

3. The provisional World Parliament and provisional World Government shall establish a World Environmental Protection Agency, which shall include in the scope of its responsibilities the implementation of this resolution and the supervision of the establishment of the recognition of animal rights throughout the world. (See WLA#9 summary or full text, first adopted 1987, 3rd session, revised 2004, 8th session.)

4. Until a more fully operative democratic world federation is established, the World Environmental Protection Agency is responsible to the provisional World Parliament, and to any provisional World Cabinet that is created by the provisional World Parliament. The World Environmental Protection Agency has a Board of Trustees of twenty-five members, to be appointed by the provisional World Cabinet, to be drawn from all parts of the Earth, and to include no fewer than five well-known advocates of animal rights. The Board of Trustees shall determine the organization and functioning of the World Environmental Protection Agency in accordance with the terms of this resolution and in conformance with the *Constitution for the Federation of Earth,* while at all times responsible to the Cabinet and Parliament. No nation may have veto powers in the decisions of the World Environmental Protection Agency.

5. At subsequent sessions of the provisional World Parliament, the Parliament will review implementation of this resolution, and will take further action as appropriate.

Document Four

Note: This document was adopted as world statutory code (World Legislative Act Number 9) by the third session of the Provisional World Parliament, convened in conformance with Article 19 of the *Earth Constitution*, in the Hilton Fontainebleau Hotel, Miami Beach, Florida, United States, in June 1987.

Amendments were adopted at the eighth (2004) session of the Parliament. It clearly shows the route to global protection of our planetary environment that is mandated by the *Earth Constitution*.

World Legislative Act #9

Global Ministry of Environment

Short title:

Environment Ministry

WHEREAS:

Thirty-four years after the first United Nations Conference on the Environment, held at Stockholm, Sweden, in 1970, many global environmental problems are evident, and some of them are worsening progressively;

There are serious problems in our world in terms of:

• Lack of industrial safety;
• Pollution;
• Improper selection of technology;
• Unequal distribution of the benefits of technological development;

Many problems of the environment affect humanity as a whole, for example:

1. Deforestation,
2. Loss of top soil,
3. Acid rain and snow,
4. Worsening climate,
5. Increase of carbon-dioxide in the atmosphere,
6. Ozone depletion,
7. Toxic wastes,
8. Extinction of species,
9. Noise pollution,

10. Degradation of mountains,
11. Widespread hunger, resulting from agricultural disruptions,
12. Pollution of major river systems,
13. Export of hazardous wastes and pollutants to the "third world".

The Earth is the only world we have, and environmental problems disregard boundaries;

Most problems of the environment are supra national, and therefore require a global or trans-national approach to identify and find solutions to those problems of the environment which need to be solved on a global basis, and by the provisional World Parliament.

The Earth Federation must protect Nature for its unique value in the health and recovery of humans.

THEREFORE:

Article 1. This third session of the provisional World Parliament hereby establishes a Global Ministry of Environment. The Global Ministry of Environment (GME) is authorized to do the following:

1.1. Identify the major issues of environment disruptions and problems;

1.2. Monitor environmental dangers;

1.3. Solve world environmental problems on a global or transnational scale;

1.4. Co-ordinate all efforts before problems and situations become irreversible;

1.5. Identify the major causes of animals and plants becoming extinct;

1.6. Identify possible preventions and remedies to threats of extinction; and

1.7. Implement remedies and preventive measures to prevent extinctions.

Article 2. The Global Ministry of Environment shall work with agencies of the Integrative Complex to solve Global Environmental Problems according to the following directives:

2.1. The increase of carbon-dioxide in the atmosphere

2.1.1. The GME shall coordinate with the World Hydrocarbon Resource Board to reduce the consumption of fossil fuels. The GME shall plan large-scale measures to control pollution, and to protect the eco-system as the basis of human existence;

2.1.2. Until the Energy Ministry is established, the GME shall receive plans, including grant proposals for sustainable solar, hydrogen, electromagnetic, biological and other energy sources;

2.1.3. The GME will coordinate with the <u>Emergency Earth Rescue Administration</u> and the Agency for Technological and Environmental Assessment for the world-wide program of re-forestation and afforestation, with emphasis on fast growing trees having economic value, avoiding monocultures;

2.1.4. The GME shall report semi-annually to the World Executive on the Emergency Earth Rescue Administration actions to re-mineralize forest lands to promote and protect the healthy growth of all forests.

2.2. Oceans

2.2.1. This Act re-confirms international convention regulations that tankers carrying oil must be doubly protected, unless legally emptied and withdrawn from use. The GME shall report semi-annually to the World Oceans and Seabeds Authority regarding commercial and government compliance with oil tanker regulations.

2.2.2. The GME shall work with the <u>Commission for Legislative Review</u> to draft world legislation that sewage from cities must be adequately treated before discharged into rivers and oceans. The plan shall include estimates for Earth Federation subsidies of municipal sewage treatment systems for cities and populated areas that have not been able to develop adequate sewage treatment systems under national and international programs.

2.2.3. The GME shall work with the Commission for Legislative Review to draft world legislation to fully protect from harmful exploitation the Arctic and Antarctic regions.

2.2.4. The oceans and seabeds are the property of all humanity, under jurisdiction and management of the <u>World Oceans and Seabeds Authority (WOSA)</u>. The GME shall coordinate with the WOSA to ensure the protection of the oceans and seabeds.

2.2.5. The GME will coordinate with the Emergency Earth Rescue Administration and the Agency for Technological and Environmental Assessment for the world-wide program of ocean and lake re-mineralization, with emphasis on blends of minerals that encourage phytoplankton growth of species that do not cause de-oxyfication of the oceans, lakes and atmosphere. The GME shall report semi-annually to the World Executive on the Emergency Earth Rescue Administration actions to re-mineralize the oceans , including reports on oxygen levels of both the ocean and atmosphere at numerous recording points.

2.2.6. The GME shall coordinate with the WOSA to otherwise protect the oceans and seabeds against pollution;

2.3. Forests

2.3.1. The GME shall recommend the particular assortment of properly selected trees and plants to the Emergency Earth Rescue Administration (EERA) in the massive world-wide reforestation and afforestation program, being careful not to upset the eco-system The GME will assess the impact of native and introduced species in the operations of the EERA, to reduce harmful interactions in the EERA operations. The GME shall assess the effect on both local native flora and local native fauna. When feasible, the GME will recommend native flora. However, in cases where extinction prevents reintroduction of native species, the GME may recommend use of introduced species, if introduced species do not further damage the ecology.

2.3.2. Until the Energy Ministry is established, the GME shall work with the Commission for Legislative Review to draft world legislation to assist people who depend on trees for fuel to transition to non-hydrocarbon energy sources, in order to avoid excessive cutting of trees for firewood, and burning of brush for kindling or clearance. The GME shall encourage composting of brush, rather than the burning of brush, unless composting interferes with natural fire cycles required for ecosystem sustenance;

2.3.3. The GME shall coordinate with other agencies of the Earth Federation to promote family planning as part of the global development program;

2.4. Acid Rain

2.4.1. The GME shall determine pollution control standards in manufacturing to reduce oxides of nitrogen and sulphur; The GME shall plan large-scale measures to control pollution, and to protect the eco-system as the basis of human existence.

2.4.2. The GME shall determine pollution control standards and measures to control and eliminate causes of acid rain in transportation. In particular, the GME shall assess full costs of hydrocarbon combustion, to eliminate hydrocarbons as fuels, while there are still hydrocarbons available for lubricants and plastics for both present and future generations of people.

2.5. Mountains

2.5.1. This Act designates high mountains, such as the Himalayas, the Andes and the Alps, as Areas of World Protection. In particular, high mountains above the timberline, above the arable regions and above the regions customarily inhabited are under protection and jurisdiction of the Earth Federation.

2.5.2. The GME will monitor uses of high mountains to conserve and protect both the mountain environments and the areas downstream, which are of transnational concern.

2.5.3. This Act recognizes the value of certain high mountain areas in equatorial regions as potential sites for future spaceports. In particular, the equatorial Andean region is most suitable for spaceports. This Act discourages land speculation in this region. For the purpose of eminent domain for spaceport development, the Earth Federation will compensate landowners with title to no more than the current August 15th 2004 land value assessments on the market in the equatorial Andean area.

2.6. The Global Ministry of Environment shall protect endangered animals and plants;
    The Ministry shall use the various conservation categories of the International Union of Conservation of Nature and Natural Resources (ICUN) [ed. World Conservation Union]; and Mace & Lande (1991);

2.7. Review Pertinent International Convention Law. The Ministry shall review international convention law regarding the environment for integration and codification into World Law, submitting proposals to Commission for Legislative Review:

2.7.1. Basel Convention (www.basel.int)

2.7.2. Biodiversity Convention (www.biodiv.org)

2.7.3. Climate Change Convention & Kyoto Protocol (www.unfccc.org)

2.7.4. Convention on International Trade in Endangered Species or Wild Fauna and Flora (CITES) (www.cites.org)

2.7.5. London Dumping Convention (www.londonconvention.org)

2.7.6. Migratory Species Convention (www.cms.int)

2.7.7. Montreal Protocol (www.unep.org/ozone)

2.7.8. Ramsar Wetlands Convention (www.ramsar.org) .

Article 3. Further Detailed Steps to be Taken

3.01. The GME shall determine the damage of used radiological, chemical and biological weapons and affected areas. The GME will attempt to develop technology to remove radiological, chemical and biological wastes from affected areas.

3.02. The GME shall coordinate with the World Disarmament Agency to sequester or render harmless radiological, chemical and biological materials to protect the environment.

3.03. The Ministry of Environment will coordinate with a Space Administration to protect the environment, including the environment of outer space, the moon, asteroids and planets. The provisional World Parliament or World Parliament will establish the Space Administration under separate legislation.

3.04. The GME may coordinate or cooperation with environmental organizations and governmental authorities to exchange information;

3.05. The Global Ministry of Environment may coordinate with the environmental agencies of the United Nations system.

3.06. In coordination with the <u>World University System</u>, and in particular with the Institute on Governmental Procedures and World Problems, the GME may establish training centers;

3.07. The GME shall develop and implement energy conservation, recycling and energy-equivalency standards so that energy will be saved;

3.08. The GME shall work with the Commission for Legislative Review to draft world legislation to conserve and distribute surplus agricultural food stocks, such as in the USA and the European Community. Until a Ministry of Food, Agriculture and Nutrition is developed, the GME shall monitor food stocks. The GME may permit destruction of spoiled crops only. Intentional destruction of surplus agricultural food stocks without a permit is prohibited (class 3 felony)

The world legislation shall include provisions to prevent food surplus distributions from disrupting local economies.

3.09. The GME may monitor wet-lands to protect from industrial uses, and from developmental encroachment. This Act recognizes the international convention for the protection of wetlands.

3.10. The GME shall work with the Commission for Legislative Review to draft world legislation to give preference to the use of trains and buses as means of public transport;

Article Four • Guidelines for the Specific Action Program of the Ministry of Environment

4.1. This Act promotes environmental education at every level of society in cooperation with the Ministry of Education.

4.2. Developers and governmental agencies shall select appropriate technology, whether large or small, for development projects.

4.3. A major project is defined as a development activity that might adversely affect the global environment on a large scale, such as the building of a large dam on a major transnational river, or the enlargement of port facilities on a seacoast. The mining of hydrocarbons is a major project, unless the hydrocarbons retrieved are naturally at the surface. This Act requires prior environmental assessment for any major project that may affect the global environment. Utilizing public or private funds for any major project that may affect the environment without first obtaining environmental assessment is unlawful (class 3 felony). This Act requires permits from the GME for major projects. Beginning or continuing a major project without a GME permit is unlawful (class 3 felony)

Projects that begin or are already continuing within 12 months of the adoption of this world legislation are special cases that the GME may address outside of World Court.

The GME shall work with the Commission for Legislative Review to draft world legislation to regulate major projects.

This Act promotes selection of appropriate technology for development projects, whether major projects or small scale projects;

4.4. The establishment of an international conservation agency under the Ministry of Environment must include a program and standards for the recycling of materials;

4.5. Each session of the provisional World Parliament shall revise the action program of the Ministry of Environment. The GME shall deliver an annual report at each session, or at least annually.

Article Five • Creation of the Global Ministry of Environment

Within three months after the approval of this Act by the provisional World Parliament, the Global Ministry of Environment shall begin operation. The Environment Ministry has the authority to supervise the determinations and implementation of this Act. The Environment Ministry is responsible to the provisional World Parliament, as well as to the provisional World Cabinet.

The GME shall receive assessments from the Agency for Technological and Environmental Assessment and other agencies of the Integrative Complex.

Article Six • Composition of the Global Ministry of Environment

This Act composes a Governing Council for the Global Ministry of Environment of from 15 to 95 Trusteeship Council Members, composing a Council of which a maximum of 32 members may come from any single continent of Earth, and a maximum of 12 members from any single country. At no time can more than one-third of the Council members be from any single continent.

6.1.1. The provisional World Parliament shall nominate six Parliamentary Members;

6.1.2. Each Agency of the Integrative Complex shall nominate one member, for a total of 7 Agency Members from the Integrative Complex;

6.1.3. The Attorneys General Office and the World Ombudsen shall each nominate one member;

6.1.4. The first 25 nations to preliminarily ratify or finally ratify the *Earth Constitution* may each nominate a Member. After more than 25 countries have accepted Lines of Credit, then for the election of successive terms for Directors, each national government shall nominate one candidate and the total of 25 Directors shall be elected by a combined vote of the national governments.

6.1.5. Each of the twenty World Electoral and Administrative Regional Ministers shall appoint a Member;

6.1.6. The first 35 non-national sources of funding to the Earth Federation Funding Corporation eligible to name a Director to the EFFC, may also name a Trusteeship Council Member. After more than 35 non-national sources have accepted Lines of Credit, then for the election of successive terms for Directors, each no-national source shall nominate one candidate and the total of 35 Directors shall be elected by a combined vote of the non-national sources. These posts continue until the full operative stage of world government, at which time the posts will sunset;

6.2. Trusteeship Council Members hold office for three years. Agencies, countries or organizations may re-elect Members.

6.3. By simple majority vote, the provisional World Parliament may expel Members for cause.

6.4. The original nominating agency, country or organization for Members fills respective vacancies in the Trusteeship Council. 6.5. The provisional World Parliament or World Parliament shall elect a Minister for Environment from among their own members. The Minister for Environment shall nominate a Senior Administrator from the Civil Service lists. If these lists have not yet been compiled, the Minister may make any appointment, subject to approval or disapproval by the simple majority vote of Trusteeship Council and the provisional World Parliament, voting separately.

6.6. The Trusteeship Council shall decide the further form of organization and the functions of the Global Ministry of Environment, in accordance with the aims and specifications of this Act, and in accordance with the *Earth Constitution*. The Trusteeship Council is responsible to the provisional World Parliament and to the provisional World Cabinet.

Document Five

Note: This resolution was adopted at the sixth session of the Provisional World Parliament in Bangkok, Thailand, March, 2003. Its intent is to make clear that fears of overweening bureaucracy as well as fears of totalitarian government are unfounded as far as the Earth Constitution is concerned.

Resolution on the Spirit of Global Government under the *Constitution for the Federation of Earth*

We, the delegates of the Sixth Provisional World Parliament at Bangkok, meeting under the auspices of the *Constitution for the Federation of Earth* in March 2003, do hereby affirm the following resolution:

In the light of the fact that many people today express a fear of what they call "big government", a sentiment that makes them hesitate before the idea of world government out of concern that local autonomy and individuality may be diminished,

In the light of the fact that many people today express a fear of what they call "bureaucracy", a sentiment that individual freedoms may be curtailed under a global federal bureaucracy that might require permits for everything and anything that people wish to do,

In the light of the fact that some nation-states today express a fear that world government might diminish their integrity and autonomy as individual nations, which they now claim is defended under the concept of "national sovereignty",

WE WISH TO EMPHASIZE that the *Constitution for the Federation of Earth* is carefully written to eliminate these potential dangers of world government. The Preamble of the Constitution asserts that "the principle of unity in diversity is the basis for a new age when war shall be outlawed and peace prevail; and when basic human rights and responsibilities shall be shared by all without discrimination." The Constitution is written with the protection of individuals and the integrity of nations in mind, and creates a separate branch of government known as the World Ombudsmus to explicitly prevent world government from violating the rights and freedoms of individuals, groups and nations.

At this Provisional World Parliament, we assembled delegates wish to emphasize these principles embodied in the world constitution by formulating a guideline for future legislation:

The foundation of a secure future for humanity and our natural environment is genuine democracy for all citizens of the planet. This means the empowerment of citizens from the local level to the global level through a social infrastructure providing education and other institutions aimed at making possible effective participation of citizens in democratic decision making.

We wish to emphasize that world government must be a federal system that preserves sufficient local autonomy for citizens to concretely work for justice and the redress of grievances on all levels from local, to national, to global. They must be free to pass local laws to address their particular concerns within the larger democratic framework of a world government that ensures universal political, economic and social rights to all.

Citizens must be encouraged by world government to recognize and challenge undemocratic institutions and practices at every level. The *Constitution* as quoted above emphasizes responsibilities as well as rights. World government must encourage a broad range of active citizen involvement in democratic processes. Active citizenship and taking responsibility is not fully accomplished through periodic voting, but through attending public forums, organizing, signing petitions, protesting, street theatre, civil disobedience, writing articles and editorials, contributing money, teaching, supporting and establishing alternative media, and many other ways. The active involvement and critical questioning upon which the democratic process depends both permits and encourages each citizen to take active responsibility for good government.

Similarly, nation-states must be protected from unwanted imperialism by other nations-states, or by world government itself, whether this takes the forms of cultural, economic or power based attempts at coercion. The integrity and autonomy of individual nation-states can only be effectively protected by the democratic authority of the whole of humanity, which is the only legitimate sovereign on Earth. Under the principle of unity in diversity, a truly federal system emphasizing the diversity of individuals, peoples, and nations is to be promoted and protected. This resolution emphatically states that future legislation enacted under the *Constitution for the Federation of Earth* should conform to the principles outlined herein.

Document Six

Note: This document was authored and introduced by Eugenia Almand, JD, Secretary, Provisional World Parliament. It was deliberated and adopted at the 12th Session of the Parliament at Kolkata, India, December 28, 2010. It authorizes states in the U.S., cantons in China, or Pradesh in India to join the Earth Federation as independent nations to be represented in the House of Nations. In doing so, it significantly and appropriately increases the representation from these areas of the world within the World Parliament.

Declaration of World Federal Distinction

Whereas much of the world is already divided into various continental or sub-continental federations;

Whereas in addition to continental and sub-continental federations, there are also cases of regional military blocks that divide and endanger the peace of Earth by their very existence;

Whereas the nature of the social contract within federal union is fundamentally and essentially different from the social contract or lack thereof within any confederation, alliance or treaty system;

Whereas, up to the present, there has been confusion at some levels supposing that a nation could enter the Earth Federation by any treaty, alliance or confederation;

Whereas, up to the present there has been apparent confusion at some levels that the *Constitution for the Federation of Earth* were a proposal for a treaty, or for a new system of treaties, alliances, blocks or confederation;

This twelfth session of the World Parliament convening at Kolkata, in December 2010, under the authority of Article 19 of the *Constitution for the Federation of Earth*, hereby declares and reaffirms the principle of world federal distinction—that preliminary ratification of the *Constitution for the Federation of Earth* is an internal affair for both the respective state ratifying as well as for the Earth Federation. Unlike a treaty system, alliance or confederation, states within the Earth Federation have no exterior relation vis-à-vis the Earth Federation. From member states of the Earth Federation, there are no ambassadors appointed to represent the state, because there is no con-federal relation. For member states of the

Earth Federation, there is no exterior relation but rather a federal relation to other states of the Earth Federation, as well as to the Earth Federation itself.

This principle recognizes states and federal relation based upon world constitutional ratification, not upon military prowess, and not upon continental federation. The Earth Federation recognizes nationhood based upon ratification, not based upon prior status in any alliance, confederation, treaty system, continental federation or sub-continental union. In keeping with this principle, the constituent states, cantons, Pradesh or provinces of any continental federation (confederation or sub-continental union) may directly and preliminarily ratify the *Constitution for the Federation of Earth* without waiting for their respective continental federation (confederation or sub-continental union) to do so first. Preliminary ratification of the *Earth Constitution* does not imply or signify any alliance, confederation or treaty. Furthermore, the inclusion of any state in the Earth Federation does not terminate the powers and responsibilities that state has in relation to its respective continental federation (confederation or sub-continental union) insofar as the state's powers and responsibilities are not in violation of world law. Only in any respect that the responsibilities are in violation of world law, the obligation to the continental federation (confederation or sub-continental union) dissolves.

With this clarification of world federal distinction, the World Parliament, acting on behalf of the people of Earth, once again welcomes the nations and people of the Earth to ratify the *Earth Constitution* and truly unite as the Earth Federation.

Document Seven

Note: This document was written by Dr. Almand and Dr. Martin on behalf of the Institute on World Problems and the Earth Federation Movement for distribution at the General Review Conference of the ICC in Kampala, Uganda, June 2010. It was publically distributed as well as presented officially to the Secretariat of the General Review Conference.

Towards the Effective Rule of Law – Institute on World Problems Recommendations to the General Review Conference for the ICC. 4 June 2010

The Institute on World Problems (IOWP) recognizes common goals and multiple links between the work of the Provisional World Parliament (PWP) that has met in eleven sessions to date and the work of the International Criminal Court developing under the Rome Statute of the Assembly of States Parties (ASP). Among these common goals are the strengthening the rule of law in the world, developing a court at the world level that can hold all individuals accountable with regard to certain heinous crimes, and ending the impunity for these crimes associated with a system of nation-states often recognizing no enforceable law above themselves.

At its Seventh Session in Chennai, India in December 2003, the Parliament reviewed the Rome Statute and passed a strengthened version of the statute as World Legislative Act number 20. This act gave great independence and legitimacy to the ICC by providing the Court with a legislative basis for its operation and linking the Court with an emerging system of global institutions that point toward universality of jurisdiction and enforceability of Court decisions and orders.

If the ASP accepts the common goals indentified above, then the IOWP urges the decision-makers at the ASP to reexamine aspects of the principle of complementarity that appear to defeat these goals. The judicial systems of nations, of course, need to become and remain the first level of responsibility for addressing crimes against humanity, genocide, war crimes, or other serious offences covered by the Rome Statute. However, as the ICC now recognizes, these judicial systems need to develop into legal conformity with the provisions of the Rome Statute and attain to a consistency of procedures and practices that ultimately hold all individuals everywhere equally responsible before the law and subject to consistent, fair, and objective constraints of the due process of law.

This development of the rule of consistent, coherent law in the world requires an ICC that is truly independent and universal in its jurisdiction and not dependent for its operations on a variety of nation-state actors with differing internal political agendas, differing versions of due process, and differing responses to subpoenas, court initiatives, or court orders. Complementarity in its positive form requires coherent judicial and legal response at the national level prior to judicial action at the supranational level by the ICC. However, complementarity becomes seriously flawed and an impediment to strengthening the rule of enforceable law over individuals in the world if it is construed as requiring ICC *dependence* on national actors for the gathering of evidence, the carrying out of subpoenas, investigation, or the carrying out of court decisions.

The IOWP recommends that decision-makers within the Assembly of States Parties consider two courses of action directed toward strengthening the ICC toward a truly independent status and thereby strengthening the regime of coherent criminal law for the world that moves in the direction of becoming universal over all individuals, consistent, and enforceable. The first course of action would be to link the ICC formally or informally with the work of the Provisional World Parliament, specifically with World Legislative Act #20, and the upcoming review of this act at the Twelfth Session of the PWP scheduled to meet in Kolkata, India, December 27-31, 2010. This linking process would allow the court to access the strengthened wording of the Parliament version of the Rome Statute thereby empowering it further in the direction of universality and independence of the political variables within nation-state actors.

It would also associate the Court with parliamentary legislative practices and procedures at the supranational level that ultimately must be developed to provide the legitimacy and framework for statutes implemented by any court system. As the U.N. Universal Declaration of Human Rights makes clear under Articles 7, 21.3, and 28, the protection of human rights through the rule of law in the world ultimately requires an emerging judicial, legislative, and executive framework applying equally to all citizens of the Earth.

The second course of action that the IOWP recommends to decision-makers within the Assembly of States Parties is more far reaching and calls upon the goal expressed in the U.N. Universal Declaration of Human Rights, Article 28: "Everyone is entitled to a social and international order in which the rights and freedoms set forth in this Declaration can be fully realized." It should be clear that any such viable international order would need to develop not only a universal judicial system beginning with the ICC, but to move toward developing world legislative and executive processes required to lend universal legitimacy and enforceability to court functions.

In the light of these facts, the IOWP recommends that the Assembly of States Parties begin developing mechanisms that allow the ASP to evolve in the direction of becoming a legislative house (a "house of nations") within an emerging world parliament. The fact that the ASP has already developed the Rome Statute body of legislation suggests a nascent legislative role for the ASP. This needs to be developed toward a horizon that ultimately no longer sees the ASP as a treaty of sovereign nation-states but as an emerging House of Nations within a world parliament system that would ultimately include a complementary House of Peoples, directly elected.

The IOWP believes that acting on these recommendations could provide the ICC and the ASP with an emerging framework of goals that lift the work of these bodies out of an *ad hoc* response to a variety of horrendous situations in which atrocities are being carried out with apparent impunity in various parts of the world toward a program that coherently and consistently develops the ideal of the rule of democratically legislated, judicially administered, and impartially enforced laws over individuals everywhere upon the Earth.

Respectfully submitted on behalf of the Institute on World Problems,

Eugenia Almand, J.D.   *Glen T. Martin, Ph.D.*

Document Eight

Note: This Resolution was deliberated and adopted at the 12th Session of the Provisional World Parliament Kolkata, India, December 28, 2010. It was formulated to make clear that every one of the many rights specified in the *Earth Constitution* carries with it correlative responsibilities and duties. The citizens of the Earth Federation will be encouraged in every possible way to participate in government at the local, regional, and planetary levels.

Declaration of Citizen and Government Responsibilities under the Earth Constitution

Prologue: A dynamic and vibrant democracy necessarily requires the existence of *citizenship within a community of rights and responsibilities*. When democracy exists in human affairs, the persons whose dignity, rights, equality, and consent are thus institutionalized are transformed from mere individuals forced to obey arbitrary laws by police or military authorities to *citizens* morally responsible to one another and to the society as a whole. A community of rights and responsibilities emerges that is a very special form of human association. Every one of one's rights becomes complemented by duties and obligations to other persons and the community. If a citizen has a right, then this automatically and necessarily means that government and other citizens have duties with respect to that citizen and the community of which that citizen is a part. One cannot assign responsibilities or duties without simultaneously recognizing corresponding rights. The two features of democracy form an inseparable conceptual and practical whole.

To be part of an institutional framework that recognizes one's human dignity is to be politically recognized as a *citizen*, not merely a subject. Our rights embodied in a democratic political framework necessarily engender moral duties to society. We become co-participants in the ongoing development of events, laws, and institutions, and thus morally responsible to our fellow citizens, the common good, and future generations. Loyalty to a genuine *community of rights and responsibilities* becomes a living force that binds the consent of the governed together within a community of mutual duties and obligations. Democracy not only recognizes our inalienable dignity as human beings, but it raises us to an even higher level of dignity by making us responsible to society and to our fellow citizens within a community of rights and duties. The honest and trustworthy exercise of responsibilities entails understandings and skill development that require education for citizens. Rights cannot be adequately protected unless both citizens and those in government are adequately educated to perform their responsibilities.

This resolution, therefore, draws upon the framework and content of the *Earth Constitution* (e.g. Articles 8.2.1, 12, and 13), as well as existing World Legislative Acts and Resolutions of the Provisional World Parliament (e.g., WLAs 26, 32, and the Resolution on the Spirit of Global Government), and supplements these in the spirit and letter of the *Constitution* by emphasizing both the conceptual framework of citizen and government responsibilities and the obligations of both citizens and government to educate themselves in the concepts and skills of communicative dialogue directed toward mutual understanding that constitute practical corollaries of the principle of respect for the dignity of all persons within the authentic democratic rule of law. (For purposes of future reference, this nexus of concepts shall be called "the responsibility principle.")

1. The first principle of authentic democracy, therefore, *is the dignity of all persons as human beings.* This means persons cannot be manipulated, dominated, deceived, or dehumanized as if they were mere things. Torture is prohibited, as is imprisonment without proper due process of law, as are lying and deceit to the population. The deceitful use of people to achieve ends to which they are not a party is prohibited to any government that approximates genuine democracy. All these kinds of activities dehumanize people, turning them into mere things to be manipulated, and violate our inherent human dignity. This inherent dignity must be institutionalized in concrete systems of rights, due process procedures, and other democratic protections.

1.1 It is the responsibility of all agents and representatives of the Earth Federation to respect the dignity of every human being in both word and deed. This dignity is presupposed by democracy itself and by the dialogical and communicative process that is the foundation of authentic democracy. It is also the responsibility of all educational institutions receiving support from the Earth Federation (as outlined in WLA # 26) to encourage a dialogical framework of educational development that presupposes this dignity and equality of all participants. To the extent that both citizens and representatives of the Earth Federation develop within an open, honest, and transparent framework of discussion and communicative dialogue, human dignity will become ever-more widely recognized and respected.

1.2 Corporate entities do not have dignity and cannot have the rights that adhere to natural persons. Corporations can properly be granted conditional powers but not rights. Conditional powers and specific corporate mandates are granted through the procedures of democratic government. "Inalienable rights" (*Earth Constitution,* Article 12) can only be protected by government with regard to natural persons, just as only natural persons can have human dignity. Corporate entities or "legal personhood" necessarily involves only a grant of conditional powers by government and a correlative *responsibility* and accountability to government for the exercise of those powers.

2. The second principle of democracy is the idea that *all people have human rights that are inalienable.* This derives from our inviolable human dignity. This does not necessarily suggest the idea that *a priori* attributes somehow inhere in a human individual from birth. It means, rather, that constitutions such as the *Earth Constitution* must specify those rights that are *beyond the power of government to touch.* Democratic freedom is not worth much if government can suspend or alter fundamental protections of persons through the passage of laws or suspension of due process requirements.

It is the responsibility of all agents and representatives of the Earth Federation to recognize and respect those rights designated by the *Earth Constitution* as inalienable. It is also the responsibility of all the aforementioned educational institutions to assist students to develop awareness of these rights and their functions within a democratic system premised on tolerance, mutual respect, and open dialogue and debate. In addition, it is the responsibility of all corporations and businesses worldwide to respect and honor these rights. It is the responsibility of all citizens within the Earth Federation to respect these rights in all other persons and to recognize the inseparability of these rights with corresponding duties.

3. The third principle of democracy *is universal political equality within a context of reasonable economic equality.* This is implicit in the first two principles and means that democracy cannot function unless all adult human beings, who are subject to laws and decisions that affect them, have a right to a basic political equality of voice allowing them to participate in this decision-making process. In cases of large populations, this participation often takes the form of voting for representatives who make decisions on behalf of the population, within a context of citizen oversight and transparency.

It is the responsibility of the agents, representatives, and laws of the Earth Federation to promote reasonable political and economic equality among the citizens of the Federation. We recognize that Articles 12 and 13 of the *Earth Constitution* address this responsibility very effectively. Vast differences in wealth, education, or social status translate into unreasonable inequality of political influence. It is the responsibility of government, educational institutions, businesses, and private individuals to recognize the essential function of reasonable equality within democratic government and to promote this in word and deed.

4. The fourth principle of democracy is the existence of a *public space necessary for genuine communication*. The free exchange of ideas and the development of a genuinely communicative dimension are essential to any notion that the people are the source of legitimate authority in government. Communicative public space is to be distinguished from the early-modern liberal democratic idea, promoted by John Stuart Mill and others, of a "free marketplace of ideas." Ideas do not fit well into the capitalist model of supply and demand, and their truth or wisdom certainly is not a matter of the whims of popular consumption and taste. Communicative public space requires institutionalized spaces for discussion that are free from dog-eat-dog political competition and sloganeering as well as from corporate public relations and advertising propaganda. The capacity for reasoned discourse and debate, intimately connected with our human dignity, must find ample space within any society claiming to be a democracy.

It is the responsibility of the agents, representatives, and laws of the Earth Federation to promote development and maintenance of ample public space allowing for genuine communication and dialogue within all the localities of the Federation as well as among the peoples of Earth. One especially important mechanism for this will be the development and protection of a free internet, email, blog, and website system available to all citizens of the Earth Federation. It is the responsibility of the aforementioned educational institutions to take a leadership role in the promotion of institutions and cultures revolving around authentic, open, and transparent dialogue, debate, and communicative interaction locally, nationally, and within our planetary venue.

5. The fifth principle of democracy is the idea that *government only functions legitimately with the consent of the governed and active participation of the governed in formulating the laws under which they live*. Governmental authority to legislate and enforce laws is predicated on an unforced consent to these laws by the population. This means that consent must not be "manufactured" or engineered through government propaganda, intimidation, pressure to conformity, a corporate controlled media system, or any other method, but must be the product of free exchange of ideas within a democratic framework. As this is sometimes expressed, ultimate sovereignty belongs to the people, and only their free consent can create legitimate political obligation to respect and obey the laws. The people have the right to withdraw allegiance from any government that seriously violates their consent, dignity, equality, or human rights.

It is the responsibility of the agents, representatives, and laws of the Earth Federation to protect the transparency and integrity of the law-making process so that there is no doubt among reasonable citizens of the Earth Federation that they have consented in principle to the laws made in their name. Even minorities whose opinion is overruled every time a majority decision is taken should be able to recognize and respect the integrity of the *process* through which the decision has been made and hence consent to the laws themselves. It is the responsibility of the aforementioned educational institutions to assist students in developing a dialogical and communicative ability through which they can both participate in the process of giving consent to the laws made in their name as well as critically evaluate and appreciate the integrity and transparency of the democratic processes informing the Earth Federation government. It is the responsibility of the Earth Federation Civil Service Administration Article (8.2.1) to build into civil service training and certification standards of dialogical competency that must be met by all persons receiving civil service certification.

6. The sixth principle of democracy requires a constitutional-legal framework and community spirit that *reduces as much as possible the use of force in human affairs*. It entirely eliminates war, which is always the antithesis of democracy and internally destroys the democracy of countries as well as the communicative intelligence of citizens. Democracy also works to eliminate force in the form of political violence (such as repression or arrest of those with dissenting ideas). The legitimate use of force by democratic government requires effective legal restraints and systems of accountability for police and government officials. It also requires the principle of *minimum use of force necessary* in arresting lawbreakers and otherwise keeping order as well as careful avoidance of the use of force against any and all innocent bystanders. It absolutely prohibits the use or threat of force, fear, or intimidation as a form of political control of the population or against law-abiding nonviolent dissenters.

6.1 It is the responsibility of all agents, representatives, and laws of the Earth Federation to reduce as much as possible the use of force within human affairs, to eliminate war entirely, and to create the institutions necessary for the adjudication, reconciliation, or mediation between conflicting individuals, corporate entities, or governmental units within the Earth Federation. It is the responsibility of the aforementioned educational institutions, as addressed in WLA # 26, to promote reflection on the deleterious effects of violence in human affairs and the need for a communicative framework that necessarily requires both the absence of violence and the threat of violence. It is also their responsibility to educate citizens in the principles and techniques of communicative dialogue.

6.2 The responsibility to promote communicative dialogue and mutual understanding is also emphasized in WLA #32, the Conflict Resolution Act, which is directed toward minimizing violence in human affairs. It is the responsibility not only of the Department of Conflict Resolution and all other governmental agencies, but of all the citizens of the Earth Federation to promote the tolerance, mutual respect, and communicative openness that are indispensible for the effective and substantial reduction of the use or threat of force and violence from human affairs. This responsibility necessarily requires universal education and training in the processes of communicative dialogue and mutual understanding.

7. The seventh principle of democracy is *representation of the common good of the whole*. Within a framework of freedom, citizens soon develop a loyal community of rights and duties in which the common good of the whole becomes a matter of utmost importance. Democratic government that represents them must embody this concern. The notion of the common good of the whole logically includes the idea that the good of future generations must be taken into account. Legitimate government does not represent the interests of a segment of the population. Concern for the environment, for the general and widespread prosperity of citizens, for preservation of resources for future generations, and for protecting the rights and political voice of all citizens equally are understood as representing the common good.

It is the responsibility of all agents, representatives, and laws of the Earth Federation to consider the impact of their ideas, actions, and laws on the common good as this can be formulated with suitable and reasonable variations for the local, national or mundial (world) levels. This responsibility also applies to the aforementioned educational institutions as well as citizens of the Earth Federation. WLA # 26 requires pedagogical frameworks allowing students to reflect on and develop a "good government index" and thereby reflect on the concept of the common good, what this implies, and how it relates to individuals, businesses, and governmental responsibilities. The concept of the common good necessarily includes development of a global framework that promotes, institutionalizes, and makes possible all of the above six principles and sets of responsibilities enumerated within this document.

Document Nine

Note: This document was deliberated and adopted at the Eighth Session of the Provisional World Parliament at Lucknow, India, August 2004. It demonstrates the principle articulated in Document Eight that the Earth Federation Government will make every effort to include citizens even in governing at the global level. It establishes a Global People's Assembly system for the Earth as well as other features designed to enhance participation in the world government established with the ratification of the *Earth Constitution*.

World Legislative Act #29: the Elections Act

To inaugurate enabling legislation for the World Boundaries and Elections Administration, including provisions for a Global Peoples Assembly.

Short title: Elections Act

Whereas, the People of Earth have great need for the electoral processes and popular decision making processes as defined in the *Earth Constitution* Article 2. Section 9; Article 4 Sections 5 & 7; Article 5, Section C.;

Whereas, the *Earth Constitution* has adequate provisions for both representative democracy and for direct democracy; defined in Article 8, Section C., for a World Boundaries and Elections Administration to meet this need;

Whereas, the People of Earth are already working on the processes for decision making in numerous non-governmental and para-governmental organizations around the world;

This eighth session of the provisional World Parliament, meeting in August 2004 at Gomptinagar, City Montessori School, Lucknow, Uttar Pradesh, India, hereby adopts this Act to inaugurate enabling legislation for the World Boundaries and Elections Administration (WBEA), including provisions for a Global Peoples Assembly.

1. Basic Administrative Structure

As per the *Earth Constitution*, Article 8 C-2., a Cabinet Minister and a Senior Administrator, or a Vice President and a Senior Administrator, together with a World Boundaries and Elections Commission, direct the

World Boundaries and Elections Administration. One commissioner each from ten World Electoral and Administrative Magna-Regions, plus the Cabinet Minister and the Senior Administrator composes the commission.

As soon as the first operative stage is reached, the House of Counselors shall nominate the Commissioners from qualified members of a Global Peoples Assembly, and then the World Presidium may appoint from the nominations for five year terms. During the stage of provisional world government, the Global Peoples Assembly may make the nominations directly. The Presidium can then appoint nominees for three year terms, or until the next session of provisional World Parliament, whichever is longer. Commissioners may serve consecutive terms.

2. Administrative Functions. The functions of the World Boundaries and Elections Administration (WBEA) include the following, in conformance with the *Earth Constitution*, Article 8, C-1:

2.01. To define the boundaries for the basic World Electoral and Administrative Districts, the World Electoral and Administrative Regions and Magna-Regions, and the Continental Divisions, for submission to the World Parliament for approval by legislative action.

2.02. To make periodic adjustments every ten or five years, as needed, of the boundaries for the World Electoral and Administrative Districts, the World Electoral and Administrative Regions and Magna-Regions, and of the Continental Divisions, subject to approval by the World Parliament.

2.03. To define the detailed procedures for the nomination and election of Members of the World Parliament to the House of Peoples and to the House of Counselors, subject to approval by the World Parliament.

2.04. To conduct the elections for Members of the World Parliament to the House of Peoples and to the House of Counselors.

2.05. Before each World Parliamentary Election, to prepare Voters' Information Booklets which shall summarize major current public issues, and shall list each candidate for elective office together with standard information about each candidate, and give space for each candidate to state respective views on the defined major issues as well as on any other major issue of choice;

Voter Information Booklets shall include information on any initiatives or referendums which are to be voted upon; to distribute the Voter's Information Booklets for each World Electoral District, or suitable group of Districts; The WBEA shall seek the advice of the Institute on Governmental Procedures and World Problems, the Agency for Research and Planning, and the Agency for Technological and Environmental Assessment in preparing the booklets.

2.06. To define the rules for world political parties and political representation, subject to approval by the World Parliament, and subject to review and recommendations of the World Ombudsmus. **2.07.** To define the detailed procedures for legislative initiative and referendum by the Citizens of Earth, and to conduct voting on supra-national or global initiatives and referendums in conjunction with world parliamentary elections.

2.08. To conduct plebiscites when requested by other Organs of the World Government, and to make recommendations for the settlement of boundary disputes.

2.09. To conduct a global census every five years, and to prepare and maintain complete demographic analyses for Earth. In addition to pre-stipulated functions, the World Boundaries and Elections Administration shall perform the following duties:

2.10. To create and maintain a world electoral registry, to manage the electoral process.

2.11. To directly stimulate and promote popular participation in world government affairs on a worldwide basis. In particular, to support a Global Peoples Assembly (GPA), to include peoples committees and peoples councils on a wide variety of different issues. The Global Peoples Assembly may include all citizens of Earth who express a desire to participate in the Assembly in conformance with world law.

2.12. To eventually construct and maintain dedicated facilities for the Global Peoples Assembly (GPA) in every Administrative District on Earth, with facilities of ample capacity for all world citizens projected to participate.

2.13. To directly stimulate and promote a diverse range of approaches to the world decision making processes, to include Internet, radio, television, and other technology decision making systems in the overall decision processes.

3. Boundaries

The provisional World Parliament adopts the Newcombe Plan for World Districts and Regions. directing the Commission for Legislative Review to make adjustments as necessary to bring the plan up to date and within constitutional limits. The provisional World Parliament recommends the World Parliament to immediately review the districting plan, particularly if the districting is not brought fully within constitutional limits by the first operative stage of world government. (The Newcombe Plan is presented as an addendum to this legislation.)

4. Registry.

To make measured elections, a voter registry is necessary. The voter registry shall include identifying information and a three part number. One number part consisting of four digits shall identify the voter's primary electoral district of residence. A second part consisting of six digits (00.00.00) shall record the birth date, in day.month.year Common Era format. The third number part consisting of twelve digits is randomly generated from among available registry numbers.

The <u>World Service Authority</u>, together with the <u>World Citizens Registry</u>, shall operate the Registry. As the World Service Authority is already operating with a numbered registry system, the World Citizen Registry shall make recommendations to the World Service Authority and to the WBEA Commission for integrating the two systems within the World Electoral and Boundaries Administration. The World Service Authority shall report to the WBEA regarding its operations, including integration process. The budget proposal shall include a budget proposal in Earth credits for upgrading its system to the sixteen digit format. The budget proposal shall include projected itemized costs in Earth credits for registering the following numbers of citizens:

4.1. 2,500,000...........(FEC, Art 17, Sec C1a)
4.2. 301,000,000 .....(FEC, Art 17, Sec C1b)
4.3. 600,000,000..... .(FEC, Art 17, Sec C1c)
4.4. 3,000,000,000 ...(FEC, Art 17, Sec D1)
4.5. 5,500,000,000.....(FEC, Art 17, Sec E1)
4.6. 7,000,000,000 ..(approximate Earth population in five years' time?)

5. Nomination and Election of Members to the World Parliament
The World Boundaries and Elections Commission (WBEC) shall plan details for the nomination and election of delegate Members of the World Parliament to the House of Peoples and to the House of Counselors. To facilitate this process, the WBEC shall request electoral procedure proposals from the Global Peoples Assembly and from peoples committees, peoples councils and other groups promoting world parliament and world electoral processes. The WBEC may adjust submitted electoral procedure proposals as appropriate. Upon thorough definition, the WBEC shall submit the plans to the provisional World Parliament and World Parliament.

This Act requires a solemn undertaking in support of the *Earth Constitution* from any world citizen who will be a candidate in any campaign for the House of Peoples or House of Counselors.

6. Conducting Elections

The World Boundaries and Elections Administration shall conduct measured elections as soon as feasible. To facilitate this process, the World Boundaries and Elections Commission may request coordination assistance from the Global Peoples Assembly and from Peoples Committees, Peoples Councils and other groups promoting world parliament and world electoral processes.

As soon as feasible, the World Boundaries and Elections Commission shall begin allocations, in Earth credit or Earth currency, from its budget for the purpose of conducting measured elections.

7. Voter Information Office

This Act establishes the Voter Information Office to include not only campaign positions of candidates, but also printed versions of world legislation, the Earth Constitution, world governmental reports and bulletins, projections, commentaries, Institute for Economic Democracy literature and other materials. The Office may include a section dedicated for political parties, though the WBEA does not finance the printing costs for participating parties. Participating parties will have a quota of space in the party section, according to conditions decided by the WBEA.

The first office of the Voter Information Office is in Lucknow, India. The WBEC may establish Magna-Regional offices in Washington, D.C., in USA and in Tokyo, Japan, or in other locations, as conditions permit. As soon as feasible, the WBEC will establish a Regional Office within each World Region and a District Office within each World District.

8. Rules for Political Parties

Political parties that wish to participate in the Electoral Process must ratify the Earth Constitution. The WBEA shall determine further rules of procedure for political parties, subject to approval by the World Parliament.

9. Campaign Limits – Candidates may receive campaign contributions only from world citizens (natural persons) or from the public electoral campaign budget of the WBEA. Campaign contributions are limited to one thousand Earth Hours of credits or currency (&1000) per person contributing. The WBEA may match campaign contributions in accordance with its budget and rules established by the WBEA and approved by the World Parliament.

10. Legislative Initiatives

Initiatives are electoral processes that have originated directed from the People. By initiative signed by at least 200,000 citizens, the People may initiate World Parliamentary debate directly. The People turn in the signed initiative to the World Boundaries and Elections Commission. The WBEC presents the initiative at the provisional World Parliament or World Parliament. Initiatives shall conform to the basic professional legislative drafting guidelines adopted by the provisional World Parliament. This Act recommends world citizens to ensure conformity with guidelines before circulating initiative for citizens' signatures, as the WBEC may discard ambiguous or incomprehensible initiatives.

11. Legislative Referendums

World Referendums are electoral processes that have originated from the World Parliament, but that are voted upon directly by the People. During the provisional stage of world government and the first operative stage of world government, the provisional World Parliament or World Parliament may conduct referendums, or until an operative electoral voter registry is established in a World Electoral and Administrative District, the provisional World Parliament or World Parliament may conduct referendums outside of the general elections and measured voting process. As soon as feasible, world citizens will vote upon legislative referendums during general elections, or in special election, within a measurable vote.

12. Plebiscites

World Plebiscites are electoral processes that have originated either directly from the People, or from the provisional World Parliament or from the World Parliament. World Plebiscites are voted upon by the People. However, the WBEA may conduct World Plebiscites at sub-jurisdictional levels, as defined in the *Earth Constitution*.

13. Census. During the provisional stage of world government, the electoral process may operate using census data acquired before provisional world government. Sources may include national government census figures, local government census figures, population research reports or reports from other sources, such as United Nations Population Fund. As soon as feasible after the beginning of the first operative stage of world government, the World Boundaries and Elections Commission shall submit a collaborative action plan to the World Parliament, including proposed means to conduct the periodic 5 year census.

14. Global Peoples Assembly (GPA)

The Global Peoples Assembly is a global para-governmental agency and process, comprising both non-governmental and governmental functions, emerging to improve democratic process at a global level, encouraging popular participation in making world citizen decisions.

14.1 Functions of the Global Peoples Assembly, its subsidiary and partner organizations, include the following:

14.1.1. to endorse, promote or reject endorsement of candidates to any House of the Provisional World Parliament or World Parliament. Endorsement or rejection of endorsement by the GPA is not binding on candidates, but may carry significant political weight;

14.1.2. to recommend that the World Parliament deliberate specified issues or subjects of legislation;

14.1.3. to generate necessary world citizens Initiatives and Plebiscites for election by the People of Earth in measured world elections conducted by the World Boundaries and Elections Administration, if the Global Peoples Assembly does not perceive recommendations to be adequate;

14.1.4. to discuss pending decisions and past decisions of the World Parliament;

14.1.5. to discuss pending decisions and past decision of the People via world initiatives, world referendums and world plebiscites;

14.1.6. to form citizens commissions to investigate electoral procedures, systems or subsystems that may have been subverted by faulty or fraudulent electronic count or other means, or the secrecy of which may have been compromised. (The individuals vote is secret, but not the actual counting of votes, which is a public function.); and

14.1.7. to discuss and review its own functioning, making corrections as necessary to ensure broad popular participation in the world political process.

14.2 Membership and Partner Organizations

14.2.1. Participating members. A Delegate's Council shall register any person as a participating member who declares sympathy with the goals of GPAM if the registering person has participated within the last two years in a Local Peoples Assembly (LPA), Regional Peoples Assembly (RPA), or Global Peoples Assembly GPA), or other GPAM activity. This includes participation in an endorsed or co-sponsored event or activity. This entitles a participating member to join in GPAM debates and to vote on GPAM issues in person or by mail or electronic means. Participants in a GPAM directed activity not responding to two consecutive requests to vote or debate over two or more weeks are determined temporarily inactive for purposes of quorum rules for that activity.

14.2.2. Contributing members. Participating members may become contributing members via a GPAM fiscal agent, and may register as a member of an LPA, RPA, GPA or GPAM itself. Participating members are automatically contributing members of higher level assemblies and of GPAM. The Delegates Council policy may determine the division of participating membership dues among these entities (LPA, RPA, GPA or GPAM.)

14.2.3. Partner Organizations. A partner organization is a non-profit entity, such as a national or international non-governmental (NGO), community-based organization, professional or labour organization, or governmental entity in sympathy with the goals of GPAM. A participating organization is a partner organization which periodically hosts an assembly to choose delegates and conduct other GPAM business. Partner organizations are encouraged to become participating organizations by hosting assemblies.

14.3. Delegates Council.

14.3.1. Initial Arrangements

Volunteers shall organize the first Delegates Council. All groups that the first Delegates Council recognizes as peoples assemblies or possible affiliates are entitled to one delegate in the next higher jurisdictional level of the People's Assembly. The Delegates Council shall make recommendations as to Delegates Council size, specific responsibilities of Delegates, Delegates Council manner of replacement, and Delegates' compensation, if any, and submit this to the vote of the plenary of the Global Peoples Assembly. The Delegates Council shall have representation from at least all twenty World Electoral and Administrative Regions of Earth, though to begin, it may have less.

14.3.2. Liaisons and Delegates

Numbers of Delegates. This Act encourages broad participation in the Global Peoples Assembly. This Act recommends the Credentials Committee to find additional adjacent space and electronically link the assembly, if feasible.

If there are too many delegates to function effectively or equitably, due to facility capacity restrictions, the Credentials Committee may reduce the number of delegates to a particular assembly by only accepting delegates from regional assemblies, or from regional groupings of assemblies, and from larger assemblies or populations:

14.3.2.1. A smaller assembly with at least 10 participating members may elect or nominate 1 delegate to attend a larger assembly, at least 100 participating, then 2 delegates, at least 1000 participating then 3 delegates, etc. This method may be modified as needed by replacing "10" by any number x, so that an assembly with at least xn participating members has n delegates.

14.3.2.2. An assembly may use a method for extra delegates based on area population size, say 1 extra delegate for a population over 100,000, 2 for over 1,000,000, 3 for over 10,000,000, etc.

14.3.2.3. An assembly may elect or nominate delegates based on financial support, for example, the assembly may nominate m extra delegates for at least y/m contributing members, by choosing an appropriate number y.

14.3.2.4. Assemblies or organizations may designate participating members as liaisons to other assemblies and organizations. Delegates are liaisons who are designated to sit on the Delegates Council by their assemblies or non-participating partner organizations. This Act requires that an executive or governing council delegate of a partner organization obtain respective authorization from the partner organization, but need not officially represent the views of that organization. The Delegates Council will request alternates or replacements for inactive delegates.

14.3.2.5. Partner organizations may designate a single delegate, but partner delegates shall constitute less than 50% of all delegates. In order to accomplish this, or for other purposes this Act adopts a uniform method to allow large assemblies to have more than one delegate.

14.3.2.6. Subject to availability of resources, GPAM may subsidize travel and other expenses for delegates who request financial aid, according to need and past or potential level of participation.

14.3.3. Voting. The Delegates Council and other groups of the Global Peoples Assembly will seek consensus, with 2/3 of those present required for decisions on resolutions, internal initiatives, policy, Charter and Bylaws. Consensus and electoral decisions take effect immediately, but if a ratification vote fails at a future GPAM Plenary, the respective assembly must revoke or change the decision as advised. By simple majority vote, Delegates, liaisons or partner members may submit proposed decisions, along with pro and con statements, to the participating members for an advisory vote. Other contested decisions, including elections and procedural decisions, are by majority vote.

Robert's Rules of Order Newly Revised, latest edition is the basic manual for procedure of the Global Peoples Assembly and the Delegates Council, unless the Delegates Council or Global Peoples Assembly decides otherwise. To ease access to Robert's Rules, the Delegates Council or Global Peoples Assembly may decide to use the 1917 edition of Robert's Rules of Order Newly Revised, from public domain.

14.3.4. Meetings

The Delegates Council shall meet at GPAs, and shall strive to meet in person at least annually and electronically at least quarterly. For voting purposes, a quorum shall be 25% of all delegates.

14.3.5 Leadership

The Delegates Council shall elect officers to conduct business and organize meetings. These officers shall include President, Vice-President, Secretary, and Treasurer, who serve for up to two terms of two years each. The Delegates Council make create other leadership positions and groups as needed, with duties and terms of office.

14.3.6. Credentials Committee. The Delegates Council shall form a Credentials Committee to compile a list of qualified assemblies and partner organizations and to maintain a database of participating members and of current delegates, and alternates. This committee shall also solicit potential assemblies and partner organizations and issue qualification guidelines with approval of the Delegates Council. The Credentials Committee shall determine the activity of participating members for quorum purposes.

The Credentials Committee shall form a list of recommended candidates to serve in elections to the House of Peoples and to the Hour of Counselors in general world government elections. The Credentials Committee may elaborate commentary on World Parliament candidates coming from the World Districts and Regional Assemblies.

A candidate for World Parliament may run for office without endorsement from the Credentials Committee, if all qualifications are met, as defined in the Earth Constitution.

14.3.7. Internal Initiatives. An internal initiative is a initiative emerging from the Global Peoples Assembly and affecting the Global Peoples Assembly. An assembly that sponsors an internal initiative may circulate its proposal to the active GPAM participants for feedback and revision by that assembly. 10% of the participating membership must endorse the final version of this internal initiative before it goes to the Delegates Council. The Delegates Council must then act on the initiative, possibly after amendments, with acceptance requiring a 2/3 vote of those present. If acceptance fails, the Delegates Council will refer the internal initiative, with pro and con statements, to a GPAM Plenary for deliberation and an up or down 2/3 vote of those present. Internal Initiatives must be consistent with the Earth Constitution.

14.4. GPAM Plenary Sessions

14.4.1. Voting on Policy. Simple majority vote of the Global Peoples Assembly Plenary decides resolutions, general policy decisions, internal initiatives, and changes to Bylaws or Charter, as submitted by the Delegates Council, The Delegates Council may attempt to rephrase failed motions for reconsideration at a future Global Peoples Assembly Plenary. A GPAM Plenary may be an in-person session at a GPA, or it may be conducted by the Delegates Council with mail or electronic ballot from participating members. A Plenary may also propose a resolution, policy decision, or Bylaw or Charter Change for consideration by the Delegates Council.

14.4.2. Voting for Candidates.

The "Borda Count" is recognized by mathematical authorities as less subject to unexpected results or to manipulation than most other voting methods. First each voter ranks all the candidates (or choices) from highest to lowest preference, possibly ranking some equally. The least preferred candidate gets no votes, the next candidate gets 1 vote, the next 2 votes, etc. For example, if there are 5 candidates, then the candidates ranked most to least preferred, get 4,3,2,1,0 votes respectively. The candidate with the most votes wins.

If there are n candidates, the most preferred candidate gets n-1 votes, the next n-2 votes, etc. If m positions are to be filled, then the highest m recipients of votes are elected. If several candidates are ranked equally, then each gets an equal number of votes. Thus if the 2nd and 3rd candidates are ranked equally in the 5 candidate example, the voting allocation would be 4, 2.5, 2.5, 1, 0.

If the Delegates Council has forwarded nominees for multiple at-large offices, then election is by a Borda count. However, the Plenary Session has the option, by majority vote, of rejecting all candidates for individual offices or of slates of candidates for multiple openings.

14.4.3. Other Procedures. Procedural issues not addressed by the Bylaws will be governed by Robert's Rules of Order Newly Revised, latest edition.

14.5. Financial Arrangements

14.5.1. Fiscal Agents. GPAM shall initially affiliate with fiscal agents in different countries or regions for handling membership fees and possibly other tasks, such as fundraising or communications. A fiscal agent is a non-profit organization that receives a percentage of the membership fees and other monies raised, to be negotiated according to agreed tasks.

GPAM may form its own entities to handle financial matters, consistent with world legislation.

15. Dedicated Facilities for the Global Peoples Assemblies

The Global Peoples Assemblies may meet in rented or offered facilities, as necessary. The provisional World Parliament recommends the World Parliament to construct dedicated facilities, such as a Magna-Forum in each Magna-Region (10 Magna Regions). This Act recommends a Magna-Forum facility with capacity to host 25,000 people during the first operative stage of World Government, and beyond. If the people by plebiscite in a magna-region decide that larger facilities are necessary, the Agencies of the Integrative Complex will study the environmental and social impact of larger facilities' requirements, to assess the optimum location for the larger facility. If there are not significant environmental or social impact problems projected by the larger facility, the World Parliament may allocate the funds for the larger facility. Global equity is a determining factor in the decision for placement of forums. Therefore, if one magna-region has a larger magna-forum built, this may be a precedent for the building of larger magna-forum facilities in other magna-regions.

This Act recommends the World Parliament to construct a Regional-Forum facility in each World Region, with capacity to host 5 to 10,000 people during the first operative stage of world government, and 25,000 people during the second operative stage and full operative stage of world government.

This Act recommends World Parliament to construct a District Forum facility with capacity to host 1000 people during the provisional stage of world government, 5,000 people during the first operative stage of world government, 10,000 people during the second operative stage of world government, and 25,000 people during the full operative stage of World Government.

Each constructed forum facility shall have full access for disabled persons.

Each constructed forum facility shall have a crèche with professional child development personnel, for attending infants and children up to 14 years of age, while parents or custodians are attending the Global Peoples Assembly.

16. Internet Programs

This Act promotes the development of Internet programs and projects to create a better and stronger world democratic process. Internet programs include wikis, non-governmental organization web pages, para-governmental web pages, other web pages, skypes, list serves, e-groups, electronic polling mechanisms, and instantaneous translation services.

17. Radio and Television

This Act authorizes the Agency for Research and Planning to assign public radio and television frequencies for each District, Region and other jurisdictional levels of the Earth Federation. The frequencies assigned shall include dedicated frequencies for broadcast of each District, Region and other jurisdictional level of the Global Peoples Assembly.

18. Other Technology systems may supplement.

To reach world citizens who live in rural areas, under conditions of poverty, or who otherwise do not have access to Internet, television or radio, the WBEA shall expend a portion of its budget to reach and include participation from world citizens who otherwise would not be able to participate. This may include other technology systems, such as paper dissemination of voter information booklets. The WBEA shall recommend a budget portion in its first proposed budgets. Upcoming sessions of the provisional World Parliament or World Parliament may determine the exact portions.

19. Children's Participation

This Act commends the Children's World Parliament and the World Parliament of Youth. This Act recognizes the great importance for the education of youth in civic responsibility.

The World Boundaries and Elections Commission shall include budgetary provisions for youth participation and parliamentary training in the annual budget of the WBEA.

20. The Syntegrity Project

On a semi-annual basis, or as often as feasible, the WBEA shall sponsor syntegrations to analyze weaknesses in the structure of the WBEA system and sub-systems, to find recommendations for improvement, and for other purposes. WBEA shall pay for syntegrations from its operating budget.

21. Budget

The World Boundaries and Elections Commission shall prepare an annual budget to be submitted to the sessions of the provisional World Parliament and World Parliament, including proposals for operation of each program of the WBEA and in particular an elections budget. The provisional World Parliament and World Parliament may make adjustments to budgetary requests, to efficiently strengthen the overall program for Earth Federation. Upon budget approval by the provisional World Parliament or World Parliament, the Central Bank of the World Treasury shall disburse funds monthly to the WBEA for its operations.

The WBEA shall make budget requests and report expenditures in terms of Earth credits or Earth currency.

22. Reporting

The World Boundaries and Elections Administration shall make an annual report to the World Parliament and to the Presidium.

23. Further Provisions

The World Parliament may at any time define further the responsibilities, functioning and organization of the World Boundaries and Elections Administration, consistent with the provisions of Article VIII and other provisions of the *Earth Constitution*.

Document Ten

Note: this document was deliberated and adopted at the 12th session of the Provisional World Parliament in Kolkata, India, December 28, 2010. Its purpose is to further strengthen the possibility of citizen participation in government even to the point of nonviolent civil disobedience. It does this by requiring juries and courts to *hear the reasons* for the disobedience, a right that is now often denied to those who commit civil disobedience in the U.S. and some other countries.

World Legislative Act #44

Nonviolent Civil Disobedience Act

Whereas, the Parliament recognizes that peace with justice within the Earth Federation is not a final condition descending from governmental institutions and authorities alone, but rather constitutes a dynamic process requiring active involvement of the citizenry,

Whereas, the Parliament recognizes and encourages citizen participation in creating a peaceful and just world order that may be accomplished in a variety of nonviolent ways such as voting, writing letters or editorials, contributing money, attending public events, teaching, signing petitions, gathering to protest, etc., and that participants may feel that nonviolent violation of the law is necessary to the effectiveness, or to register the seriousness of, their protests;

We members of the Provisional World Parliament at 11th session, hereby enact the following rules by which the courts shall treat nonviolent civil disobedience.

1. Civil disobedience is defined as the public violation of the law for a moral purpose.

2. The statutes violated by civil disobedience protests shall govern the charges brought against the violators, for example, the statutes governing trespass on Earth Federation property or those governing the defacing or damage to property. Violators of the law are subject to prosecution under the statutes violated as would be any individual.

3. However, the courts shall treat as an ameliorating or extenuating circumstance the fact that the violation of the law was done for the moral purpose of publicly protesting actions, laws, or policies of government considered wrongful or unjust by the protestors. The court shall allow at trial the purposes for which the illegal act was committed. The court shall take these purposes into consideration in both the court charge to the jury and in assigning penalties.

4. In cases of damage to or defacing of public property, the court shall distinguish the kind of property that was damaged or defaced. For example, was the property part of an illegal project on behalf of the government, one prohibited by the *Earth Constitution*, such as infrastructure surrounding the building or maintenance of a nuclear weapon or the maintenance of illegal weapons of war at a military installation? Or was the property damaged, on the other hand, useful public property of benefit to a common good that was needlessly diminished through the act of civil disobedience? Did the damage cause significant environmental damage or risk to the public, such as risk of detonation of prohibited weapons?

5. The courts shall allow defense in cases of nonviolent civil disobedience to use the reasons for committing the civil disobedience as part of the defense, raising the social, political, environmental, moral, or human rights issues appropriate to this act of civil disobedience.

6. The court shall write civil disobedience issues so raised into the court record.

7. The decisions and deliberations of the court become part of the body of legal cases that future courts may draw upon or review in making decisions.

Document Eleven

Note: this document was submitted by Glen T. Martin to the 12th Session of the Provisional World Parliament meeting at Kolkata, India, December 29, 2010. It was deliberated and unanimously adopted after several friendly amendments. The amended version is given here. Its purpose is for the EFM to have available a conceptual model of the Earth Federation as this is envisioned by the *Earth Constitution* in order to help people envision the positive transformation of the world system that will take place upon ratification of the *Constitution.*

Conceptual Model of the Earth Federation

Prologue

We delegates of the 12th session of the Provisional World Parliament, meeting in Kolkata, India December 27-31, 2010, have certified this conceptual model in order to encourage the citizens of Earth to envision concretely the holistic world system founded by the *Constitution for the Federation of Earth*. The Preamble to the *Earth Constitution* rightly states that *"the principle of unity in diversity is the basis for a new age when war shall be outlawed and peace prevail; when the earth's total resources shall be equitably used for human welfare; and when basic human rights and responsibilities shall be shared by all without discrimination."* This principle of unity in diversity names the paradigm shift behind the *Earth Constitution*.

The principle of unity in diversity epitomizes the new paradigm emerging from the scientific revolutions of the 20th century. Previously the world had been modeled as a *machine* characterized by universal causal determinism and composed of isolated, independent parts called atoms that, in living systems, often acted in competition with one another. This was reflected in outdated social theories such as the doctrine of capitalist competition or the dogma of survival of the fittest. The new paradigm sees the world and human society more accurately on the model of an *organism* in which the parts interact within a dynamic whole that transcends the sum of its individual components.

On the human level this implies a social ecology of interdependence and mutual relationships among the many parts within a unity that transcends the sum of its interdependent parts. Hence, the diversity of persons, nations, cultures, ethnicities, and races in the world involves a complex multiplicity of interdependent relationships and "worlds within worlds," all necessary to one another and inseparable at the deepest levels. Unity in diversity implies authentic global democracy, mutual respect and cooperation among all peoples, the ending of war and militarism, and universal sustainable prosperity.

The unity of the whole involves the social ecological wholeness of human life on Earth itself, which is itself part of the natural unity of our planetary ecosystem. Parts and whole are both real and necessary to one another. Our common human nature, our common ability to use language, our common human characteristics and mannerisms, our common ability for love, compassion and mutual recognition, and our universal human rights and dignity express the unity of the whole. There can be no true protection and appreciation of this wonderful diversity of the parts unless this is embraced, respected, and protected through true unities. As with natural ecology, a multiplicity of scientific disciplines have demonstrated that in human civilization the one and the many are necessary and complementary to one another.

The *fragmentation* of the system of sovereign nation-states recognizing no enforceable law above themselves and its tandem system of global capitalism in which the rich corporations, banks, and nations exploit poor people and nations worldwide has been replaced by a *holistic* world system under the *Earth Constitution*. The paradigm shift to a holistic world system established on the principle of unity in diversity has clearly predictable consequences for peace, prosperity, justice, freedom, and environmental sustainability, just as the present fragmented world system has definite consequences for each of these domains – consequences that we see all around us in the form of war, poverty, injustice, slavery, and environmental destruction. The parliament hopes that this document will aid the people of Earth to understand more deeply the terrible consequences of fragmentation and the absolute need to ratify and implement a holistic world system under the *Earth Constitution* within the very near future.

The fragmentation of the present world disorder parallels the fragmented, linear thinking deriving largely from that outdated paradigm. The *Constitution* is a product of the discipline of "systems thinking" that has developed within many 20th century sciences. Systems thinking discerns wholes. It examines interrelationships and dynamic patterns, such as those that today cause the horrible consequences of the present world order in terms of militarism, poverty, and environmental destruction. Systems thinking understands that most human behavior is a product of the systems within which we live. Changing our world system from fragmentation to holism will profoundly transform human attitudes and behavior (Senge 2006; Meadows 2008).

The *Constitution* is not only a product of a deep understanding of the holistic unity in diversity of our world system. It will require creative and insightful systems thinkers to enliven it, both before ratification and once ratified, into a dynamic system of democratic responsiveness to an ever-evolving complex set of world relationships. The dynamic, holistic structure of the *Constitution* itself will help foster creative systems thinking within the emerging Earth Federation.

The *Constitution* was created through a process of four World Constituent Assemblies composed of world citizens from around the globe. These visionary world citizens met four times in the Assemblies, and interacted continuously between meetings, from 1968 to 1991 to produce this document serving as a foundation for a decent world system premised on the paradigm of the *unity in diversity* of genuine democracy. The *Constitution* is the foundation stone for genuine world democracy based on the principle of *all*. All human beings everywhere are included for the first time in history. This is the only proper response to the fact that human rights are universal; human dignity is universal; the human longing for freedom, justice, equality, peace, and prosperity is universal.

The *Constitution* also offers a *founded* world system for the first time in history, not one that has haphazardly evolved from earlier outdated assumptions. It creates an integrated world system in which the Earth Federation is open to an evolving future guided by the vision embodied in the *Constitution* of peace, prosperity, justice, freedom, and sustainability. No longer locked into antiquated self-destructive economic and political assumptions and the fragmented thinking that produced them, the people of Earth will be able to move nonviolently forward toward a decent future for everyone. These founding ideals are built into the structure of the emerging Earth Federation within an open, self-correcting system directed toward their actualization within an ever-changing environment.

Article 19 of the *Earth Constitution,* gives the people of Earth the mandate and the duty to begin the process of building the Earth Federation now, of elaborating the ministries, agencies, and organs specified by the *Constitution* from day one. There is no need to wait for ratification. We call this pledge the "act of civil obedience" in which we leave the immoral condition of citizens of some so-called sovereign nation under the war system and commit to living according to the peaceful rule of democratic law under the emerging Earth Federation.

Many members of the World Constitution and Parliament Association (WCPA) and the organizations within the Earth Federation Movement (EFM) (going all the way back to the initial signatories of the *Constitution* at Innsbruck, Austria, in 1977) have pledged recognition of the *Constitution* as the law for planet Earth and therefore have begun living the transformed world system that it represents. Within the limits of the resources available to us, we activated the World Parliament under the heading of "Provisional World Parliament" in order to distinguish before and after phases of the development of viable world law. During the 1980s we created a bench of the World Supreme Court, which put all nuclear weapons producing nations on trial for this criminal act.

We have also worked to begin various ministries specified by the *Constitution*, and have created a number of agencies through the Provisional World Parliament (specified later in this document). We have been seeking pledges or gifts of world territory (out from under any sovereign nation and ruled under the *Earth Constitution* and the Provisional World Parliament). We have designed and are actively promoting a universal Earth Currency with nations and leaders around the world. And we have established the Institute on World Problems specified in Article 8.4 of the *Constitution*. The Institute is also a non-profit 501C3 organization in the U.S., but its mandate, mission, and authority derive directly from the *Earth Constitution*.

The *Constitution* itself demands (on both moral and legal grounds) that world citizens begin living and creating the transformed world system immediately. Self-government (by the people, for the people, and of the people) will never happen unless it begins here and now. We can no longer defer to the illegitimate system of militarized, warring nation-states. We the people must begin taking democratic responsibility for the governing of our planet.

Since 1982, the Provisional World Parliament has met eleven times under the authority of Article 19 of the *Constitution*. The Parliament, through passing some 47 provisional world legislative acts (WLAs) and a number of resolutions articulating the spirit and meaning of the emerging Earth Federation, has been elaborating the details and specific legislation necessary to enable, activate, and concretize the framework provided by the *Constitution*. By reading this legislation and resolutions, it is not difficult to discern the kind of world order being developed by the Parliament through its ten sessions to date, as well as the dynamic systems thinking that has significantly informed the work of the Parliament. All the many thousands of world citizens who have committed the "act of civil obedience" are bound by the world legislation enacted by the Provisional World Parliament. We are building the new world system within the rotten shell of the old system of war, poverty, injustice, slavery, and unsustainability.

By reading the Resolution on Good Government and its Essential Tasks under the Earth Federation passed by the eighth session of the Parliament we can see clearly the kind of transformed world system that is being promoted by the Parliament under the authority of the *Earth Constitution,* and the outlines of the world that many thousands of WCPA members everywhere on Earth are living as we speak. Just as we see all around us the horrific empirical consequences of the present world order, so in the work of the Provisional World Parliament we see peace structured into law, equality structured into law, the common good structured into law, the welfare of future generations structured into law, and individual freedom structured into law. (All this material can be found on-line at www.worldproblems.net and in the three volume set entitled *Emerging World Law – Key documents and Decisions of the Global Constituent Assemblies and the Provisional World Parliament,* edited by Eugenia Almand and Glen T. Martin.)

Fortunately, Article 17 of the *Earth Constitution* specifies four stages of implementation until the full force of the Federation of Earth is realized, from the building of provisional world government prior to ratification to three stages of ratification and implementation. This not only make the process of transformation of the world's system practical and doable, it allows the flexibility and creativity needed for growth toward mature living in peace, prosperity, justice, freedom, and sustainability. We model the future by living it now. We grow from our failures as well as successes. The *Constitution* and the hundreds of thousands around the world within the Earth Federation Movement allow for this process of growth. The future and the present are dynamically linked in this way.

The institutional assumptions structuring our present world disorder for centuries have led to a world of perpetual wars, slavery, exploitation, worldwide poverty, disease, human misery, and environmental destruction. The institutional assumptions behind genuine democracy for humankind premised on the *unity in diversity* of all are entirely different, and the consequences of the resulting world system will be entirely different. The kind of world we live in is not the product of some mythical, greedy, and aggressive "human nature" but rather the product of the institutions, assumptions, and systems by which we organize our social lives. Common sense, practical laws, and ratification of the *Earth Constitution* in the present will lead to a vastly better world for all peoples in the relatively near future, just as these have been transforming the lives and practices of hundreds of thousands of people around the world since 1977.

A Peace System

Historically, many thinkers from the 17th century to the present have understood the world system of militarized sovereign nation-states as inherently a *war system*. War is not an occasional failure of this system but an intrinsic characteristic of the fact that there is no enforceable world law over nations and individuals that can mandate demilitarization and bring to justice those who violate the peaceful democratic rule of law. In consequence, nations operate on the basis of power politics involving the implicit or explicit use of coercion to promote their variety of perceived self-interests. The result is a world of chaos, injustice, and violence that today wastes more than one trillion U.S. dollars per year on militarism while the basic needs of the majority of human beings remain unmet. The result is a collection of 192 more or less autonomous entities who deny our basic interdependence on this Earth and who utterly lack the ability to join together sufficiently to deal with global crises such as climate crisis or worldwide diminishing resources.

People say war cannot be eliminated, and this is truly so under the institutional paradigm within which the world remains currently trapped. However, under the *Constitution*, the nations of the Earth Federation are federated under the common rule of enforceable laws and sovereignty is shared by governmental authorities from the local to the national and the world level. The most fundamental component for creating a world peace system is *global democracy itself*, for democracy institutionalizes processes of nonviolent change and embraces all citizens within a regime of political participation within which their voices are heard and their rights are protected.

At the global level such a regime would abolish the fragmentation of militarized sovereign nation-states in lethal and secretive competition with one another while mitigating the fragmented identifications of people worldwide with their local religion, ethnicity, race, culture, or other grouping. Non-military global democracy would also eliminate the military-industrial complex in which tremendous profits are made from producing munitions and military machines and which promotes overwhelming incentives for war and perpetual violence.

For this reason the World Parliament created under the *Constitution* is the first and foremost component of a world peace system. The House of Peoples represents all people on Earth through representatives elected from 1000 electoral districts worldwide apportioned according to population. The House of Nations represents all nations with one to three representatives (depending on population) appointed or elected by the nations themselves. And the House of Counselors (composed of 200 representatives, 10 from each of 20 magna-regions worldwide) represents the people of Earth as a whole and the common good for the entire planet.

The world democracy created under the World Parliament composed of these three houses, therefore, will embrace all races, religions, and other groupings in global dialogue and decision-making. The House of Nations will embrace all nations large and small, ending imperialism and exploitation of weaker nations by powerful nations. And the House of Counselors, with experts on all aspects of our civilization from the environment to demilitarization to cultural conflicts to principles of sustainable development, will provide wisdom and expertise to the Parliament in the service of the common good of humanity and the planet.

The *Earth Constitution* converts today's system of fragmented individualism (of nations, corporations, and persons) to a *global social contract*. A global social contract means that all are included in the regime of collective empowerment. A planetary community is established on fundamental moral and practical principles thereby transforming (for many at least) self-interested individuals into responsible citizens. A truly democratic world system is an essential foundation stone for world peace. Every group and nation must feel that its voice is heard and that it may effectively participate in governing the Earth in cooperation with other world citizens throughout the Earth Federation. The establishment of an effective World Parliament alone creates the foundations for a genuine world peace system.

Second, under both the *Constitution* and the Provisional World Parliament, many specific features of the *Constitution* and laws passed by the Parliament establish the concrete lineaments of a world peace system. Not only does the *Earth Constitution* require a demilitarized world, the Provisional World Parliament has created detailed legislation to regulate and empower the process of disarmament. The very first World Legislative Act adopted in 1982 by the Provisional World Parliament (WLA #1) enacted a world law prohibiting the design, development, sale, transport, or deployment of weapons of mass destruction, including nuclear weapons and the missiles that deliver them.

The Parliament acting under the *Constitution* is not simply concerned with prohibiting such horrific features of our present world order. It is building the infrastructure for conversion: how to get from here to there. The World Peace Act of the Seventh Session of Parliament (WLA #13) set the parameters for a systematic and orderly conversion from the war system to a peace system. Individuals, businesses, university researchers, and government officials involved in any way in the weapons production and procurement process are systematically informed of the new world legislation and have measured grace periods within which they may desist from their illegal activities without penalty. Penalties are increased not only according to the severity of the crime (e.g., designing nuclear weapons or delivery systems, a criminal act if there ever was one) but also according to whether the criminal activity has persisted after the grace period.

A number of scholars have pointed out that private terrorism is simply war by another name. It is war waged by the weak and relatively powerless as opposed to war financed and organized by nation-states (state terrorism) and their imperial military systems. The Provisional World Parliament, at its Second Session in New Delhi, India, enacted WLA #8, creating a World Commission on Terrorism. This commission is charged not only to invite cooperation from nations and NGOs in dealing with terrorism, it is also charged to address the fundamental causes of terrorism in terms of the perceptions of gross injustices, the feeling of voicelessness among marginalized peoples, and the perception that the current world political authorities are engaged in their own terrorist war against certain groups, religions, or cultures.

The Parliament recognizes that we cannot create a decent world order with ever more war and violence, even if this is directed toward terrorists and their organizations. Only changing our institutional assumptions can change the world order in any meaningful ways. The peace system created by the *Earth Constitution* includes a multiplicity of elements working together to ensure that the system establishes enduring peace. First and foremost, we have seen, is the establishment of *effective world democracy* itself, in which people and nations from the entire planet participate in governing the planet and thereby institutionalizing the procedures for nonviolent and peaceful social change. Today's sovereign nation-state system, with its militarism and national security apparatus, defeats authentic democracy in all nations. Authentic democracy can only develop in a demilitarized world recognizing *universal* rights, duties, freedoms, and obligations.

Third, the *Constitution* sets up an effective and impartial World Judiciary with authority over all persons, including national leaders. This ensures peace from two directions: all national leaders can be indicted for violating the law (no more impunity as in today's world) and a judiciary treating everyone fairly and equally under the law diminishes the feelings of resentment that now fuel much violence and war worldwide. The World Court system has eight benches designed to deal with the variety of cases that might endanger world peace. It has benches for human rights cases, for criminal cases dealing with individuals, corporations, or groups, for public cases dealing with conflict between government and corporations or other groups, and for international conflicts between nations. World peace through world law requires an effective judiciary to deal with all forms of conflict between individuals, groups, or nations. When people see impartial justice being done on a global scale, they will understand that a peace system has truly come into the world.

Fourth, the *Constitution* creates the Earth Federation Enforcement System of the world police and world attorneys general to ensure a peaceful and nonviolent world order premised on justice and the effective enforcement of the laws against war and violence everywhere on Earth. The police will possess only weapons necessary to apprehend individuals (Article 10.1.5). All weapons of war are abolished even for the Earth Federation Government. Both Articles 2 and 10 specify that the Earth Federation will be non-military. Article 10 specifies that one of the basic functions of the enforcement system will be "conflict resolution" and states that "a basic condition for preventing outbreaks of violence, which the Enforcement System shall facilitate in every way possible, shall be to assure a fair hearing under nonviolent circumstances for any person or group having a grievance, and likewise to assure a fair opportunity for a just settlement of any grievance with due regard for the rights and welfare of all concerned."

This fundamental tenet of a peace system (institutionalized worldwide and operating as well through the World Judiciary and the World Ombudsmus) has been elaborated by the Provisional World Parliament in World Legislative Act 32 that creates a Department of Conflict Resolution within the Enforcement System in conformity with Article 10.2.8.5. This shows the transformed role of the police from protectors of ruling class property rights and oppressive national security regimes (now their chief functions within nation-states) to protector and friend of the citizens of Earth. The legislation specifies that the civil servants involved in the Department of Conflict Resolution will involve first and foremost existing groups, civic leaders, local organizations, and participation of the people in facilitating conflict resolution everywhere on Earth where people need these services.

Officials will not be allowed to carry any weapons in this Department nor do any undercover work and, according to the legislation, they must be servants and facilitators of the people locally to solve and resolve their own problems. Nothing like this is found on a planetary scale in today's militarized global war system. This is truly what a peace system for the Earth will look like. People are empowered to create peace by an Earth Federation whose mission is to serve the people of Earth through a world system founded on peace, prosperity, justice, freedom, and sustainability. The emerging Earth Federation is an integrated whole with all these basic functions integrated into a practical and effective system of democratic world government.

Fifth, the *Constitution* creates another worldwide organization answering to the World Parliament that is a vital component of the world peace system: the World Ombudsmus. This organization, with offices everywhere within the Federation, will be devoted to protecting the human rights of the citizens of Earth (as specified in Articles 12 and 13) from violation by individuals, corporations, nations, or the World Government itself. The *Earth Constitution* recognizes so-called "third generation rights" of the right to peace and the right to a protected and decent environment. If people's rights, freedoms, peaceful coexistence, and planetary environment are really protected, the causes of war will be largely eliminated. The Ombudsmus *Constitution*ally will have significant authority to act on behalf of the citizens of Earth to protect their many rights and freedoms identified by Articles 12 and 13. No nation or group will likely want to resort to violence when they see that their voices, dignity, and self-determination are respected and protected.

Sixth, the Provisional World Parliament passed a World Education Act (WLA #26) at its eighth session in Lucknow, India in 2004. The Earth Federation government will promote high quality education everywhere and require all schools that are recipient of Earth Federation aid to include programs focusing on global issues, peace studies issues, study of the *Earth Constitution*, and study of the nature and responsibilities of good government within a global democracy. Education worldwide will promote peace, mutual tolerance, the founding principle of unity in diversity, and the dynamics of conflict resolution. Pedagogy will become a fundamental component in the world peace system.

Education will be one central component of an integrated Earth Federation plan to empower all citizens of the Earth to think in terms of the principle of unity in diversity, of mutual respect and tolerance within the framework of effective global democracy, and an educated citizenry capable of global citizenship. The Parliament understands that peace will be the product of a global system with many components working together: from good leadership, to the content and attitude of the mass media, to the spirit and intent with which corporations operate, to the sense that people have of world citizenship, to the degree of fairness and prosperity apparent in the world, to the quality of worldwide education. Under the *Earth Constitution* and the Education Act of the Provisional World Parliament students will be encouraged to examine cultural forms that suppress other human beings, for example, through dress codes or other such cultural practices. Such a system cannot be entirely created *a priori* ahead of time. What can be provided ahead of time is a dynamic framework like the *Earth Constitution* that allows creativity and innovation in structuring a world peace system such as that shown by the Provisional World Parliament.

Finally, these six elements in the world peace system set up by the *Constitution* are complemented and enlivened by the several other features specified in this conceptual model. If the world is converted to a prosperity system, a justice system, a freedom system, and a sustainability system, then the grounds for war and violence will have been substantially undercut. The *Constitution* creates a dynamic world system that includes a multiplicity of agencies and branches working together under common holistic principles directed toward these goals. As one thinker put it: "A diverse system with multiple pathways and redundancies is more stable and less vulnerable to external shock than a uniform system with little diversity" (Meadows, 2008: 3-4). All these factors deriving from the holistic paradigm of unity in diversity at the heart of the *Constitution* work together to create a truly new historical era for human civilization. A stable, diverse world peace system derives from the holistic structure of the *Constitution* itself.

A Prosperity System – The New Democratic Economics

The present global economic system, like the system of sovereign nation-states, has evolved out of European civilization since the Renaissance, slowly becoming the official doctrines concerning what is "natural" politically and economically. The so-called "natural" political organization of sovereign states was recognized at the Treaty of Westphalia in 1648 and the so-called "natural" system of economic laws was described in Adam Smith's *Wealth of Nations* that appeared in 1776. In both cases the imperial arrogance of Europe began the process of imposing these "natural" systems on the rest of humankind. For centuries we have seen the triumph of the nation-state system described above as a system of perpetual wars, violence, and chaos. Today, we also witness the triumph of the system of monopoly capitalism in the form of immense poverty, scarcity, and misery for at least 60% of the people on Earth simultaneous with unimaginable wealth and power for a mere 1% of the Earth's population who own 40% of its wealth.

Impartial observers have pointed out that these few use the chaos of the present system of sovereign nations to further consolidate their wealth and power. Only by democratizing the world system can we change this horrific condition and create a prosperity system for the Earth. Authentic democracy cannot function when the few control such wealth and power. This can only be transformed when government functions on behalf of the universal rights and dignity of all the people of Earth and no longer on behalf of the ruling classes of some 192 autonomous nation-states.

The sovereign nation-state system integrated with monopoly capitalism leads to mayhem not only between countries but within countries. World Bank and IMF imposed economic "reforms" have led to economic disaster after disaster as "structural adjustment" destroys regional markets and opens countries up to predatory corporations and exploitative economic control from the imperial centers of capital. In *The Globalization of Poverty: Impacts of IMF and World Bank Reforms* (1999), economist Michael Chossudovsky chronicles the destruction of peoples worldwide under the onslaught of neocolonial greed run from the financial centers of capital.

In many cases (such as the infamous genocide in Rwanda) massive human rights violations were the direct consequence of the destruction of the economy by predatory control from abroad. Desperate people whose economies have disintegrated are likely to turn to irrational and murderous violence. Many other studies, such as Catherine Caufield's *Masters of Illusion: The World Bank and the Poverty of Nations* (1996) and Bruce Rich's *Mortgaging the Earth: The World Bank, Environmental Impoverishment, and the Crisis of Development* (1994) have shown similar results.

A main reason why the above mentioned series of events occurs and leads to breakdown of civil order and human rights violations is because the imperial centers of power define human rights in an entirely arbitrary and circumscribed manner. Human rights for them are limited to the traditional "political" rights. A poverty stricken society or government is supposed to respect freedom of speech and press, due process, voting procedures, etc. Starving people in the face of economic chaos caused by predatory economics from the imperial centers or the World Bank are supposed to respect one another's political rights. The consistent policy of the U.S. has been to treat the U.N. Universal Declaration of Human Rights (that includes economic and social rights) as "merely symbolic," having no authoritative force (Blum 2000).

A major cause of the violations of political human rights today is because people worldwide are denied their economic and social rights: the right to a living wage, to healthcare, to social security, to adequate leisure time, to educational opportunities, etc. As we have seen, these are all features intrinsic to genuine democracy. When people are economically exploited and destitute, it is pointless to speak to them about respecting political rights. The *Earth Constitution* transforms this situation through the simple mechanism of presenting two bills of rights, Articles 12 and 13. Article 13 guarantees economic, social, and environmental rights to every citizen of the Federation creating a world where economic exploitation and chaos (due to a denial of economic and social rights) do not and cannot lead to a corresponding massive violation of political rights.

The other side of this coin of human rights violations is the practice of imperial nations in training the military elites of Third World nations in what is euphemistically known as "counterinsurgency warfare." The top secret school at Fort Benning, Georgia, in the United States (formerly known as the "School of the Americas") is only one example of this systematic foreign policy run from the imperial centers of the world. The militaries of Third World countries are trained in warfare against their own populations, in murder, blackmail, disappearances, torture, and other means of repression (Hodge and Cooper 2004; Chomsky 1996: 29-34; Klein 2008). Human economic and political rights cannot be respected within the conceptual framework of *war*, for war is precisely the barbarous no-holds-barred attempt to destroy a perceived "enemy."

The real job of these military and paramilitary juntas is to protect the status quo by maintaining a "stable investment climate" for multinational corporations and their backers of the global economic *status quo* in the Pentagon and elsewhere. Protection of human rights is indeed "merely symbolic" under the system of sovereign nation-states, with its inherent domination of the weak by the strong and inherent system of global economic exploitation. Transforming the global paradigm to a non-military federation with an independent branch of government (the World Ombudsmus) serving to protect political, social, economic, and environmental rights worldwide will by and large solve the problem of human rights violations that has plagued the twentieth and twenty-first centuries (see Klein 2008).

Article 13 of the *Earth Constitution* guarantees equal opportunity for employment with wages to assure human dignity, free and adequate public education for everyone, free and adequate public health services and medical care, protection of the natural environment, conservation of essential natural resources, adequate housing, nutritious food supplies, safe drinking water, and social security for all citizens to protect against accident and to assure dignity in old age. None of these elements in a universal prosperity system can be realized under the present global economic system based on private ownership of natural resources, especially land, and accumulation of wealth for the few at the expense of the many. Global prosperity can only be actualized through effective economic and political democracy on a planetary scale.

Under genuine global democracy there can be no more economic imperialism of corporations or nations, no more sweatshops, no more economic exploitation, nor more externalization of costs to the environment and the public by businesses, and no more interference with planetary democracy through manipulations by the rich. As with the world peace system, a world prosperity system will be institutionalized and maintained by the World Parliament, the World Executive, the World Courts, the World Police, and the World Ombudsmus. For the first time in history, the *Earth Constitution* will establish the reasonable economic and political equality of all persons that are essential to effective democracy.

In short, the *Earth Constitution* creates a democratic world commonwealth directed to the common good of humanity and future generations. As we have seen, it is non-military by law (Article 2) and democratic at every level, leaving economic and political self-determination to the nations insofar as these conform to universal human rights and world law (Article 14). Hence, the three major non-democratic sources of the deep violence of today's world – sovereign nation-states, transnational corporations, and global banking cartels – are brought under the democratic control of the people of Earth through enforceable world law.

All nations joining the Earth Federation must demilitarize in accordance with a coordinated and carefully orchestrated procedure. Under Article 17, half of the immense wealth saved by this process is then used to fund the newly formed Earth Federation, the other half kept by the nations to empower sustainable development. All transnational corporations are refranchised in the service of human welfare by the World Parliament. And global banking is mundialized – socially owned by the people of Earth – to be administered through people's banks in localities worldwide.

The Earth Federation now coordinates the international actions of demilitarized nation-states through world laws legislated by the World Parliament. Conflicts are settled through the world court system and violators are subject to arrest and prosecution by the World Attorneys General and the World Police. Similarly, transnational corporations are regulated through the democratic legislation of the World Parliament. Their charters will mandate that they operate in ways that promote the general economic and environmental welfare of humanity. Their expertise and organizational infrastructures can now be used to promote universal prosperity while protecting the environment, no longer for exploitation of the most poor and vulnerable for cheap labor and resources, and no longer externalizing costs into the environment through pollution and production exclusively for private profit.

Our global monetary system today is 99% composed of privately created debt-money (Brown 2007). Because of this we live in a world of global scarcity and desperation requiring, as we have seen, massive military training for counterinsurgency warfare and massive military interventions by imperial nations designed to protect and promote the present world domination by a tiny corporate and financial elite. The *Earth Constitution* explicitly states that money must be created by the Federation as *debt-free money* addressed to the common good and planetary prosperity (Article 8.7.1.6 and 8.7.1.7).

Therefore, and perhaps most importantly, the Earth Federation issues debt-free, interest-free money to promote the prosperity, free trade, and well-being of the people of Earth while protecting the planetary environment. Individuals, corporations, state and local governments may all take advantage of very low cost development loans and lines of credit that are not premised on exploitation of the debtors in the service of private profit (Article 4). In addition, primary created (dept-free) money will be judiciously spent for global infrastructure needs by the World Parliament. Money and banking are now used in the service of the common good of the people of Earth and in protection of the "ecological fabric of life" on our planet. The rich can no longer exploit poor people and nations through a system of loans and debt that has so far created such misery for the peoples and nations of Earth.

Three key features of the corrupt oligarchy that now dominates the world economy are eliminated from the start. *First,* military Keynesianism (or militarism used to artificially pump up the economies of nations) is eliminated, since under Article 2 all militaries worldwide become illegal. The immense profitability and incentive for war based within the industrial-military complex is abolished. *Second,* legal corporate personhood is abolished. This legal deception has turned the once beneficial corporations of the world into monstrous, immortal super-humans, who use their billions of dollars and super-human legal rights to dominate the economy of our planet. *Third,* the *Constitution* also removes the ability of these corporate entities and the super-rich to influence politics, judges, and government officials through massive campaign contributions or other forms of monetary influence.

Hence, the key steps necessary to founding a truly democratic and prosperous world order take place with the ratification of the *Constitution*: the hold of the industrial-military oligarchies now dominating the planet is broken along with the hold of their associates, the banking, corporate, and massive financial oligarchies, and the monetary system of the world is placed in the service of the people of Earth. The founding of world democracy under the *Earth Constitution* accomplishes all this from its very inception.

We have seen that, during its twelve sessions to date, the Provisional World Parliament has passed some 47 World Legislative Acts designed to implement and develop the infrastructure of the Earth Federation under both the spirit and letter of the *Constitution for the Federation of Earth.* Many of these acts are directed toward elaborating a prosperity system for the Earth under the guidelines set forth in the *Earth Constitution*. These acts include the creation of a World Economic Development Organization (WLA 2), an Earth Financial Funding Corporation (WLA 7), a Provisional Office for World Revenue (WLA 17), a World Patents Act (WLA 21), a World Equity Act (WLA 22), a World Public Utilities Act (WLA 38), and an act for a World Guaranteed Annual Income (WLA 42). Together they are laying the economic foundations for a global market economy based on human rights, promotion of the common good, and a democratic world order that benefits everyone, not just the present 10 percent of humanity who today own 85 percent of all the global wealth (Brown, 2007: 271).

As early as the first session of the Parliament in 1982, when WLA 2 was passed, creating the World Economic Development Organization (WEDO), the Parliament saw through the deception of debt-based money creation. Among the means of funding for WEDO is the directive to develop the financing potential and procedures of *Earth Constitution to base finance on people's potential productive capacity in both goods and services*, rather than on past savings (defined under Article 8, Section 7, paragraphs 1.4, 1.5, 1.6, and 1.7).

From this principle of funding under the *Earth Constitution* (that is, the creation of debt-free fiat money and credit based on the potential of those funded to produce goods and services) follows all the other principles of the Provisional World Parliament that are building the infrastructure for an equitable and just world order. With government-issued debt-free money, the Earth Federation will hire tens of millions of unemployed people in the Third World to restore the environment, replant the forests of the Earth, and restore the degraded agricultural lands of the Earth. This massive effort is absolutely necessary if we are to deal effectively with global warming. The *Constitution* creates a voluntary, non-military World Service Corps (Article 4.36) that will employ many millions from poor countries and bring cash into communities worldwide, thereby revitalizing local economies.

The Earth Federation will have a common currency valued the same everywhere, ending speculation in currencies and the domination of "hard" over "soft" currencies. It will institute the principle of "equal pay for equal work," without gender or other discrimination, ending the exporting of production to low-wage areas of the world in order to maximize the rate of exploitation and profit. It will encourage in numerous ways *worker investment and cooperative management* in the firms within which they often spend their working lives. It will distribute the work burden among the working population more equitably and empower people at the grass roots level worldwide through such democratic innovations as microloans, infrastructure development, education, and healthcare.

The first premise of the Equity Act (WLA #22) of the Eighth Session of the Provisional World Parliament was to end the geometric differences in buying power between nations by equalizing wages done for equally productive work. The Act also set a standard for the Earth Currency, the universal currency of the Earth Federation that will not be subject to manipulation and speculation as is the present chaos of national currencies. The currency is valued in terms of the dual criteria of a basket of universal and necessary commodities and one hour of productive work. The introduction of the Earth Currency so defined will alone transform the global economic system in the direction of stability, equity, and justice.

The *Manifesto of the Earth Federation* explains at some length the various economic measures that can easily transform the present system of domination and exploitation into one of universal prosperity. There is no mystery about how wealth is created through a combination of land (natural resources), capital, and productive labor (J.W. Smith 2010). The real question is why two thirds of the world remains in poverty when we know so much about wealth creation. The simple economic and social measures enacted to date by the Provisional World Parliament are the foundation of a world system of universal prosperity. Together, they simply place economics on the foundation of planetary democracy.

The Parliament also passed WLA #18, creating a Provisional Office of World Revenue to handle financial matters of the Emerging Earth

Federation until the first operative stage of world government is activated. In order to end the unjust and exploitative use of patents and intellectual property rights that now allows First World corporations to control the wealth-producing process and the most advanced technologies in their own interest worldwide, the Parliament passed WLA #21, the World Patents Act, activating an office that supervises world patents and, with small changes in the current system (as explained in the *Manifesto*), will promote technology transfer and use of creative, innovative ideas for development throughout the world.

WLA #23, the Global Accounting & Auditing Standards Act, will standardize accounting worldwide according to current internationally accepted standards and help prevent corporate theft, manipulating of books, hoarding in off-shore bank accounts, and other practices that currently bedevil the world's economy and interfere with the development of general prosperity. Again, we see that changing the assumptions from the current ones of fragmentation and division to those based on the principle of *unity in diversity* can dramatically alter the deleterious consequences of current institutional arrangements.

In short, the economic principles explicit within the *Earth Constitution* and used by the Provisional World Parliament provide a genuine "New Deal" for the people of Earth. The tens of millions hired to restore the environment will have money to exchange in their local economies. In conjunction with interest-free loans or grants for building infrastructure, sanitation systems, education, healthcare, and many private and public sustainable new enterprises, local economies will "take off" in that dynamic circulation of money within communities that economists speak of as economic health. Once the militarized *nation-state* is removed (today pouring more than one trillion U.S. dollars per year down the toilet of militarism) along with gigantic corporate and banking institutions dedicated to extracting private profit from localities into foreign banks of the rich, economic well-being will not be difficult to achieve.

The *Constitution* guarantees everyone on Earth a living wage entirely sufficient to live with dignity and freedom (under Article 13). It ensures sanitation systems, essential resources, and educational systems for everyone. It provides every person on Earth with free health care, free education, and ample insurance in case of accident or old age. Provisional world legislation enacted by the Provisional World Parliament under the authority of Article 19 of the *Constitution* provides every person over age 18 with a guaranteed annual income sufficient to eliminate extreme poverty and starvation from the Earth (WLA 42).

Free quality education is essential to economic health, and such worldwide education will essentially stop the brain drain in which talented and educated persons from poor countries move to first-world jobs and salaries. Reasonable laws will also regulate intellectual property rights (IPRs) thereby disseminating inexpensive technological innovations equitably throughout the world, activating sustainable and efficient economies everywhere (see the *Manifesto of the Earth Federation*). These many elements work together as part of an integrated *prosperity system* under the *Earth Constitution*: money creation, banking, intellectual property rights, education, technology transfer, a World Service Corps, equal pay for equal work, a global living wage, and protection of economic and social rights all working together to undergird a genuine prosperity system for the Earth.

The world order can be fairly easily transformed into one of planetary peace with justice and prosperity. The present world system of scarcity and domination is a result of the principle inherent in money created as public debt to private financial elites and on a global system of maximizing private profit at the expense of the common good of the people of Earth and our planetary environment. Perhaps the most fundamental secret lies in "democratic money": money issued debt-free in the name of the productive capacity of the citizens of Earth to produce goods and services.

These principles cannot work, we have seen, unless we take this "all" seriously and universalize democracy to every person on Earth. This universalization process is the fundamental imperative of our time. Yet there is a concomitant aspect of our moral obligation today that requires us to abjure violence, war, and military service altogether and create a world order premised on substantive justice and fairness for all peoples. As an integrated whole, the world peace system and the world prosperity system created by the *Constitution* will necessarily also be a world justice system.

A Justice System

Since the time of Aristotle, thinkers have distinguished two dimensions of justice: *distributive justice* that considers how the resources of society can best be distributed, taking into consideration both the common good of society and the principle that equal rewards should follow equal accomplishments, and *corrective justice* in which society sets up a system of trials, judgments, and punishments for those who break the laws or to settle civil disputes. Historically the concept of justice has also been developed as the moral idea of fairness: the idea of treating individuals or peoples fairly or equitably. The *Earth Constitution* and the Provisional World Parliament have extensively developed all these aspects of justice. The same integrated set of governmental branches integral to the peace system and the prosperity system work to operate the justice system under the *Constitution*. With the help of many departments gathering data on world economic and social conditions, the World Parliament of some 1500 lawmakers representing all peoples, nations, and the common good of humanity studies the needs of the people of Earth and makes laws directed toward peace, universal prosperity, justice, freedom, and sustainability. All persons as individuals are held responsible to these laws.

The World Police and Attorneys General identify, indict, and apprehend suspects accused of violating world laws. We have seen that the police have only such weapons that are necessary to apprehend *individuals*. The requirement that police protect innocent bystanders is also emphasized, as is the humane and dignified treatment of those who are arrested and held for a fair and impartial trial (Article 12.13 and 12.14). The professional and highly qualified world judiciary within the Earth Federation Civil Service framework conducts impartial trials of those accused, and the World Ombudsmus carefully watches to see that human rights are protected throughout the process.

Under this system of correctional justice, no longer will the law and punishment be directed primarily toward the poor, with the overwhelming majority of those incarcerated coming from poor and disadvantaged background and subject to the kinds of laws and profiling that in effect punish the poor for being poor. Developing the spirit and intent of the *Constitution* with regard to correctional justice, the Provisional World Parliament has articulated the kinds of laws and corresponding punishments that will be fundamental to the justice system of the Earth Federation. It has worked out a system of seven classes of felonies, with corresponding punishments for conviction depending on the seriousness of the offense. (The World Penal Code is elaborated in detail in WLA # 19.) Those apprehended and tried under the Earth Federation will no longer be the poor but all persons who violate the laws regarding peace, general prosperity, justice, freedom, and sustainability.

For example, the very first world legislative act passed by the Parliament at its first session in 1982 in Brighton, England, prohibits all weapons of mass destruction and criminalizes involvement with such weapons. Under provisional world law, design, research, or testing such weapons is a class six felony, buying them a class six felony, selling a class five felony, transport, deployment, or installing a class one felony, and production, manufacture, or fabricating a class one felony. Similarly the World Peace

Act (WLA #13) passed in 2003 at the Sixth Session of the Parliament in Bangkok, Thailand, proscribes in greater detail activities related to WMDs or prohibited military activity such as finance, brokerage, lending, design of components, military software programming, impeding enforcement against proscribed military-related activities, disrupting communications, designing machine viruses, conscription, bids for war damage, etc. The act provides for permits to be issued to de-mine, decontaminate, disassemble, or convert to peaceful uses military hardware or munitions plants. WLA #15, Statute of the World Court of Human Rights, assigns procedures and penalties for the violation of human rights as does WLA #20 establishing the protocols for an Earth Federation World Court Bench for Criminal Cases.

From these examples it should be clear that those indicted, tried, and convicted will be the real criminals of the world for the first time in human history. No longer will the poor be targeted, but the violators of peace, human rights, and the integrity of our environment. The justice system will operate under a truly new paradigm, protecting the rights of those accused who must be apprehended with a minimum use of force. Those accused may include heads of nations, CEOs of multinational corporations, bankers illegally manipulating the monetary system, military generals, or wealthy and powerful persons. All individuals will be equally subject to the law and the laws prohibit many of the criminal activities that are today accepted as normal under the fragmented paradigm of nation-state sovereignty and monopoly capitalism. The rich and powerful will be for the first time in history equally subject to the law and the system of correctional justice along with everyone else.

The system of *distributive justice* under the *Earth Constitution* and Provisional World Parliament is equally transformative of the present disastrous world order. We have seen that Article 13 of the *Earth Constitution* guarantees equal opportunity for employment with wages sufficient to assure human dignity, free and adequate public education for everyone, free and adequate public health services and medical care, protection of the natural environment, conservation of essential natural resources, adequate housing, nutritious food supplies and safe drinking water, and social security for all citizens to protect against accident and assure dignity in old age. Distributive justice first and foremost recognizes universal human dignity and the right of every person to the livable income necessary to be free from extreme misery and deprivation.

Following the *Earth Constitution*, the Global Equity Act mandates the World Parliament to set a living wage for the world that assures this human dignity. Based on this living wage (entirely sufficient for a good life), the act specifies the maximum wage (inclusive of investment income) as four times the living wage. (This would make those at the higher levels very well off indeed. Our planet is very rich in resources, and there is no legitimate reason why everyone cannot be well off.) As Mahatma Gandhi predicts: no more will "the few ride on the backs of the millions." Profits for businesses beyond what is required for overhead, wages, materials, and production must be either donated to any public or private non-profit organizations or poured back into the business in a sustainable manner. Again following the *Constitution* (which specifies "better distribution of the workload of humanity") the act requires Parliament to regularly recalculate what constitutes full time work with a view to a just work week for all persons. It specifies that people receive "equal pay for equal work," taking into account individual merit, seniority, and special talents.

As we have seen, global banking is socially owned under the Earth Federation, establishing a system that makes funding available to all who have a creative, sustainable, and productive project. The resulting market system will produce not only near universal prosperity, as described above, but will produce genuine economic justice for the first time in history. Creative new ways to reward innovation, hard work, and special talents will be implemented by the World Parliament and communities worldwide to replace the destructive notion that the only incentives people require involve evermore riches even beyond what normal persons could reasonably use for a life of comfort and luxury. People will look to advancement, public awards, community appreciation, and other forms of recognition rather than simply monetary gain. These and similar principles of distributive justice will create a decent world order for the majority of persons on the Earth.

The system of correctional justice will complement the system of distributive justice. The vast majority of people will see for themselves that things are truly fair and just in the moral sense. It should be clear that the justice system also requires the peace system and the prosperity system as we have described them. This equitable system of justice will also empower the freedom system which depends on, and derives from, a just world framework.

A Freedom System

Freedom, the protection of individual human rights premised on the autonomy and dignity of the individual person, is a multi-dimensional concept that lies at the very heart of democracy. We have seen the many ways in which the several branches of the Earth Federation government work together to ensure peace, prosperity, and justice. The same is true of freedom. The Earth Federation system as a whole ensures and undergirds freedom through dozens of features working together.

Article 12 of the *Earth Constitution* specifies 18 items articulating a series of political rights and freedoms. It even includes seven items that begin with the word "freedom" – "freedom of thought and conscience, speech, press, writing, etc.; freedom of assembly, association, etc.; freedom to vote and campaign; freedom of religion or no religion; freedom for political beliefs or no political beliefs; and freedom for investigation, research, and reporting. Article 13 also includes five items that begin with the words "free" or "freedom" – freedom of choice in work or profession; free public education and equal opportunities; free public health services and medical care; freedom of self-determination for dissenters or minorities; freedom for change of residence anywhere on Earth. The *Earth Constitution* addresses multiple dimensions of human freedom (see Martin 2010).

Article 12 calls all the rights that it specifies "inalienable" and states that "it shall be mandatory for the World Parliament, the World Executive, and all organs and agencies of the World Government to honor, implement, and enforce these rights. All persons whose rights have been violated "have full recourse through the World Ombudsmus, the Enforcement System, and the World Courts." Ultimately, however, freedom is most fundamentally assured through the establishment of a *global community* under the *Earth Constitution* dedicated to human development and the actualization of human potential. No longer will people be enslaved to multinational corporations, banking cartels, or national security state domination. These impediments will be brought into line by the global founded community of rights and responsibilities deriving from legislation empowering individuals from the ground up.

Aware that the greatest danger to freedom historically has been government itself, especially the Executive Branch of government in control of police and military, the framers of the *Constitution* separated the police from the Executive branch, as we have seen, and abolished the military altogether. The Executive Branch of the Earth Federation that administers the day to day operations of many government agencies is run by a presidium of five persons, one from each continental division of the planet. The Executive has no power to declare a state of emergency and suspend the *Constitution*, and it has no power to refuse to spend the budget allocated to it by the World Parliament (Article 6.6).

The World Police and Attorneys General, we have seen, are a separate agency responsible directly to Parliament (representing the people of

Earth). The police possess only weapons necessary to apprehend individuals and, like all government officials, can be removed for cause. The World Ombudsmus, is an independent agency of government responsible to the World Parliament that can investigate and indict the police for violations of human rights. The *Constitution* provides a comprehensive system of checks and balances directed toward protecting freedom and democracy.

Article 13 of the *Earth Constitution* presents an additional 19 items articulating a series of human rights that are often referred to as "second generation rights" and "third generation rights." The rights elaborated in Article 12 constitute the traditional political freedoms deriving from the 18th century democratic revolutions: freedom of speech, assembly, press, religion, etc. The conception of second generation rights developed through the early 20th century and were famously expressed, for example, in the U.N. Universal Declaration of Human Rights of 1948.

These include the rights to decent wages, healthcare, social security, education, etc. They are predicated on the understanding that a supportive *social framework* is a necessary foundation for personal freedom and dignity. These are elaborated in Article 13 of the *Earth Constitution*. However, the *Constitution* understands that even these are insufficient for true freedom. The positive fullness of freedom can only be realized on Earth when people are also guaranteed the "third generation" rights to world peace and protection of the global environment. The *Constitution* takes freedom to a higher level than any previous historical form.

We have seen that the founding principle of the *Earth Constitution* is unity in diversity, a principle that the Federation will promote throughout the government as well as in media, education, and law. The second "broad function" of the Earth Federation specified in Article 1 of the *Constitution* states that it must "protect universal human rights, including life, liberty, security, democracy, and equal opportunities in life." The entire system of the *Constitution* is built around this and the other five broad functions specified in Article 1, the first of which (Article 1.1) is world peace, the second of which (1.2) is freedom and the protection of human rights, and the fifth of which is "to protect the environment and the ecological fabric of life." The *Constitution* is specifically designed to enhance human flourishing and freedom throughout its many dimensions.

Major impediments to human freedom and flourishing endemic to the present world chaos are removed and prevented from recurring by the integrated functions of the Earth Federation under the *Constitution*. For example, there will be no more national security state, world militarism, authoritarian regimes, rogue militarized terror groups, corporate violations of the dignity of employees, extremes of poverty and deprivation, lack of literacy and education, or lack of adequate health care. Scholars sometimes speak of the defense of first generation political rights as "negative freedom" – the removal of impediments to individual self-determination.

However, the *Constitution* will also enhance the "positive freedom" of actualization within an empowering community premised on unity in diversity. The supporting matrix of a community of rights and responsibilities, premised as well on second and third generation rights, provides the framework for the creative actualization of our individual and collective human potential. The protection of "life, security, and equal opportunities" on Earth, institutionalized through a global community of freedom (as specified in Article 1) will vastly empower the people of Earth. Freedom will no longer merely be a "freedom from" but will become the positive fullness of "freedom for." The *Earth Constitution* establishes a dynamic and powerful freedom system.

A Sustainability System

Environmental destruction (like war, poverty, injustice, and denial of freedom) is a direct consequence of our present global political and economic system. If companies have to consider the bottom line in a competitive situation where they must make a certain margin of profit or go out of business, then the incentive to *externalize* costs into the air, water, and soil to the detriment of the planetary ecosystem and future generations is tremendous. Genuine sustainability can only be achieved when the common good and the welfare of future generations are factored into the economic equation. Sustainability means that the resources taken from the Earth are either replaced fully (for example, lumber can be replaced though replanting forests) or used sparingly until ways can be found to substitute artificial resources for essential natural resources (Daly 1996).

The *Earth Constitution* contains dozens of references to "the environment" and the "ecology" of our planet, indicating that a major premise of the Earth Federation will be environmental sustainability. The *Constitution* mundializes those natural resources that are vital to the well being of humanity and that are limited in quantity or non-renewable (Article 4). Hence, they are taken out of the hands of giant corporate monopolies who today exploit them for the private profit of a few at the expense of most of humanity and future generations. The Provisional World Parliament has taken steps to enable this *Constitutional* mandate, for example, by passing the Water Act at its Eight Session. Multinational corporations have bought up water rights in India and elsewhere and used their "right to private property" to blackmail ordinary citizens who need water (see Shiva, *Water Wars: Privatization, Pollution, and Profit,* 2002).

In his book *When Corporations Rule the World* (1995), former Harvard Business School faculty member, David Korten, chronicles the devastation of our natural resources as well as the environment by multinational corporations based in the imperial centers of capital. Natural resources are essential for human well-being and need to be carefully conserved for the well-being of all the Earth's citizens as well as future generations. The Provisional World Parliament created the World Oceans and Seabeds Authority to supervise the vast riches of the oceans for the welfare of humanity, oceans now being exploited by predatory nation-states, and private corporations without any democratic governmental supervision.

With the vast power placed in human hands by engines, electricity, and specialized machines, the ecosystems of the Earth began to be destroyed at a rate far beyond the ability of nature to heal and repair damages caused by human interference. The technological revolutions of the 18th and 19th centuries continued into the electronic and digital revolutions of the 20th and 21st centuries placing such power in human hands that human activity in its present forms may well destroy the life-support systems of the entire planet and collapse the fabric of life to the point where higher forms of life can no longer survive upon the Earth. The forests of the world, for example, provide the planetary ecosystem with much of the oxygen that supports all aerobic forms of life. They bind carbon dioxide that is exhaled by most living creatures and produced by all forms of combustion. They moderate the climate, provide habitats for most of the vast bio-diversity of the Earth, and draw fresh water from the ocean coasts into the interior of continents. Yet the forests of the Earth are disappearing at the rate of an area one half the size of California each year.

In addition to forests, agricultural soils of the Earth are rapidly disappearing. Unsustainable agricultural practices are rapidly depleting topsoils of the planet to the point where vast areas have become unsuitable for agriculture and have been converted to grazing lands. Yet overgrazing worldwide is turning even these areas on every continent into desert wasteland, places that cannot be used to support most life. Runoff from the use of pesticides is poisoning water supplies and ecosystems. Billions of tons of topsoil are lost each year to erosion because of these unsustainable agricultural practices.

Regarding fresh water, the over-pumping of aquifers and overuse of water is dropping water tables worldwide, causing water crises and shortages in many areas of the world. The cities of the world, in addition, are becoming poisoners of the planet's fresh air supplies. Hundreds of millions of gasoline and internal combustion engines and other sources of air pollution spew pollutants into the air. Yet the atmosphere of the Earth is necessary to support all higher forms of life and is at the heart of the ecosystem of our planet.

These cities also produce immense amounts of polluted water, garbage, and trash wastes that are filling and poisoning countrysides, rivers, and oceans worldwide. At the same time, the human population continues to grow at the rate of 80 million new persons per year, every person of whom requires basic resources, fresh water, clean air, and agricultural and forest resources to support them throughout their life-spans, and every one of whom produces waste materials that are returned to the environment (Caldicott 1992; Renner 1996; Daly 1996; Speth 2004).

The principle of Gaia, the idea that the entire Earth (as it has evolved over its 4.6 billion year existence) forms an encompassing ecosystem, is only slowly becoming understood by large numbers of people. This awareness grows as planetary phenomena signaling the alteration of the entire global ecosystem become widely known. Phenomena such as global warming, melting of the polar ice caps, depletion of the ozone layer, collapsing of entire ocean fisheries, rapid extinction of species on a daily basis, increased planetary disasters and superstorms, and possible inversions of global ocean currents and weather patterns are well understood (Lovelock 1991).

Thoughtful human beings today have understood that human life is inseparable from the web of life on Earth. They have understood that we must alter our economic, social, and political practices rapidly to bring human civilization into harmony with the planetary web of life that sustains us. They understand that all development must be sustainable, that it must support human life in the present in ways that do not diminish the life-prospects of future generations. Today, virtually all societies and all nations are living at the expense of future generations, both of humans and other species (Caldicott 1992; Daly 1996; Speth 2004). Actualization of our life-prospects diminishes their life-prospects. At the current rate of destruction, it is even possible that we will reduce their life-prospects to zero.

The *Earth Constitution* and the work of the Provisional World Parliament have been dedicated to addressing these horrific consequences of the present world disorder. This premise of our global, democratically conceived, well-being is behind the Parliament's passage of the World Hydrogen Energy Authority (WLA #10) to spearhead research and conversion to renewable clean energy for the world, the Hydrocarbon Resource Act (WLA #16) to conserve, regulate on behalf of a clean environment, and utilize democratically the world's remaining hydrocarbon resources, and the Water Act (WLA #30) that recognizes clean water as a right of all persons and takes steps to protect the Earth's diminishing water resources, restore sources of fresh water to the Earth, and democratically apportion these resources to all persons on Earth.

Recognizing not only that the global environment is threatened but that it is already seriously damaged (as the *Manifesto of the Earth Federation* demonstrates at length), the Provisional World Parliament at its Second Session adopted WLA #6 creating the Emergency Earth Rescue Administration (EERA). The task of the EERA is to spearhead the gigantic task of restoring the environment of the Earth once the first operative stage of world government under the *Constitution* has been activated. Millions of trees will need to be planted, major initiatives will be needed to restore diminished agricultural lands, and emergency efforts will be required to reclaim sources and conditions for fresh water for the peoples of Earth.

The Parliament also passed WLA #9 creating, within the World Administration of the *Constitution*, a Global Ministry on the Environment to facilitate conversion to sustainability and staff the EERA. Such momentous tasks, absolutely necessary for a decent future for the Earth, can never be accomplished by the fragmented system of nation-states or the U.N. The U.N., which is a mere confederation of sovereign nation-states, has held three global conferences on the destruction of our planetary environment: in Rio de Janeiro, Brazil in 1992, Johannesburg, South Africa in 2002, and Copenhagen, Denmark in 2009. There is common agreement that these were all complete failures to deal with our environmental crises.

The Provisional World Parliament has created a network of practical, pragmatic, and immediately necessary laws and agencies to deal with the immense problems of global environmental restoration and conversion to sustainability. As we have seen, the very first article of the *Earth Constitution* specifies that the fifth broad function of the Earth Federation will be "to protect the environment and the ecological fabric of life from all sources of damage, and to control technological innovations whose effects transcend national boundaries, for the purpose of keeping Earth a safe, healthy and happy home for humanity." Both the *Constitution* and the Parliament are dedicated to creating a world system adequate to this task.

The *Constitution* explicitly requires the government of the Earth Federation to protect the ecological fabric of life on Earth, that is, to respect the Gaia principle with all its ramifications. Not only does the *Constitution* make this a primary mandate of the Earth Federation, but in its second bill of rights (Article 13) makes respect for the Gaia principle a right of the people of Earth themselves and a "directive principle for the world government" to actualize this right. Article 13, numbers 9, 10, and 11 read as follows. People have a right to "protection of the natural environment which is the common heritage of humanity against pollution, ecological disruption or damage which could imperil life or lower the quality of life" (9). "Conservation of those natural resources of Earth which are limited so that present and future generations may continue to enjoy life on planet Earth" (10), and "assurance for everyone of adequate housing, of adequate and nutritious food supplies, of safe and adequate water supplies, of pure air with protection of oxygen supplies and the ozone layer, and, in general, for the continuance of an environment which can sustain healthy living for all" (11).

Clearly, here again, the *Constitution* explicitly recognizes the need for human economic, political, and social institutions to conform to the Gaia principle (which is the principle of sustainability) protecting the whole of the planetary environment for future generations. The key to a sustainable civilization is not only to promote education concerning the principles of natural ecology. This effort alone is insufficient and will ultimately fail unless the anti-ecological institutions of the modern world, described above, are also transformed according to the scientific principles of natural ecology.

For this to happen, the entire human community must be joined together through the dynamic of genuine unity in diversity that constitutes a complementary principle of *social ecology* in human life uniting all people under non-military democratic world government. Only thus can the Gaia principle become a guiding principle for all human political, economic, and social processes. These principles of social ecology are inseparable from the principles of natural ecology. It is necessary to do for humanity what the natural Gaia principle does for nature. The *Constitution for the Federation of the Earth* joins the two together to create a truly ecological and sustainable world order.

Conclusion

The *Constitution* and its elaboration through the work of the Provisional World Parliament provide the *necessary* conditions for a peaceful, prosperous, and sustainable world system. Throughout our model, however, we have assumed the creative input of human beings with integrity, vision, and creative energy who must enliven the system outlined by the *Constitution* and the Parliament. The Earth Federation needs Parliamentarians, Judges, Administrators, Police, and Ombudsmen of who are capable of cooperatively working as part of an open ended, democratic learning community informed by the dynamics of systems thinking. We need dedicated people who are willing to begin living from this moment forward according to the ethical and legal principles embodied in the *Earth Constitution.*

Such persons will serve as the *sufficient* condition for actualizing the unity in diversity of this world system. Such persons in our present historical situation must also serve as the sufficient condition for the ratification and implementation of the *Constitution.* The necessary features of a holistic world system can be described in print. The sufficient conditions for its actualization depend on the love, aspirations, conscience, and intelligence of actual human beings. Within the Earth Federation Movement today, citizens all around the world are actualizing this vision and living according to the *Earth Constitution,* no longer according to the illegitimate and immoral system of warring nation-states.

Study of the *Constitution for the Federation of Earth* repays the student richly. For a model of a future world order emerges that not only transforms the fragmented and outdated paradigms of the present world disorder but shows itself to be entirely practical and imminently possible under the guidelines provided by Articles 17 and 19. The conceptual model created here by the Provisional World Parliament at its 12th session in Kolkata, India in 2010 presents only the highlights of the integrated planetary system initiated by the *Earth Constitution* and the Provisional World Parliament. We hope that the parameters of this model that we have sketched in this document may inspire people to ever more intensive study of the *Earth Constitution* and modeling of the transformed world system that it engenders.

As people begin to understand the vision, there is tremendous urgency that they also act on that vision with creativity, integrity, and energy. The *Constitution* must be ratified in a founding ratification convention according to the Protocols already developed by the Provisional World Parliament. It converts the presently failed world system to peace, prosperity, justice, freedom, and sustainability. It replaces the U.N. Charter with real democratic government keeping the valuable agencies of the U.N. as ministries of the Earth Federation.

Nothing less than the fate of humanity and our precious planet Earth are at stake. We invite your participation. We invite you to a life of "civil obedience."

Part Three

A Constitution for the Federation of Earth

As Amended at the
Fourth World Constituent Assembly
in Troia, Portugal, 1991

Originally drafted by the World Constitution Drafting Committee of 25 members as designated at the First World Constituent Assembly in Interlaken, Switzerland and Wolfach, Germany, 1968. Drafting Committee Chair: Sir Dr. Reinhart Ruge. Primary authors: H. Philip Isely, Terence P. Amerasinghe, Syed Md. Husain, D. M. Spencer, and Max Habicht.

Now Being Circulated Worldwide for Ratification
By the Nations and People of Earth

PREAMBLE

Realizing that Humanity today has come to a turning point in history and that we are on the threshold of an new world order which promises to usher in an era of peace, prosperity, justice and harmony;

Aware of the interdependence of people, nations and all life;

Aware that man's abuse of science and technology has brought Humanity to the brink of disaster through the production of horrendous weaponry of mass destruction and to the brink of ecological and social catastrophe;

Aware that the traditional concept of security through military defense is a total illusion both for the present and for the future;

Aware of the misery and conflicts caused by ever increasing disparity between rich and poor;

Conscious of our obligation to posterity to save Humanity from imminent and total annihilation;

Conscious that Humanity is One despite the existence of diverse nations, races, creeds, ideologies and cultures and that the principle of unity in diversity is the basis for a new age when war shall be outlawed and peace prevail; when the earth's total resources shall be equitably used for human welfare; and when basic human rights and responsibilities shall be shared by all without discrimination;

Conscious of the inescapable reality that the greatest hope for the survival of life on earth is the establishment of a democratic world government;

We, citizens of the world, hereby resolve to establish a world federation to be governed in accordance with this constitution for the Federation of Earth.

A CONSTITUTION FOR THE FEDERATION OF EARTH

Article 1 - Broad Functions of the Earth Federation

The broad functions of the Federation of Earth shall be:

1.1 To prevent war, secure disarmament, and resolve territorial and other disputes which endanger peace and human rights.

1.2 To protect universal human rights, including life, liberty, security, democracy, and equal opportunities in life.

1.3 To obtain for all people on earth the conditions required for equitable economic and social development and for diminishing social differences.

1.4 To regulate world trade, communications, transportation, currency, standards, use of world resources, and other global and international processes.

1.5 To protect the environment and the ecological fabric of life from all sources of damage, and to control technological innovations whose effects transcend national boundaries, for the purpose of keeping Earth a safe, healthy and happy home for humanity.

1.6 To devise and implement solutions to all problems which are beyond the capacity of national governments, or which are now or may become of global or international concern or consequence.

Article 2 - Basic Structure of Earth Federation

2.1 The Federation of Earth shall be organized as a universal federation, to include all nations and all people, and to encompass all oceans, seas and lands of Earth, inclusive of non-self governing territories, together with the surrounding atmosphere.

2.2 The World Government for the Federation of Earth shall be non-military and shall be democratic in its own structure, with ultimate sovereignty residing in all the people who live on Earth.

2.3 The authority and powers granted to the World Government shall be limited to those defined in this Constitution for the Federation of Earth, applicable to problems and affairs which transcend national boundaries, leaving to national governments jurisdiction over the internal affairs of the respective nations but consistent with the authority of the World Government to protect universal human rights as defined in this World Constitution.

2.4   The basic direct electoral and administrative units of the World Government shall be World Electoral and Administrative Districts. A total of not more than 1000 World Electoral and Administrative Districts shall be defined, and shall be nearly equal in population, within the limits of plus or minus ten percent.

2.5   Contiguous World Electoral and Administrative Districts shall be combined as may be appropriate to compose a total of twenty World Electoral and Administrative Regions for the following purposes, but not limited thereto: for the election or appointment of certain world government officials; for administrative purposes; for composing various organs of the world government as enumerated in Article 4; for the functioning of the Judiciary, the Enforcement System, and the Ombudsmus, as well as for the functioning of any other organ or agency of the World Government.

2.6   The World Electoral and Administrative Regions may be composed of a variable number of World Electoral and Administrative Districts, taking into consideration geographic, cultural, ecological and other factors as well as population.

2.7   Contiguous World Electoral and Administrative Regions shall be grouped together in pairs to compose Magna-Regions.

2.8   The boundaries for World Electoral and Administrative Regions shall not cross the boundaries of the World Electoral and Administrative Districts, and shall be common insofar as feasible for the various administrative departments and for the several organs and agencies of the World Government. Boundaries for the World Electoral and Administrative Districts as well as for the Regions need not conform to existing national boundaries, but shall conform as far as practicable.

2.9 The World Electoral and Administrative Regions shall be grouped to compose at least five Continental Divisions of the Earth, for the election or appointment of certain world government officials, and for certain aspects of the composition and functioning of the several organs and agencies of the World Government as specified hereinafter. The boundaries of Continental Divisions shall not cross existing national boundaries as far as practicable. Continental Divisions may be composed of a variable number of World Electoral and Administrative Regions.

Article 3 - Organs of the Earth Federation

The organs of the World Government shall be:

3.1   The World Parliament

3.2   The World Executive

3.3   The World Administration

3.4   The Integrative Complex

3.5   The World Judiciary

3.6   The Enforcement System

3.7   The World Ombudsmus

Article 4 - Grant of Specific Powers to the Earth Federation

The powers of the World government to be exercised through its several organs and agencies shall comprise the following:

4.1   Prevent wars and armed conflicts among the nations, regions, districts, parts and peoples of Earth.

4.2   Supervise disarmament and prevent re-armament; prohibit and eliminate the design, testing, manufacture, sale, purchase, use and possession of weapons of mass destruction, and prohibit or regulate all lethal weapons which the World Parliament may decide.

4.3   Prohibit incitement to war, and discrimination against or defamation of conscientious objectors.

4.4   Provide the means for peaceful and just solutions of disputes and conflicts among or between nations, peoples, and/or other components within the Federation of Earth.

4.5   Supervise boundary settlements and conduct plebiscites as needed.

4.6   Define the boundaries for the districts, regions and divisions which are established for electoral, administrative, judicial and other purposes of the World Government.

4.7   Define and regulate procedures for the nomination and election of the members of each House of the World Parliament, and for the nomination, election, appointment and employment of all World Government officials and personnel.

4.8   Codify world laws, including the body of international law developed prior to adoption of the world constitution, but not inconsistent therewith, and which is approved by the World Parliament.

4.9   Establish universal standards for weights, measurements, accounting and records.

4.10   Provide assistance in the event of large scale calamities, including drought, famine, pestilence, flood, earthquake, hurricane, ecological disruptions and other disasters.

4.11   Guarantee and enforce the civil liberties and the basic human rights which are defined in the Bill of Rights for the Citizens of Earth which is made a part of this World Constitution under Article 12.

4.12   Define standards and promote the worldwide improvement in working conditions, nutrition, health, housing, human settlements, environmental conditions, education, economic security, and other conditions defined under Article 13 of this World Constitution.

4.13   Regulate and supervise international transportation, communications, postal services, and migrations of people.

4.14   Regulate and supervise supra-national trade, industry, corporations, businesses, cartels, professional services, labor supply, finances, investments and insurance.

4.15   Secure and supervise the elimination of tariffs and other trade barriers among nations, but with provisions to prevent or minimize hardship for those previously protected by tariffs.

4.16   Raise the revenues and funds, by direct and/or indirect means, which are necessary for the purposes and activities of the World Government.

4.17   Establish and operate world financial, banking, credit and insurance institutions designed to serve human needs; establish, issue and regulate world currency, credit and exchange.

4.18   Plan for and regulate the development, use, conservation and re-cycling of the natural resources of Earth as the common heritage of Humanity; protect the environment in every way for the benefit of both present and future generations.

4.19   Create and operate a World Economic Development Organization to serve equitably the needs of all nations and people included within the World Federation.

4.20   Develop and implement solutions to transnational problems of food supply, agricultural production, soil fertility, soil conservation, pest control, diet, nutrition, drugs and poisons, and the disposal of toxic wastes.

4.21   Develop and implement means to control population growth in relation to the life-support capacities of Earth, and solve problems of population distribution.

4.22   Develop, protect, regulate and conserve the water supplies of Earth; develop, operate and/or coordinate transnational irrigation and other water supply and control projects; assure equitable allocation of trans-national water supplies, and protect against adverse trans-national effects of water or moisture diversion or weather control projects within national boundaries.

4.23 Own, administer and supervise the development and conservation of the oceans and sea-beds of Earth and all resources thereof, and protect from damage.

4.24 Protect from damage, and control and supervise the uses of the atmosphere of Earth.

4.25 Conduct inter-planetary and cosmic explorations and research; have exclusive jurisdiction over the Moon and over all satellites launched from Earth.

4.26 Establish, operate and/or coordinate global air lines, ocean transport systems, international railways and highways, global communication systems, and means for interplanetary travel and communications; control and administer vital waterways.

4.27 Develop, operate and/or coordinate transnational power systems, or networks of small units, integrating into the systems or networks power derived from the sun, wind, water, tides, heat differentials, magnetic forces, and any other source of safe, ecologically sound and continuing energy supply.

4.28 Control the mining, production, transportation and use of fossil sources of energy to the extent necessary to reduce and prevent damages to the environment and the ecology, as well as to prevent conflicts and conserve supplies for sustained use by succeeding generations.

4.29 Exercise exclusive jurisdiction and control over nuclear energy research and testing and nuclear power production, including the right to prohibit any form of testing or production considered hazardous.

4.30 Place under world controls essential natural resources which may be limited or unevenly distributed about the Earth. Find and implement ways to reduce wastes and find ways to minimize disparities when development or production is insufficient to supply everybody with all that may be needed.

4.31 Provide for the examination and assessment of technological innovations which are or may be of supranational consequence, to determine possible hazards or perils to humanity or the environment; institute such controls and regulations of technology as may be found necessary to prevent or correct widespread hazards or perils to human health and welfare.

4.32 Carry out intensive programs to develop safe alternatives to any technology or technological processes which may be hazardous to the environment, the ecological system, or human health and welfare.

4.33 Resolve supra-national problems caused by gross disparities in technological development or capability, capital formation, availability of natural resources, educational opportunity, economic opportunity, and wage and price differentials. Assist the processes of technology transfer under conditions which safeguard human welfare and the environment and contribute to minimizing disparities.

4.34 Intervene under procedures to be defined by the World Parliament in cases of either intra-state violence and intra-state problems which seriously affect world peace or universal human rights.

4.35 Develop a world university system. Obtain the correction of prejudicial communicative materials which cause misunderstandings or conflicts due to differences of race, religion, sex, national origin or affiliation.

4.36 Organize, coordinate and/or administer a voluntary, non-military World Service Corps, to carry out a wide variety of projects designed to serve human welfare.

4.37 Designate as may be found desirable an official world language or official world languages.

4.38 Establish and operate a system of world parks, wild life preserves, natural places, and wilderness areas.

4.39 Define and establish procedures for initiative and referendum by the Citizens of Earth on matters of supra-national legislation not prohibited by this World Constitution.

4.40 Establish such departments, bureaus, commissions, institutes, corporations, administrations, or agencies as may be needed to carry out any and all of the functions and powers of the World Government.

4.41 Serve the needs of humanity in any and all ways which are now, or may prove in the future to be, beyond the capacity of national and local governments.

Article 5 - The World Parliament

5.1   Functions and Powers of the World Parliament

The functions and powers of the World Parliament shall comprise the following:

5.1.1 To prepare and enact detailed legislation in all areas of authority and jurisdiction granted to the World Government under Article 4 of this World Constitution.

5.1.2 To amend or repeal world laws as may be found necessary or desirable.

5.1.3 To approve, amend or reject the international laws developed prior to the advent of World Government, and to codify and integrate the system of world law and world legislation under the World Government.

5.1.4 To establish such regulations and directions as may be needed, consistent with this world constitution, for the proper functioning of all organs, branches, departments, bureaus, commissions, institutes, agencies or parts of the World Government.

5.1.5 To review, amend and give final approval to each budget for the World Government, as submitted by the World Executive; to devise the specific means for directly raising funds needed to fulfill the budget, including taxes, licenses, fees, globally accounted social and public costs which must be added into the prices for goods and services, loans and credit advances, and any other appropriate means; and to appropriate and allocate funds for all operations and functions of the World Government in accordance with approved budgets, but subject to the right of the Parliament to revise any appropriation not yet spent or contractually committed.

5.1.6 To create, alter, abolish or consolidate the departments, bureaus, commissions, institutes, agencies or other parts of the World Government as may be needed for the best functioning of the several organs of the World Government, subject to the specific provisions of this World Constitution.

5.1.7 To approve the appointments of the heads of all major departments, commissions, offices, agencies and other parts of the several organs of the World Government, except those chosen by electoral or civil service procedures.

5.1.8 To remove from office for cause any member of the World Executive, and any elective or appointive head of any organ, department, office, agency or other part of the World Government, subject to the specific provisions in this World Constitution concerning specific offices.

5.1.9 To define and revise the boundaries of the World Electoral and Administrative Districts, the World Electoral and Administrative Regions and Magna Regions, and the Continental Divisions.

5.1.10 To schedule the implementation of those provisions of the World Constitution which require implementation by stages during the several stages of Provisional World Government, First Operative Stage of World Government, Second Operative Stage of World Government, and Full Operative Stage of World Government, as defined in Articles 17 and 19 of this World Constitution.

5.1.11 To plan and schedule the implementation of those provisions of the World Constitution which may require a period of years to be accomplished.

5.2   Composition of the World Parliament

5.2.1 The World Parliament shall be composed of three houses, designated as follows:

*   The House of Peoples, to represent the people of Earth directly and equally;

*   The House of Nations, to represent the nations which are joined together in the Federation of Earth; and a

*   House of Counselors with particular functions to represent the highest good and best interests of humanity as a whole.

5.2.2 All members of the World Parliament, regardless of House, shall be designated as Members of the World Parliament.

5.3   The House of Peoples

5.3.1 The House of Peoples shall be composed of the peoples delegates directly elected in proportion to population from the World Electoral and Administrative Districts, as defined in Article 2.4.

5.3.2 Peoples delegates shall be elected by universal adult suffrage, open to all persons of age 18 and above.

5.3.3 One peoples delegate shall be elected from each World Electoral and Administrative District to serve a five year term in the House of Peoples. Peoples delegates may be elected to serve successive terms without limit. Each peoples delegate shall have one vote.

5.3.4 A candidate for election to serve as a peoples delegate must be at least 21 years of age, a resident for at least one year of the electoral district from which the candidate is seeking election, and shall take a pledge of service to humanity.

5.4   The House of Nations

5.4.1 The House of Nations shall be composed of national delegates elected or appointed by procedures to be determined by each national government on the following basis:

5.4.1.1 One national delegate from each nation of at least 100,000 population, but less than 10,000,000 population.

5.4.1.2 Two national delegates from each nation of at least 10,000,000 population, but less than 100,000,000 population.

5.4.1.3 Three national delegates from each nation of 100,000,000 population or more.

5.4.2 Nations of less than 100,000 population may join in groups with other nations for purposes of representation in the House of Nations.

5.4.3 National delegates shall be elected or appointed to serve for terms of five years, and may be elected or appointed to serve successive terms without limit. Each national delegate shall have one vote.

5.4.4 Any person to serve as a national delegate shall be a citizen for at least two years of the nation to be represented, must be at least 21 years of age, and shall take a pledge of service to humanity.

5.5 The House of Counselors

5.5.1 The House of Counselors shall be composed of 200 counselors chosen in equal numbers from nominations submitted from the twenty World Electoral and Administrative Regions, as defined in Article 2.5. and 2.6., ten from each Region.

5.5.2 Nominations for members of the House of Counselors shall be made by the teachers and students of universities and colleges and of scientific academies and institutes within each world electoral and administrative region. Nominees may be persons who are off campus in any walk of life as well as on campus.

5.5.3 Nominees to the House of Counselors from each World Electoral and Administrative Region shall, by vote taken among themselves, reduce the number of nominees to no less than two times and no more than three times the number to be elected.

5.5.4 Nominees to serve as members of the House of Counselors must be at least 25 years of age, and shall take a pledge of service to humanity. There shall be no residence requirement, and a nominee need not be a resident of the region from which nominated or elected.

5.5.5 The members of the House of Counselors from each region shall be elected by the members of the other two houses of the World Parliament from the particular region.

5.5.6 Counselors shall be elected to serve terms of ten years. One-half of the members of the House of Counselors shall be elected every five years. Counselors may serve successive terms without limit. Each Counselor shall have one vote.

5.6 Procedures of the World Parliament

5.6.1 Each house of the World Parliament during its first session after general elections shall elect a panel of five chairpersons from among its own members, one from each of five Continental Divisions. The chairpersons shall rotate annually so that each will serve for one year as chief presiding officer, while the other four serve as vice-chairpersons.

5.6.2 The panels of Chairpersons from each House shall meet together, as needed, for the purpose of coordinating the work of the Houses of the World Parliament, both severally and jointly.

5.6.3 Any legislative measure or action may be initiated in either House of Peoples or House of Nations or both concurrently, and shall become effective when passed by a simple majority vote of both the House of Peoples and of the House of Nations, except in those cases where an absolute majority vote or other voting majority is specified in this World Constitution.

5.6.4 In case of deadlock on a measure initiated in either the House of Peoples or House of Nations, the measure shall then automatically go to the House of Counselors for decision by simple majority vote of the House of Counselors, except in the cases where other majority vote is required in this World Constitution. Any measure may be referred for decision to the House of Counselors by a concurrent vote of the other two houses.

5.6.5 The House of Counselors may initiate any legislative measure, which shall then be submitted to the other two houses and must be passed by simple majority vote of both the House of Peoples and House of Nations to become effective, unless other voting majority is required by some provision of this World Constitution.

5.6.6 The House of Counselors may introduce an opinion or resolution on any measure pending before either of the other two houses; either of the other houses may request the opinion of the House of Counselors before acting upon a measure.

5.6.7 Each house of the World Parliament shall adopt its own detailed rules of procedure, which shall by consistent with the procedures set forth in this World Constitution, and which shall be designed to facilitate coordinated functioning of the three houses.

5.6.8 Approval of appointments by the World Parliament or any house thereof shall require simple majority votes, while removals for cause shall require absolute majority votes.

5.6.9 After the full operative stage of World Government is declared, general elections for members of the World Parliament to the House of Peoples shall be held every five years. The first general elections shall be held within the first two years following the declaration of the full operative stage of World Government.

5.6.10 Until the full operative stage of World Government is declared, elections for members of the World Parliament to the House of Peoples may be conducted whenever feasible in relation to the campaign for ratification of this World Constitution.

5.6.11 Regular sessions of the House of Peoples and House of Nations of the World Parliament shall convene on the second Monday of January of each and every Year.

5.6.12 Each nation, according to its own procedures, shall appoint or elect members of the World Parliament to the House of Nations at least thirty days prior to the date for convening the World Parliament in January.

5.6.13 The House of Peoples together with the House of Nations shall elect the members of the World Parliament to the House of Counselors during the month of January after the general elections. For its first session after general elections, the House of Counselors shall convene on the second Monday of March, and thereafter concurrently with the other two houses.

5.6.14 Bi-elections to fill vacancies shall be held within three months from occurrence of the vacancy or vacancies.

5.6.15 The World Parliament shall remain in session for a minimum of nine months of each year. One or two breaks may be taken during each year, at times and for durations to be decided by simple majority vote of the House of Peoples and House of Nations sitting jointly.

5.6.16 Annual salaries for members of the World Parliament of all three houses shall be the same, except for those who serve also as members of the Presidium and of the Executive Cabinet.

5.6.17 Salary schedules for members of the World Parliament and for members of the Presidium and of the Executive Cabinet shall be determined by the World Parliament.

Article 6 - The World Executive

6.1 Functions and Powers of the World Executive

6.1.1 To implement the basic system of world law as defined in the World Constitution and in the codified system of world law after approval by the World Parliament.

6.1.2 To implement legislation enacted by the World Parliament.

6.1.3　To propose and recommend legislation for enactment by the World Parliament.

6.1.4　To convene the World Parliament in special sessions when necessary.

6.1.5　To supervise the World Administration and the Integrative Complex and all of the departments, bureaus, offices, institutes and agencies thereof.

6.1.6　To nominate, select and remove the heads of various organs, branches, departments, bureaus, offices, commissions, institutes, agencies and other parts of the World Government, in accordance with the provisions of this World Constitution and as specified in measures enacted by the World Parliament.

6.1.7　To prepare and submit annually to the World Parliament a comprehensive budget for the operations of the World Government, and to prepare and submit periodically budget projections over periods of several years.

6.1.8　To define and propose priorities for world legislation and budgetary allocations.

6.1.9 To be held accountable to the World Parliament for the expenditures of appropriations made by the World Parliament in accordance with approved and longer term budgets, subject to revisions approved by the World Parliament.

6.2　Composition of the World Executive

The World Executive shall consist of a Presidium of five members, and of an Executive Cabinet of from twenty to thirty members, all of whom shall be members of the World Parliament.

6.3　The Presidium

6.3.1　The Presidium shall be composed of five members, one to be designated as President and the other four to be designated as Vice Presidents. Each member of the Presidium shall be from a different Continental Division.

6.3.2　The Presidency of the Presidium shall rotate each year, with each member in turn to serve as President, while the other four serve as Vice Presidents. The order of rotation shall be decided by the Presidium.

6.3.3　The decisions of the Presidium shall be taken collectively, on the basis of majority decisions.

6.3.4　Each member of the Presidium shall be a member of the World Parliament, either elected to the House of Peoples or to the House of Counselors, or appointed or elected to the House of Nations.

6.3.5 Nominations for the Presidium shall be made by the House of Counselors. The number of nominees shall be from two to three times the number to be elected. No more than one-third of the nominees shall be from the House of Counselors or from the House of Nations, and nominees must be included from all Continental Divisions.

6.3.6 From among the nominees submitted by the House of Counselors, the Presidium shall be elected by vote of the combined membership of all three houses of the World Parliament in joint session. A plurality vote equal to at least 40 percent of the total membership of the World Parliament shall be required for the election of each member to the Presidium, with successive elimination votes taken as necessary until the required plurality is achieved.

6.3.7 Members of the Presidium may be removed for cause, either individually or collectively, by an absolute majority vote of the combined membership of the three houses of the World Parliament in joint session.

6.3.8 The term of office for the Presidium shall be five years and shall run concurrently with the terms of office for the members as Members of the World Parliament, except that at the end of each five year period, the Presidium members in office shall continue to serve until the new Presidium for the succeeding term is elected. Membership in the Presidium shall be limited to two consecutive terms.

6.4   The Executive Cabinet

6.4.1 The Executive Cabinet shall be composed of from twenty to thirty members, with at least one member from each of the ten World Electoral and Administrative Magna Regions of the world.

6.4.2 All members of the Executive Cabinet shall be Members of the World Parliament.

6.4.3 There shall be no more than two members of the Executive Cabinet from any single nation of the World Federation. There may be only one member of the Executive Cabinet from a nation from which a Member of the World Parliament is serving as a member of the Presidium.

6.4.4 Each member of the Executive Cabinet shall serve as the head of a department or agency of the World Administration or Integrative Complex, and in this capacity shall be designated as Minister of the particular department or agency.

6.4.5 Nominations for members of the Executive Cabinet shall be made by the Presidium, taking into consideration the various functions which Executive Cabinets members are to perform. The Presidium shall nominate no more than two times the number to be elected.

6.4.6 The Executive Cabinet shall be elected by simple majority vote of the combined membership of all three houses of the World Parliament in joint session.

6.4.7 Members of the Executive Cabinet either individually or collectively may be removed for cause by an absolute majority vote of the combined membership of all three houses of the World Parliament sitting in joint session.

6.4.8 The term of office in the Executive Cabinet shall be five years, and shall run concurrently with the terms of office for the members as Members of the World Parliament, except that at the end of each five year period, the Cabinet members in office shall continue to serve until the new Executive Cabinet for the succeeding term is elected. Membership in the Executive Cabinet shall be limited to three consecutive terms, regardless of change in ministerial position.

6.5 Procedures of the World Executive

6.5.1 The Presidium shall assign the ministerial positions among the Cabinet members to head the several administrative departments and major agencies of the Administration and of the Integrative Complex. Each Vice President may also serve as a Minister to head an administrative department, but not the President. Ministerial positions may be changed at the discretion of the Presidium. A Cabinet member or Vice President may hold more than one ministerial post, but no more than three, providing that no Cabinet member is without a Ministerial post.

6.5.2 The Presidium, in consultation with the Executive Cabinet, shall prepare and present to the World Parliament near the beginning of each year a proposed program of world legislation. The Presidium may propose other legislation during the year.

6.5.3 The Presidium, in consultation with the Executive Cabinet, and in consultation with the World Financial Administration, (see Article 8, Sec. 7.1.9.) shall be responsible for preparing and submitting to the World Parliament the proposed annual budget, and budgetary projections over periods of years.

6.5.4 Each Cabinet Member and Vice President as Minister of a particular department or agency shall prepare an annual report for the particular department or agency, to be submitted both to the Presidium and to the World Parliament.

6.5.5 The members of the Presidium and of the Executive Cabinet at all times shall be responsible both individually and collectively to the World Parliament.

6.5.6 Vacancies occurring at any time in the World Executive shall be filled within sixty days by nomination and election in the same manner as specified for filling the offices originally.

6.6   Limitations on the World Executive

6.6.1 The World Executive shall not at any time alter, suspend, abridge, infringe or otherwise violate any provision of this World Constitution or any legislation or world law enacted or approved by the World Parliament in accordance with the provisions of this World Constitution.

6.6.2 The World Executive shall not have veto power over any legislation passed by the World Parliament.

6.6.3 The World Executive may not dissolve the World Parliament or any House of the World Parliament.

6.6.4 The World Executive may not act contrary to decisions of the World Courts.

6.6.5 The World Executive shall be bound to faithfully execute all legislation passed by the World Parliament in accordance with the provisions of this World Constitution, and may not impound or refuse to spend funds appropriated by the World Parliament, nor spend more funds than are appropriated by the World Parliament.

6.6.6 The World Executive may not transcend or contradict the decisions or controls of the World Parliament, the World Judiciary or the Provisions of this World Constitution by any device of executive order or executive privilege or emergency declaration or decree.

Article 7 - The World Administration

7.1   Functions of the World Administration

7.1.1 The World Administration shall be organized to carry out the detailed and continuous administration and implementation of world legislation and world law.

7.1.2 The World Administration shall be under the direction of the World Executive, and shall at all times be responsible to the World Executive.

7.1.3 The World Administration shall be organized so as to give professional continuity to the work of administration and implementation.

7.2   Structure and Procedures of the World Administration

7.2.1   The World Administration shall be composed of professionally organized departments and other agencies in all areas of activity requiring continuity of administration and implementation by the World Government.

7.2.2   Each Department or major agency of the World Administration shall be headed by a Minister who shall be either a member of the Executive Cabinet or a Vice President of the Presidium.

7.2.3   Each Department or major agency of the World Administration shall have as chief of staff a Senior Administrator, who shall assist the Minister and supervise the detailed work of the Department or agency.

7.2.4   Each Senior Administrator shall be nominated by the Minister of the particular Department or agency from among persons in the senior lists of the World Civil Service Administration, as soon as senior lists have been established by the World Civil Service Administration, and shall be confirmed by the Presidium. Temporary qualified appointments shall be made by the Ministers, with confirmation by the Presidium, pending establishment of the senior lists.

7.2.5   There shall be a Secretary General of the World Administration, who shall be nominated by the Presidium and confirmed by absolute majority vote of the entire Executive Cabinet.

7.2.6   The functions and responsibilities of the Secretary General of the World Administration shall be to assist in coordinating the work of the Senior Administrators of the several Departments and agencies of the World Administration. The Secretary General shall at all times be subject to the direction of the Presidium, and shall be directly responsible to the Presidium.

7.2.7   The employment of any Senior Administrator and of the Secretary General may be terminated for cause by absolute majority vote of both the Executive Cabinet and Presidium combined, but not contrary to civil service rules which protect tenure on grounds of competence.

7.2.8 Each Minister of a Department or agency of the World Administration, being also a Member of the World Parliament, shall provide continuous liaison between the particular Department or agency and the World Parliament, shall respond at any time to any questions or requests for information from the Parliament, including committees of any House of the World Parliament.

7.2.9 The Presidium, in cooperation with the particular Ministers in each case, shall be responsible for the original organization of each of the Departments and major agencies of the World Administration.

7.2.10 The assignment of legislative measures, constitutional provisions and areas of world law to particular Departments and agencies for administration and implementation shall be done by the Presidium in consultation with the Executive Cabinet and Secretary General, unless specifically provided in legislation passed by the World Parliament.

7.2.11 The Presidium, in consultation with the Executive Cabinet, may propose the creation of other departments and agencies to have ministerial status; and may propose the alteration, combination or termination of existing Departments and agencies of ministerial status as may seem necessary or desirable. Any such creation, alteration, combination or termination shall require a simple majority vote of approval of the three houses of the World Parliament in joint session.

7.2.12 The World Parliament by absolute majority vote of the three houses in joint session may specify the creation of new departments or agencies of ministerial status in the World Administration, or may direct the World Executive to alter, combine, or terminate existing departments or agencies of ministerial status.

7.2.13 The Presidium and the World Executive may not create, establish or maintain any administrative or executive department or agency for the purpose of circumventing control by the World Parliament.

7.3 Departments of the World Administration

Among the Departments and agencies of the World Administration of ministerial status, but not limited thereto and subject to combinations and to changes in descriptive terminology, shall be those listed under this Section. Each major area of administration shall be headed by a Cabinet Minister and a Senior Administrator, or by a Vice President and a Senior Administrator.

7.3.1 Disarmament & War Prevention.

7.3.2 Population.

7.3.3 Food and Agriculture.

7.3.4 Water Supplies and Waterways.

7.3.5   Health and Nutrition.

7.3.6   Education.

7.3.7   Cultural Diversity and the Arts.

7.3.8   Habitat and Settlements.

7.3.9 Environment and Ecology.

7.3.10   World Resources.

7.3.11   Oceans and Seabeds.

7.3.12   Atmosphere and Space.

7.3.13   Energy.

7.3.14   Science and Technology.

7.3.15   Genetic Research & Engineering.

7.3.16   Labor and Income.

7.3.17   Economic & Social Development.

7.3.18   Commerce & Industry

7.3.19   Transportation and Travel.

7.3.20   Multi-National Corporations.

7.3.21   Communications & Information.

7.3.22   Human Rights.

7.3.23   Distributive Justice.

7.3.24   World Service Corps.

7.3.25   World Territories, Capitals & Parks.

7.3.26   Exterior Relations.

7.3.27   Democratic Procedures.

7.3.28   Revenue.

Article 8 - The Integrative Complex

8.1   Definition

8.1.1 Certain administrative, research, planning and facilitative agencies of the World Government which are particularly essential for the satisfactory functioning of all or most aspects of the World Government, shall be designated as the Integrative Complex. The Integrative Complex shall include the agencies listed under this Section, with the proviso that other such agencies may be added upon recommendation of the Presidium followed by decision of the World Parliament.

8.1.1.1 The World Civil Service Administration.

8.1.1.2 The World Boundaries and Elections Administration.

8.1.1.3 The Institute on Governmental Procedures and World Problems.

8.1.1.4 The Agency for Research and Planning.

8.1.1.5   The Agency for Technological and Environmental Assessment.

8.1.1.6   The World Financial Administration.

8.1.1.7   Commission for Legislative Review.

8.1.2   Each agency of the Integrative Complex shall be headed by a Cabinet Minister and a Senior Administrator, or by a Vice President and a Senior Administrator, together with a Commission as provided hereunder. The rules of procedure for each agency shall be decided by majority decision of the Commission members together with the Administrator and the Minister or Vice President.

8.1.3   The World Parliament may at any time define further the responsibilities, functioning and organization of the several agencies of the Integrative Complex, consistent with the provisions of Article 8 and other provisions of the World Constitution.

8.1.4   Each agency of the Integrative Complex shall make an annual report to the World Parliament and to the Presidium.

8.2   The World Civil Service Administration

8.2.1   The functions of the World Civil Service Administration shall be the following, but not limited thereto:

8.2.1.1 To formulate and define standards, qualifications, tests, examinations and salary scales for the personnel of all organs, departments, bureaus, offices, commissions and agencies of the World Government, in conformity with the provisions of this World Constitution and requiring approval by the Presidium and Executive Cabinet, subject to review and approval by the World Parliament.

8.2.1.2   To establish rosters or lists of competent personnel for all categories of personnel to be appointed or employed in the service of the World Government.

8.2.1.3   To select and employ upon request by any government organ, department, bureau, office, institute, commission, agency or authorized official, such competent personnel as may be needed and authorized, except for those positions which are made elective or appointive under provisions of the World Constitution or by specific legislation of the World Parliament.

8.2.2   The World Civil Service Administration shall be headed by a ten member commission in addition to the Cabinet Minister or Vice President and Senior Administrator. The Commission shall be composed of one commissioner from each of ten World Electoral and Administrative Magna-Regions. The persons to serve as

Commissioners shall be nominated by the House of Counselors and then appointed by the Presidium for five year terms. Commissioners may serve consecutive terms.

8.3 The World Boundaries and Elections Administration

8.3.1 The functions of the World Boundaries and Elections Administration shall include the following, but not limited thereto:

8.3.1.1 To define the boundaries for the basic World Electoral and Administrative Districts, the World Electoral and Administrative Regions and Magna-Regions, and the Continental Divisions, for submission to the World Parliament for approval by legislative action.

8.3.1.2 To make periodic adjustments every ten or five years, as needed, of the boundaries for the World Electoral and Administrative Districts, the World Electoral and Administrative Regions and Magna-Regions, and of the Continental Divisions, subject to approval by the World Parliament.

8.3.1.3 To define the detailed procedures for the nomination and election of Members of the World Parliament to the House of Peoples and to the House of Counselors, subject to approval by the World Parliament.

8.3.1.4 To conduct the elections for Members of the World Parliament to the House of Peoples and to the House of Counselors.

8.3.1.5 Before each World Parliamentary Election, to prepare Voters' Information Booklets which shall summarize major current public issues, and shall list each candidate for elective office together with standard information about each candidate, and give space for each candidate to state his or her views on the defined major issues as well as on any other major issue of choice; to include information on any initiatives or referendums which are to be voted upon; to distribute the Voter's Information Booklets for each World Electoral District, or suitable group of Districts; and to obtain the advice of the Institute on Governmental Procedures and World Problems, the Agency for Research and Planning, and the Agency for Technological and Environmental Assessment in preparing the booklets.

8.3.1.6 To define the rules for world political parties, subject to approval by the World Parliament, and subject to review and recommendations of the World Ombudsmus.

8.3.1.7 To define the detailed procedures for legislative initiative and referendum by the Citizens of Earth, and to conduct voting on supra- national or global initiatives and referendums in conjunction with world parliamentary elections.

8.3.1.8 To conduct plebiscites when requested by other Organs of the World Government, and to make recommendations for the settlement of boundary disputes.

8.3.1.9 To conduct a global census every five years, and to prepare and maintain complete demographic analyses for Earth.

8.3.2 The World Boundaries and Elections Administration shall be headed by a ten member commission in addition to the Senior Administrator and the Cabinet Minister or Vice President. The commission shall be composed of one commissioner each from ten World Electoral and Administrative Magna-Regions. The persons to serve as commissioners shall be nominated by the House of Counselors and then appointed by the World Presidium for five year terms. Commissioners may serve consecutive terms.

8.4   Institute on Governmental Procedures and World Problems

8.4.1 The functions of the Institute on Governmental Procedures and World Problems shall be as follows, but not limited thereto:

8.4.1.1 To prepare and conduct courses of information, education and training for all personnel in the service of the World Government, including Members of the World Parliament and of all other elective, appointive and civil service personnel, so that every person in the service of the World Government may have a better understanding of the functions, structure, procedures and inter-relationships of the various organs, departments, bureaus, offices, institutes, commissions, agencies and other parts of the World Government.

8.4.1.2 To prepare and conduct courses and seminars for information, education, discussion, updating and new ideas in all areas of world problems, particularly for Members of the World Parliament and of the World Executive, and for the chief personnel of all organs, departments and agencies of the World Government, but open to all in the service of the World Government.

8.4.1.3 To bring in qualified persons from private and public universities, colleges and research and action organizations of many countries, as well as other qualified persons, to lecture and to be resource persons for the courses and seminars organized by the Institute on Governmental Procedures and World Problems.

8.4.1.4 To contract with private or public universities and colleges or other agencies to conduct courses and seminars for the Institute.

8.4.2 The Institute on Governmental Procedures and World Problems shall be supervised by a ten member commission in addition to the Senior Administrator and Cabinet Minister or Vice President. The commission shall be composed of one commissioner each to be named by the House of Peoples, the House of Nations, the House of Counselors, the Presidium, the Collegium of World Judges, The World Ombudsmus, The World Attorneys General Office, the Agency for Research and Planning, the Agency for Technological and Environmental Assessment, and the World Financial Administration. Commissioners shall serve five year terms, and may serve consecutive terms.

8.5 The Agency for Research and Planning

8.5.1 The functions of the Agency for Research and Planning shall be as follows, but not limited thereto:

8.5.1.1 To serve the World Parliament, the World Executive, the World Administration, and other organs, departments and agencies of the World Government in any matter requiring research and planning within the competence of the agency.

8.5.1.2 To prepare and maintain a comprehensive inventory of world resources.

8.5.1.3 To prepare comprehensive long-range plans for the development, conservation, re-cycling and equitable sharing of the resources of Earth for the benefit of all people on Earth, subject to legislative action by the World Parliament.

8.5.1.4 To prepare and maintain a comprehensive list and description of all world problems, including their inter-relationships, impact time projections and proposed solutions, together with bibliographies.

8.5.1.5 To do research and help prepare legislative measures at the request of any Member of the World Parliament or of any committee of any House of the World Parliament.

8.5.1.6 To do research and help prepare proposed legislation or proposed legislative programs and schedules at the request of the Presidium or Executive Cabinet or of any Cabinet Minister.

8.5.1.7 To do research and prepare reports at the request of any other organ, department or agency of the World Government.

8.5.1.8 To enlist the help of public and private universities, colleges, research agencies, and other associations and organizations for various research and planning projects.

8.5.1.9 To contract with public and private universities, colleges, research agencies and other organizations for the preparation of specific reports, studies and proposals.

8.5.1.10 To maintain a comprehensive World Library for the use of all Members of the World Parliament, and for the use of all other officials and persons in the service of the World Government, as well as for public information.

8.5.2 The Agency for Research and Planning shall be supervised by a ten member commission in addition to the Senior Administrator and Cabinet Minister or Vice President. The commission shall be composed of one commissioner each to be named by the House of Peoples, the House of Nations, the House of Counselors, the Presidium, the Collegium of World Judges, the Office of World Attorneys General, World Ombudsmus, the Agency for Technological and Environmental Assessment, the Institute on Governmental Procedures and World Problems, and the World Financial Administration. Commissioners shall serve five year terms, and may serve consecutive terms.

8.6 The Agency for Technological and Environmental Assessment

8.6.1 The functions of the agency for Technological and Environmental Assessment shall include the following, but not limited thereto:

8.6.1.1 To establish and maintain a registration and description of all significant technological innovations, together with impact projections.

8.6.1.2 To examine, analyze and assess the impacts and consequences of technological innovations which may have either significant beneficial or significant harmful or dangerous consequences for human life or for the ecology of life on Earth, or which may require particular regulations or prohibitions to prevent or eliminate dangers or to assure benefits.

8.6.1.3 To examine, analyze and assess environmental and ecological problems, in particular the environmental and ecological problems which may result from any intrusions or changes of the environment or ecological relationships which may be caused by technological innovations, processes of resource development, patterns of human settlements, the production of energy, patterns of economic and industrial development, or other man-made intrusions and changes of the environment, or which may result from natural causes.

8.6.1.4 To maintain a global monitoring network to measure possible harmful effects of technological innovations and environmental disturbances so that corrective measures can be designed.

8.6.1.5 To prepare recommendations based on technological and environmental analyses and assessments, which can serve as guides to the World Parliament, the World Executive, the World Administration, the Agency for Research and Planning, and to the other organs, departments and agencies of the World Government, as well as to individuals in the service of the World Government and to national and local governments and legislative bodies.

8.6.1.6 To enlist the voluntary or contractual aid and participation of private and public universities, colleges, research institutions and other associations and organizations in the work of technological and environmental assessment.

8.6.1.7 To enlist the voluntary or contractual aid and participation of private and public universities and colleges, research institutions and other organizations in devising and developing alternatives to harmful or dangerous technologies and environmentally disruptive activities, and in devising controls to assure beneficial results from technological innovations or to prevent harmful results from either technological innovations or environmental changes, all subject to legislation for implementation by the World Parliament.

8.6.2 The Agency for Technological and Environmental Assessment shall be supervised by a ten member commission in addition to the Senior Administrator and Cabinet Minister or Vice President. The commission shall be composed of one commissioner from each of ten World Electoral and Administrative Magna-Regions. The persons to serve as commissioners shall be nominated by the House of Counselors, and then appointed by the World Presidium for five year terms. Commissioners may serve consecutive terms.

8.7 The World Financial Administration

8.7.1 The functions of the World Financial Administration shall include the following, but not limited thereto:

8.7.1.1 To establish and operate the procedures for the collection of revenues for the World Government, pursuant to legislation by the World Parliament, inclusive of taxes, globally accounted social and public costs, licenses, fees, revenue sharing arrangements, income derived from supra-national public enterprises or projects or resource developments, and all other sources.

8.7.1.2 To operate a Planetary Accounting Office, and thereunder to make cost/benefit studies and reports of the functioning and activities of the World Government and of its several organs, departments, branches, bureaus, offices, commissions, institutes, agencies and other parts or projects. In making such studies and reports, account shall be taken not only of direct financial costs and benefits, but also of human, social, environmental, indirect, long-term and other costs and benefits, and of actual or possible hazards and damages. Such studies and reports shall also be designed to uncover any wastes, inefficiencies, misapplications, corruptions, diversions, unnecessary costs, and other possible irregularities.

8.7.1.3 To make cost/benefit studies and reports at the request of any House or committee of the World Parliament, and of the Presidium, the Executive Cabinet, the World Ombudsmus, the Office of World Attorneys General, the World Supreme Court, or of any administrative department or any agency of the Integrative Complex, as well as upon its own initiative.

8.7.1.4 To operate a Planetary Comptroller's Office and thereunder to supervise the disbursement of the funds of the World Government for all purposes, projects and activities duly authorized by this World Constitution, the World Parliament, the World Executive, and other organs, departments and agencies of the World Government.

8.7.1.5 To establish and operate a Planetary Banking System, making the transition to a common global currency, under the terms of specific legislation passed by the World Parliament.

8.7.1.6 Pursuant to specific legislation enacted by the World Parliament, and in conjunction with the Planetary Banking System, to establish and implement the procedures of a Planetary Monetary and Credit System based upon useful productive capacity and performance, both in goods and services. Such a monetary and credit system shall be designed for use within the Planetary Banking System for the financing of the activities and projects of the World Government, and for all other financial purposes approved by the World Parliament, without requiring the payment of interest on bonds, investments or other claims of financial ownership or debt.

8.7.1.7 To establish criteria for the extension of financial credit based upon such considerations as people available to work, usefulness, cost/benefit accounting, human and social values, environmental health and esthetics, minimizing disparities, integrity, competent management, appropriate technology, potential production and performance.

8.7.1.8   To establish and operate a Planetary Insurance System in areas of world need which transcend national boundaries and in accordance with legislation passed by the World Parliament.

8.7.1.9   To assist the Presidium as may be requested in the technical preparation of budgets for the operation of the World Government.

8.7.2   The World Financial Administration shall be supervised by a commission of ten members, together with a Senior Administrator and a Cabinet Minister or Vice President. The commission shall be composed of one commissioner each to be named by the House of Peoples, the House of Nations, the House of Counselors, the Presidium, the Collegium of World Judges, the Office of Attorneys General, the World Ombudsmus, the Agency for Research and Planning, the Agency for Technological and Environmental Assessment, and the Institute on Governmental Procedures and World Problems. Commissioners shall serve terms of five years, and may serve consecutive terms.

8.8   Commission for Legislative Review

8.8.1   The functions of the Commission for Legislative Review shall be to examine World Legislation and World Laws which the World Parliament enacts or adopts from the previous Body of International Law for the purpose of analyzing whether any particular legislation or law has become obsolete or obstructive or defective in serving the purposes intended; and to make recommendations to the World Parliament accordingly for repeal or amendment or replacement.

8.8.2   The Commission for Legislative Review shall be composed of twelve members, including two each to be elected by the House of Peoples, the House of Nations, the House of Counselors, the Collegium of World Judges, the World Ombudsmus and the Presidium. Members of the Commission shall serve terms of ten years, and may be re-elected to serve consecutive terms. One half of the Commission members after the Commission is first formed shall be elected every five years, with the first terms for one half of the members to be only five years.

Article 9 - The World Judiciary

9.1   Jurisdiction of the World Supreme Court

9.1.1   A World Supreme Court shall be established, together with such regional and district World Courts as may subsequently be found necessary. The World Supreme Court shall comprise a number of benches.

9.1.2 The World Supreme Court, together with such regional and district World Courts as may be established, shall have mandatory jurisdiction in all cases, actions, disputes, conflicts, violations of law, civil suits, guarantees of civil and human rights, constitutional interpretations, and other litigations arising under the provisions of this World Constitution, world legislation, and the body of world law approved by the World Parliament.

9.1.3 Decisions of the World Supreme Court shall be binding on all parties involved in all cases, actions and litigations brought before any bench of the World Supreme Court for settlement. Each bench of the World Supreme Court shall constitute a court of highest appeal, except when matters of extra-ordinary public importance are assigned or transferred to the Superior Tribunal of the World Supreme Court, as provided in Section 5 of Article 9.

9.2 Benches of the World Supreme Court

The benches of the World Supreme Court and their respective jurisdictions shall be as follows:

9.2.1 Bench for Human Rights: To deal with issues of human rights arising under the guarantee of civil and human rights provided by Article 12 of this World Constitution, and arising in pursuance of the provisions of Article 13 of this World Constitution, and arising otherwise under world legislation and the body of world law approved by the World Parliament.

9.2.2 Bench for Criminal Cases: To deal with issues arising from the violation of world laws and world legislation by individuals, corporations, groups and associations, but not issues primarily concerned with human rights.

9.2.3 Bench for Civil Cases: To deal with issues involving civil law suits and disputes between individuals, corporations, groups and associations arising under world legislation and world law and the administration thereof.

9.2.4 Bench for Constitutional Cases: To deal with the interpretation of the World Constitution and with issues and actions arising in connection with the interpretation of the World Constitution.

9.2.5 Bench for International Conflicts: To deal with disputes, conflicts and legal contest arising between or among the nations which have joined in the Federation of Earth.

9.2.6 Bench for Public Cases: To deal with issues not under the jurisdiction of another bench arising from conflicts, disputes, civil suits or other legal contests between the World Government and corporations, groups or individuals, or between national governments and corporations, groups or individuals in cases involving world legislation and world law.

9.2.7 Appellate Bench: To deal with issues involving world legislation and world law which may be appealed from national courts; and to decide which bench to assign a case or action or litigation when a question or disagreement arises over the proper jurisdiction.

9.2.8 Advisory Bench: To give opinions upon request on any legal question arising under world law or world legislation, exclusive of contests or actions involving interpretation of the World Constitution. Advisory opinions may be requested by any House or committee of the World Parliament, by the Presidium, any Administrative Department, the Office of World Attorneys General, the World Ombudsmus, or by any agency of the Integrative Complex.

9.2.9 Other benches may be established, combined or terminated upon recommendation of the Collegium of World Judges with approval by the World Parliament; but benches number one through eight may not be combined nor terminated except by amendment of this World Constitution.

9.3 Seats of the World Supreme Court

9.3.1 The primary seat of the World Supreme Court and all benches shall be the same as for the location of the Primary World Capital and for the location of the World Parliament and the World Executive.

9.3.2 Continental seats of the World Supreme Court shall be established in the four secondary capitals of the World Government located in four different Continental Divisions of Earth, as provided in Article 15.

9.3.3 The following permanent benches of the World Supreme Court shall be established both at the primary seat and at each of the continental seats: Human Rights, Criminal Cases, Civil Cases, and Public Cases.

9.3.4 The following permanent benches of the World Supreme Court shall be located only at the primary seat of the World Supreme Court: Constitutional Cases, International Conflicts, Appellate Bench, and Advisory Bench.

9.3.5 Benches which are located permanently only at the primary seat of the World Supreme Court may hold special sessions at the other continental seats of the World Supreme Court when necessary, or may establish continental circuits if needed.

9.3.6   Benches of the World Supreme Court which have permanent continental locations may hold special sessions at other locations when needed, or may establish regional circuits if needed.

9.4   The Collegium of World Judges

9.4.1   A Collegium of World Judges shall be established by the World Parliament. The Collegium shall consist of a minimum of twenty member judges, and may be expanded as needed but not to exceed sixty members.

9.4.2   The World Judges to compose the Collegium of World Judges shall be nominated by the House of Counselors and shall be elected by plurality vote of the three Houses of the World Parliament in joint session. The House of Counselors shall nominate between two and three times the number of world judges to be elected at any one time. An equal number of World Judges shall be elected from each of ten World Electoral and Administrative Magna-Regions, if not immediately then by rotation.

9.4.3   The term of office for a World Judge shall be ten years. Successive terms may be served without limit.

9.4.4   The Collegium of World Judges shall elect a Presiding Council of World Judges, consisting of a Chief Justice and four Associate Chief Justices. One member of the Presiding Council of World Judges shall be elected from each of five Continental Divisions of Earth. Members of the Presiding Council of World Judges shall serve five year terms on the Presiding Council, and may serve two successive terms, but not two successive terms as Chief Justice.

9.4.5   The Presiding Council of World Judges shall assign all World Judges, including themselves, to the several benches of the World Supreme Court. Each bench for a sitting at each location shall have a minimum of three World Judges, except that the number of World Judges for benches on Continental Cases and International Conflicts, and the Appellate Bench, shall be no less than five.

9.4.6   The member judges of each bench at each location shall choose annually a Presiding Judge, who may serve two successive terms.

9.4.7   The members of the several benches may be reconstituted from time to time as may seem desirable or necessary upon the decision of the Presiding Council of World Judges. Any decision to re-constitute a bench shall be referred to a vote of the entire Collegium of World Judges by request of any World Judge.

9.4.8   Any World Judge may be removed from office for cause by an absolute two thirds majority vote of the three Houses of the World Parliament in joint session.

9.4.9   Qualifications for Judges of the World Supreme Court shall be at least ten years of legal or juristic experience, minimum age of thirty years, and evident competence in world law and the humanities.

9.4.10   The salaries, expenses, remunerations and prerogatives of the World Judges shall be determined by the World Parliament, and shall be reviewed every five years, but shall not be changed to the disadvantage of any World Judge during a term of office. All members of the Collegium of World Judges shall receive the same salaries, except that additional compensation may be given to the Presiding Council of World Judges.

9.4.11   Upon recommendation by the Collegium of World Judges, the World Parliament shall have the authority to establish regional and district world courts below the World Supreme Court, and to establish the jurisdictions thereof, and the procedures for appeal to the World Supreme Court or to the several benches thereof.

9.4.12   The detailed rules of procedure for the functioning of the World Supreme Court, the Collegium of World Judges, and for each bench of the World Supreme Court, shall be decided and amended by absolute majority vote of the Collegium of World Judges.

9.5 The Superior Tribunal of the World Supreme Court

9.5.1   A Superior Tribunal of the World Supreme Court shall be established to take cases which are considered to be of extra-ordinary public importance. The Superior Tribunal for any calendar year shall consist of the Presiding Council of World Judges together with one World Judge named by the Presiding Judge of each bench of the World Court sitting at the primary seat of the World Supreme Court. The composition of the Superior Tribunal may be continued unchanged for a second year by decision of the Presiding Council of World Judges.

9.5.2   Any party to any dispute, issue, case or litigation coming under the jurisdiction of the World Supreme Court, may apply to any particular bench of the World Supreme Court or to the Presiding Council of World Judges for the assignment or transfer of the case to the Superior Tribunal on the grounds of extra-ordinary public importance. If the application is granted, the case shall be heard and disposed of by the Superior Tribunal. Also, any bench taking any particular case, if satisfied that the case is of extra-ordinary public importance, may of its own discretion transfer the case to the Superior Tribunal.

Article 10 - The Enforcement System

10.1   Basic Principles

10.1.1   The enforcement of world law and world legislation shall apply directly to individual, and individuals shall be held responsible for compliance with world law and world legislation regardless of whether the individuals are acting in their own capacity or as agents or officials of governments at any level or of the institutions of governments, or as agents or officials of corporations, organizations, associations or groups of any kind.

10.1.2   When world law or world legislation or decisions of the world courts are violated, the Enforcement System shall operate to identify and apprehend the individuals responsible for violations.

10.1.3   Any enforcement action shall not violate the civil and human rights guaranteed under this World Constitution.

10.1.4   The enforcement of world law and world legislation shall be carried out in the context of a non-military world federation wherein all member nations shall disarm as a condition for joining and benefiting from the world federation, subject to Article 17, Sec. 3.8 and 4.6 The Federation of Earth and World Government under this World Constitution shall neither keep nor use weapons of mass destruction.

10.1.5   Those agents of the enforcement system whose function shall be to apprehend and bring to court violators of world law and world legislation shall be equipped only with such weapons as are appropriate for the apprehension of the individuals responsible for violations.

10.1.6   The enforcement of world law and world legislation under this World Constitution shall be conceived and developed primarily as the processes of effective design and administration of world law and world legislation to serve the welfare of all people on Earth, with equity and justice for all, in which the resources of Earth and the funds and the credits of the World Government are used only to serve peaceful human needs, and none used for weapons of mass destruction or for war making capabilities.

10.2   The Structure for Enforcement: World Attorneys General

10.2.1   The Enforcement System shall be headed by an Office of World Attorneys General and a Commission of Regional World Attorneys.

10.2.2 The Office of World Attorneys General shall be comprised of five members, one of whom shall be designated as the World Attorney General and the other four shall each be designated an Associate World Attorney General.

10.2.3 The Commission of Regional World Attorneys shall consist of twenty Regional World Attorneys.

10.2.4 The members to compose the Office of World Attorneys General shall be nominated by the House of Counselors, with three nominees from each Continental Division of Earth. One member of the Office shall be elected from each of five Continental Divisions by plurality vote of the three houses of the World Parliament in joint session.

10.2.5 The term of office for a member of the Office of World Attorneys General shall be ten years. A member may serve two consecutive terms. The position of World Attorney General shall rotate every two years among the five members of the Office. The order of rotation shall be decided among the five members of the Office.

10.2.6 The Office of World Attorneys General shall nominate members for the Commission of twenty Regional World Attorneys from the twenty World Electoral and Administrative Regions, with between two and three nominees submitted for each Region. From these nominations, the three Houses of the World Parliament in joint session shall elect one Regional World Attorney from each of the twenty Regions. Regional World Attorneys shall serve terms of five years, and may serve three consecutive terms.

10.2.7 Each Regional World Attorney shall organize and be in charge of an Office of Regional World Attorney. Each Associate World Attorney General shall supervise five Offices of Regional World Attorneys.

10.2.8 The staff to carry out the work of enforcement, in addition to the five members of the Office of World Attorneys General and the twenty Regional World Attorneys, shall be selected from civil service lists, and shall be organized for the following functions:

10.2.8.1 Investigation.

10.2.8.2 Apprehension and arrest.

10.2.8.3 Prosecution.

10.2.8.4 Remedies and correction.

10.2.8.5 Conflict resolution.

10.2.9 Qualifications for a member of the Office of World Attorneys General and for the Regional World Attorneys shall be at least thirty years of age, at least seven years legal experience, and education in law and the humanities.

10.2.10 The World Attorney General, the Associate World Attorneys General, and the Regional World Attorneys shall at all times be responsible to the World Parliament. Any member of the Office of World Attorneys General and any Regional World Attorney can be removed from office for cause by a simple majority vote of the three Houses of the World Parliament in joint session.

10.3 The World Police

10.3.1 That section of the staff of the Office of World Attorneys General and of the Offices of Regional World Attorneys responsible for the apprehension and arrest of violators of world law and world legislation, shall be designated as World Police.

10.3.2 Each regional staff of the World Police shall be headed by a Regional World Police Captain, who shall be appointed by the Regional World Attorney.

10.3.3 The Office of World Attorneys General shall appoint a World Police Supervisor, to be in charge of those activities which transcend regional boundaries. The World Police Supervisor shall direct the Regional World Police Captains in any actions which require coordinated or joint action transcending regional boundaries, and shall direct any action which requires initiation or direction from the Office of World Attorneys General.

10.3.4 Searches and arrests to be made by World Police shall be made only upon warrants issued by the Office of World Attorneys General or by a Regional World Attorney.

10.3.5 World Police shall be armed only with weapons appropriate for the apprehension of the individuals responsible for violation of world law.

10.3.6 Employment in the capacity of World Police Captain and World Police Supervisor shall be limited to ten years.

10.3.7 The World Police Supervisor and any Regional World Police Captain may be removed from office for cause by decision of the Office of World Attorneys General or by absolute majority vote of the three Houses of the World Parliament in joint session.

10.4 The Means of Enforcement

10.4.1 Non-military means of enforcement of world law and world legislation shall be developed by the World Parliament and by the Office of World Attorneys General in consultation with the Commission of Regional World Attorneys, the Collegium of

World Judges, the World Presidium, and the World Ombudsmus. The actual means of enforcement shall require legislation by the World Parliament.

10.4.2 Non-military means of enforcement which can be developed may include: Denial of financial credit; denial of material resources and personnel; revocation of licenses, charters, or corporate rights; impounding of equipment; fines and damage payments; performance of work to rectify damages; imprisonment or isolation; and other means appropriate to the specific situations.

10.4.3 To cope with situations of potential or actual riots, insurrection and resort to armed violence, particular strategies and methods shall be developed by the World Parliament and by the Office of World Attorneys General in consultation with the Commission of Regional World Attorneys, the Collegium of World Judges, the Presidium and the World Ombudsmus. Such strategies and methods shall require enabling legislation by the World Parliament where required in addition to the specific provisions of this World Constitution.

10.4.4 A basic condition for preventing outbreaks of violence which the Enforcement System shall facilitate in every way possible, shall be to assure a fair hearing under non-violent circumstances for any person or group having a grievance, and likewise to assure a fair opportunity for a just settlement of any grievance with due regard for the rights and welfare of all concerned.

Article 11 - The World Ombudsmus

11.1 Functions and Powers of the World Ombudsmus

The functions and powers of the World Ombudsmus, as public defender, shall include the following:

11.1.1 To protect the People of Earth and all individuals against violations or neglect of universal human and civil rights which are stipulated in Article 12 and other sections of this World Constitution.

11.1.2 To protect the People of Earth against violations of this World Constitution by any official or agency of the World Government, including both elected and appointed officials or public employees regardless of organ, department, office, agency or rank.

11.1.3 To press for the implementation of the Directive Principles for the World Government as defined in Article 13 of this World Constitution.

11.1.4 To promote the welfare of the people of Earth by seeking to assure that conditions of social justice and of minimizing disparities are achieved in the implementation and administration of world legislation and world law.

11.1.5 To keep on the alert for perils to humanity arising from technological innovations, environmental disruptions and other diverse sources, and to launch initiatives for correction or prevention of such perils.

11.1.6 To ascertain that the administration of otherwise proper laws, ordinances and procedures of the World Government do not result in unforeseen injustices or inequities, or become stultified in bureaucracy or the details of administration.

11.1.7 To receive and hear complaints, grievances or requests for aid from any person, group, organization, association, body politic or agency concerning any matter which comes within the purview of the World Ombudsmus.

11.1.8 To request the Office of World Attorneys General or any Regional World Attorney to initiate legal actions or court proceedings whenever and wherever considered necessary or desirable in the view of the World Ombudsmus.

11.1.9 To directly initiate legal actions and court proceedings whenever the World Ombudsmus deems necessary.

11.1.10 To review the functioning of the departments, bureaus, offices, commissions, institutes, organs and agencies of the World Government to ascertain whether the procedures of the World government are adequately fulfilling their purposes and serving the welfare of humanity in optimum fashion, and to make recommendations for improvements.

11.1.11 To present an annual report to the World Parliament and to the Presidium on the activities of the World Ombudsmus, together with any recommendations for legislative measures to improve the functioning of the World Government for the purpose of better serving the welfare of the People of Earth.

11.2 Composition of the World Ombudsmus

11.2.1 The World Ombudsmus shall be headed by a Council of World Ombudsen of five members, one of whom shall be designated as Principal World Ombudsan, while the other four shall each be designated as an Associate World Ombudsan.

11.2.2 Members to compose the Council of World Ombudsen shall be nominated by the House of Counselors, with three nominees from each Continental Division of Earth. One member of the Council shall be elected from each of five Continental Divisions by plurality vote of the three Houses of the World Parliament in joint session.

11.2.3 The term of office for a World Ombudsan shall be ten years. A World Ombudsan may serve two successive terms. The position of Principal World Ombudsan shall be rotated every two years. The order of rotation shall be determined by the Council of World Ombudsen.

11.2.4 The Council of World Ombudsen shall be assisted by a Commission of World Advocates of twenty members. Members for the Commission of World Advocates shall be nominated by the Council of World Ombudsen from twenty World Electoral and Administrative Regions, with between two and three nominees submitted for each Region. One World Advocate shall be elected from each of the twenty World Electoral and Administrative Regions by the three Houses of the World Parliament in joint session. World Advocates shall serve terms of five years, and may serve a maximum of four successive terms.

11.2.5 The Council of World Ombudsen shall establish twenty regional offices, in addition to the principal world office at the primary seat of the World Government. The twenty regional offices of the World Ombudsmus shall parallel the organization of the twenty Offices of Regional World Attorney.

11.2.6 Each regional office of the World Ombudsmus shall be headed by a World Advocate. Each five regional offices of the World Ombudmus shall be supervised by an Associate World Ombudsan.

11.2.7 Any World Ombudsan and any World Advocate may be removed from office for cause by an absolute majority vote of the three Houses of the World Parliament in joint session.

11.2.8 Staff members for the World Ombudsmus and for each regional office of the World Ombudsmus shall be selected and employed from civil service lists.

11.2.9 Qualifications for World Ombudsan and for World Advocate shall be at least thirty years of age, at least five years legal experience, and education in law and other relevant education.

Article 12 - Bill of Rights for the Citizens of Earth

The inhabitants and citizens of Earth who are within the Federation of Earth shall have certain inalienable rights defined hereunder. It shall be mandatory for the World Parliament, the World Executive, and all organs and agencies of the World Government to honor, implement and enforce these rights, as well as for the national governments of all member nations in the Federation of Earth to do likewise. Individuals or groups suffering violation or neglect of such rights shall have full recourse through the World Ombudsmus, the Enforcement System and the World Courts for redress of grievances. The inalienable rights shall include the following:

12.1 Equal rights for all citizens of the Federation of Earth, with no discrimination on grounds of race, color, caste, nationality, sex, religion, political affiliation, property, or social status.

12.2 Equal protection and application of world legislation and world laws for all citizens of the Federation of Earth.

12.3 Freedom of thought and conscience, speech, press, writing, communication, expression, publication, broadcasting, telecasting, and cinema, except as an overt part of or incitement to violence, armed riot or insurrection.

12.4 Freedom of assembly, association, organization, petition and peaceful demonstration.

12.5 Freedom to vote without duress, and freedom for political organization and campaigning without censorship or recrimination.

12.6 Freedom to profess, practice and promote religious or religious beliefs or no religion or religious belief.

12.7 Freedom to profess and promote political beliefs or no political beliefs.

12.8 Freedom for investigation, research and reporting.

12.9 Freedom to travel without passport or visas or other forms of registration used to limit travel between, among or within nations.

12.10 Prohibition against slavery, peonage, involuntary servitude, and conscription of labor.

12.11 Prohibition against military conscription.

12.12 Safety of person from arbitrary or unreasonable arrest, detention, exile, search or seizure; requirement of warrants for searches and arrests.

12.13 Prohibition against physical or psychological duress or torture during any period of investigation, arrest, detention or imprisonment, and against cruel or unusual punishment.

12.14 Right of habeas corpus; no ex-post-facto laws; no double jeopardy; right to refuse self-incrimination or the incrimination of another.

12.15 Prohibition against private armies and paramilitary organizations as being threats to the common peace and safety.

12.16 Safety of property from arbitrary seizure; protection against exercise of the power of eminent domain without reasonable compensation.

12.17 Right to family planning and free public assistance to achieve family planning objectives.

12.18 Right of privacy of person, family and association; prohibition against surveillance as a means of political control.

Article 13 - Directive Principles for the Earth Federation

It shall be the aim of the World Government to secure certain other rights for all inhabitants within the Federation of Earth, but without immediate guarantee of universal achievement and enforcement. These rights are defined as Directive Principles, obligating the World Government to pursue every reasonable means for universal realization and implementation, and shall include the following:

13.1 Equal opportunity for useful employment for everyone, with wages or remuneration sufficient to assure human dignity.

13.2 Freedom of choice in work, occupation, employment or profession.

13.3 Full access to information and to the accumulated knowledge of the human race.

13.4 Free and adequate public education available to everyone, extending to the pre-university level; Equal opportunities for elementary and higher education for all persons; equal opportunity for continued education for all persons throughout life; the right of any person or parent to choose a private educational institution at any time.

13.5 Free and adequate public health services and medical care available to everyone throughout life under conditions of free choice.

13.6 Equal opportunity for leisure time for everyone; better distribution of the work load of society so that every person may have equitable leisure time opportunities.

13.7 Equal opportunity for everyone to enjoy the benefits of scientific and technological discoveries and developments.

13.8 Protection for everyone against the hazards and perils of technological innovations and developments.

13.9 Protection of the natural environment which is the common heritage of humanity against pollution, ecological disruption or damage which could imperil life or lower the quality of life.

13.10 Conservation of those natural resources of Earth which are limited so that present and future generations may continue to enjoy life on the planet Earth.

13.11 Assurance for everyone of adequate housing, of adequate and nutritious food supplies, of safe and adequate water supplies, of pure air with protection of oxygen supplies and the ozone layer, and in general for the continuance of an environment which can sustain healthy living for all.

13.12 Assure to each child the right to the full realization of his or her potential.

13.13 Social Security for everyone to relieve the hazards of unemployment, sickness, old age, family circumstances, disability, catastrophes of nature, and technological change, and to allow retirement with sufficient lifetime income for living under conditions of human dignity during older age.

13.14 Rapid elimination of and prohibitions against technological hazards and manmade environmental disturbances which are found to create dangers to life on Earth.

13.15 Implementation of intensive programs to discover, develop and institute safe alternatives and practical substitutions for technologies which must be eliminated and prohibited because of hazards and dangers to life.

13.16 Encouragement for cultural diversity; encouragement for decentralized administration.

13.17 Freedom for peaceful self-determination for minorities, refugees and dissenters.

13.18 Freedom for change of residence to anywhere on Earth conditioned by provisions for temporary sanctuaries in events of large numbers of refugees, stateless persons, or mass migrations.

13.19 Prohibition against the death penalty.

Article 14 - Safeguards and Reservations

14.1 Certain Safeguards

The World Government shall operate to secure for all nations and peoples within the Federation of Earth the safeguards which are defined hereunder:

14.1.1 Guarantee that full faith and credit shall be given to the public acts, records, legislation and judicial proceedings of the member nations within the Federation of Earth, consistent with the several provisions of this World Constitution.

14.1.2 Assure freedom of choice within the member nations and countries of the Federation of Earth to determine their internal political, economic and social systems consistent with the guarantees and protections given under this World Constitution to assure civil liberties and human rights and a safe environment for life, and otherwise consistent with the several provisions of this World Constitution.

14.1.3 Grant the right of asylum within the Federation of Earth for persons who may seek refuge from countries or nations which are not yet included within the Federation of Earth.

14.1.4 Grant the right of individuals and groups, after the Federation of Earth includes 90 percent of the territory of Earth, to peacefully leave the hegemony of the Federation of Earth and to live in suitable territory set aside by the Federation neither restricted nor protected by the World Government, provided that such territory does not extend beyond five percent of Earth's habitable territory, is kept completely disarmed and not used as a base for inciting violence or insurrection within or against the Federation of Earth or any member nation, and is kept free of acts of environmental or technological damage which seriously affect Earth outside such territory.

14.2 Reservation of Powers

The powers not delegated to the World Government by this World Constitution shall be reserved to the nations of the Federation of Earth and to the people of Earth.

Article 15 - World Federal Zones and the World Capitals

15.1 World Federal Zones

15.1.1 Twenty World Federal Zones shall be established within the twenty World Electoral and Administrative Regions, for the purposes of the location of the several organs of the World Government and of the administrative departments, the world courts, the offices of the Regional World Attorneys, the offices of the World Advocates, and for the location of other branches, departments, institutes, offices, bureaus, commissions, agencies and parts of the World Government.

15.1.2 The World Federal Zones shall be established as the needs and resources of the World Government develop and expand. World Federal Zones shall be established first within each of five Continental Divisions.

15.1.3 The location and administration of the World Federal Zones, including the first five, shall be determined by the World Parliament.

15.2 The World Capitals

15.2.1 Five World Capitals shall be established in each of five Continental Divisions of Earth, to be located in each of the five World Federal Zones which are established first as provided in Article 15 of this World Constitution.

15.2.2 One of the World Capitals shall be designated by the World Parliament as the Primary World Capital, and the other four shall be designated as Secondary World Capitals.

15.2.3 The primary seats of all organs of the World Government shall be located in the Primary World Capital, and other major seats of the several organs of the World Government shall be located in the Secondary World Capitals.

15.3 Locational Procedures

15.3.1 Choices for location of the twenty World Federal Zones and for the five World Capitals shall be proposed by the Presidium, and then shall be decided by a simple majority vote of the three Houses of the World Parliament in joint session. The Presidium shall offer choices of two or three locations in each of the twenty World Electoral and Administrative Regions to be World Federal Zones, and shall offer two alternative choices for each of the five World Capitals.

15.3.2 The Presidium in consultation with the Executive Cabinet shall then propose which of the five World Capitals shall be the Primary World Capital, to be decided by a simple majority vote of the three Houses of the World Parliament in joint session.

15.3.3 Each organ of the World Government shall decide how best to apportion and organize its functions and activities among the five World Capitals, and among the twenty World Federal Zones, subject to specific directions from the World Parliament.

15.3.4 The World Parliament may decide to rotate its sessions among the five World Capitals, and if so, to decide the procedure for rotation.

15.3.5 For the first two operative stages of World Government as defined in Article 17, and for the Provisional World Government as defined in Article 19, a provisional location may be selected for the Primary World Capital. The provisional location need not be continued as a permanent location.

15.3.6 Any World Capital or World Federal Zone may be relocated by an absolute two-thirds majority vote of the three Houses of the World Parliament in joint session.

15.3.7 Additional World Federal Zones may be designated if found necessary by proposal of the Presidium and approval by an absolute majority vote of the three Houses of the World Parliament in joint session.

Article 16 - World Territories and Exterior Relations

16.1 World Territory

16.1.1 Those areas of the Earth and Earth's moon which are not under the jurisdiction of existing nations at the time of forming the Federation of Earth, or which are not reasonably within the province of national ownership and administration, or which are declared to be World Territory subsequent to establishment of the Federation of Earth, shall be designated as World Territory and shall belong to all of the people of Earth.

16.1.2 The administration of World Territory shall be determined by the World Parliament and implemented by the World Executive, and shall apply to the following areas:

16.1.2.1 All oceans and seas having an international or supra-national character, together with the seabeds and resources thereof, beginning at a distance of twenty kilometers offshore, excluding inland seas of traditional national ownership.

16.1.2.2 Vital straits, channels, and canals.

16.1.2.3 The atmosphere enveloping Earth, beginning at an elevation of one kilometer above the general surface of the land, excluding the depressions in areas of much variation in elevation.

16.1.2.4 Man-made satellites and Earth's moon.

16.1.2.5 Colonies which may choose the status of World Territory; non-independent territories under the trust administration of nations or of the United Nations; any islands or atolls which are unclaimed by any nation; independent lands or countries which choose the status of World Territory; and disputed lands which choose the status of World Territory.

16.1.3 The residents of any World Territory, except designated World Federal Zones, shall have the right within reason to decide by plebiscite to become a self-governing nation within the Federation of Earth, either singly or in combination with other World Territories, or to unite with an existing nation with the Federation of Earth.

16.2   Exterior Relations

16.2.1   The World Government shall maintain exterior relations with those nations of Earth which have not joined the Federation of Earth. Exterior relations shall be under the administration of the Presidium, subject at all times to specific instructions and approval by the World Parliament.

16.2.2   All treaties and agreements with nations remaining outside the Federation of Earth shall be negotiated by the Presidium and must be ratified by a simple majority vote of the three Houses of the World Parliament.

16.2.3   The World Government for the Federation of Earth shall establish and maintain peaceful relations with other planets and celestial bodies where and when it may become possible to establish communications with the possible inhabitants thereof.

16.2.4   All explorations into outer space, both within and beyond the solar system in which Planet Earth is located, shall be under the exclusive direction and control of the World Government, and shall be conducted in such manner as shall be determined by the World Parliament.

Article 17 - Ratification and Implementation

17.1   Ratification of the World Constitution

This World Constitution shall be submitted to the nations and people of Earth for ratification by the following procedures:

17.1.1   The World Constitution shall be transmitted to the General Assembly of the United Nations Organization and to each national government on Earth, with the request that the World Constitution be submitted to the national legislature of each nation for preliminary ratification and to the people of each nation for final ratification by popular referendum.

17.1.2   Preliminary ratification by a national legislature shall be accomplished by simple majority vote of the national legislature.

17.1.3   Final ratification by the people shall be accomplished by a simple majority of votes cast in a popular referendum, provided that a minimum of twenty-five percent of eligible voters of age eighteen years and over have cast ballots within the nation or country or within World Electoral and Administrative Districts.

17.1.4   In the case of a nation without a national legislature, the head of the national government shall be requested to give preliminary ratification and to submit the World Constitution for final ratification by popular referendum.

17.1.5 In the event that a national government, after six months, fails to submit the World Constitution for ratification as requested, then the global agency assuming responsibility for the worldwide ratification campaign may proceed to conduct a direct referendum for ratification of the World Constitution by the people. Direct referendums may be organized on the basis of entire nations or countries, or on the basis of existing defined communities within nations.

17.1.6 In the event of a direct ratification referendum, final ratification shall be accomplished by a majority of the votes cast whether for an entire nation or for a World Electoral and Administrative District, provided that ballots are cast by a minimum of twenty-five percent of eligible voters of the area who are over eighteen years of age.

17.1.7 For ratification by existing communities within a nation, the procedure shall be to request local communities, cities, counties, states, provinces, cantons, prefectures, tribal jurisdictions, or other defined political units within a nation to ratify the World Constitution, and to submit the World Constitution for a referendum vote by the citizens of the community or political unit. Ratification may be accomplished by proceeding in this way until all eligible voters of age eighteen and above within the nation or World Electoral and Administrative District have had the opportunity to vote, provided that ballots are cast by a minimum of twenty-five percent of those eligible to vote.

17.1.8 Prior to the Full Operative Stage of World Government, as defined under Section 5 of Article 17, the universities, colleges and scientific academies and institutes in any country may ratify the World Constitution, thus qualifying them for participation in the nomination of Members of the World Parliament to the House of Counselors.

17.1.9 In the case of those nations currently involved in serious international disputes or where traditional enmities and chronic disputes may exist among two or more nations, a procedure for concurrent paired ratification shall be instituted whereby the nations which are parties to a current or chronic international dispute or conflict may simultaneously ratify the World Constitution. In such cases, the paired nations shall be admitted into the Federation of Earth simultaneously, with the obligation for each such nation to immediately turn over all weapons of mass destruction to the World Government, and to turn over the conflict or dispute for mandatory peaceful settlement by the World Government.

17.1.10 Each nation or political unit which ratifies this World Constitution, either by preliminary ratification or final ratification, shall be bound never to use any armed forces or weapons of mass destruction against another member or unit of the Federation of Earth, regardless of how long it may take to achieve full disarmament of all the nations and political units which ratify this World Constitution.

17.1.11 When ratified, the Constitution for the Federation of Earth becomes the supreme law of Earth. By the act of ratifying this Earth Constitution, any provision in the Constitution or Legislation of any country so ratifying, which is contrary to this Earth Constitution, is either repealed or amended to conform with the Constitution for the Federation of Earth, effective as soon as 25 countries have so ratified. The amendment of National or State Constitutions to allow entry into World Federation is not necessary prior to ratification of the Constitution for the Federation of Earth.

17.2 Stages of Implementation

17.2.1 Implementation of this World Constitution and the establishment of World Government pursuant to the terms of this World Constitution, may be accomplished in three stages, as follows, in addition to the stage of a Provisional World Government as provided under Article 19:

17.2.1.1 First Operative Stage of World Government.

17.2.1.2 Second Operative Stage of World Government.

17.2.1.3 Full Operative Stage of World Government.

17.2.2 At the beginning and during each stage, the World Parliament and the World Executive together shall establish goals and develop means for the progressive implementation of the World Constitution, and for the implementation of legislation enacted by the World Parliament.

17.3 First Operative Stage of World Government

17.3.1 The first operative stage of World Government under this World Constitution shall be implemented when the World Constitution is ratified by a sufficient number of nations and/or people to meet one or the other of the following conditions or equivalent:

17.3.1 Preliminary or final ratification by a minimum of twenty-five nations, each having a population of more than 100,000.

17.3.1.1 Preliminary or final ratification by a minimum of ten nations above 100,000 population, together with ratification by direct referendum within a minimum of fifty additional World Electoral and Administrative Districts.

17.3.1.2 Ratification by direct referendum within a minimum of 100 World Electoral and Administrative Districts, even though no nation as such has ratified.

17.3.1.3 The election of Members of the World Parliament to the House of Peoples shall be conducted in all World Electoral and Administrative Districts where ratification has been accomplished by popular referendum.

17.3.2 The Election of Members of the World Parliament to the House of Peoples may proceed concurrently with direct popular referendums both prior to and after the First Operative Stage of World Government is reached.

17.3.4 The appointment or election of Members of the World Parliament to the House of Nations shall proceed in all nations where preliminary ratification has been accomplished.

17.3.5 One-fourth of the Members of the World Parliament to the House of Counselors may be elected from nominees submitted by universities and colleges which have ratified the World Constitution.

17.3.6 The World Presidium and the Executive Cabinet shall be elected according to the provisions in Article 6, except that in the absence of a House of Counselors, the nominations shall be made by the members of the House of Peoples and of the House of Nations in joint session. Until this is accomplished, the Presidium and Executive Cabinet of the Provisional World Government as provided in Article 19, shall continue to serve.

17.3.7 When composed, the Presidium for the first operative stage of World Government shall assign or re-assign Ministerial posts among Cabinet and Presidium members, and shall immediately establish or confirm a World Disarmament Agency and a World Economic and Development Organization.

17.3.8 Those nations which ratify this World Constitution and thereby join the Federation of Earth, shall immediately transfer all weapons of mass destruction as defined and designated by the World Disarmament Agency to that Agency. (See Article 19, Sections 19.1.4 and 19.5.5).The World Disarmament Agency shall immediately immobilize all such weapons and shall proceed with dispatch to dismantle, convert to peacetime use, re-cycle the materials thereof or otherwise destroy all such weapons. During the first operative stage of World Government, the ratifying nations may retain armed forces equipped with weapons other than weapons of mass destruction as defined and designated by the World Disarmament Agency.

17.3.9 Concurrently with the reduction or elimination of such weapons of mass destruction and other military expenditures as can be accomplished during the first operative stage of World Government, the member nations of the Federation of Earth shall pay annually to the Treasury of the World Government amounts equal to one-half the amounts saved from their respective national military budgets during the last year before joining the Federation, and shall continue such payments until the full operative stage of World Government is reached. The World Government shall use fifty percent of the funds thus received to finance the work and projects of the World Economic Development Organization.

17.3.10 The World Parliament and the World Executive shall continue to develop the organs, departments, agencies and activities originated under the Provisional World Government, with such amendments as deemed necessary; and shall proceed to establish and begin the following organs, departments and agencies of the World Government, if not already underway, together with such other departments, and agencies as are considered desirable and feasible during the first operative stage of World Government:

173.10.1 The World Supreme Court;

173.10.2 The Enforcement System;

173.10.3 The World Ombudsmus;

173.10.4 The World Civil Service Administration;

173.10.5 The World Financial Administration;

173.10.6 The Agency for Research and Planning;

173.10.7 The Agency for Technological and Environmental Assessment;

173.10.8 An Emergency Earth Rescue Administration, concerned with all aspects of climate change and related factors;

173.10.9 An Integrated Global Energy System, based on environmentally safe sources;

173.10.10 A World University System, under the Department of Education;

173.10.11 A World Corporations Office, under the Department of Commerce and Industry;

173.10.12 The World Service Corps;

173.10.13 A World Oceans and Seabeds Administration.

17.3.11 At the beginning of the first operative stage, the Presidium in consultation with the Executive Cabinet shall formulate and put forward a proposed program for solving the most urgent world problems currently confronting humanity.

17.3.12 The World Parliament shall proceed to work upon solutions to world problems. The World Parliament and the World Executive working together shall institute through the several organs, departments and agencies of the World Government whatever means shall seem appropriate and feasible to accomplish the implementation and enforcement of world legislation, world law and the World Constitution; and in particular shall take certain decisive actions for the welfare of all people on Earth, applicable throughout the world, including but not limited to the following:

17.3.12.1 Expedite the organization and work of an Emergency Earth Rescue Administration, concerned with all aspects of climate change and climate crises;

17.3.12.2 Expedite the new finance, credit and monetary system, to serve human needs;

17.3.12.3 Expedite an integrated global energy system, utilizing solar energy, hydrogen energy, and other safe and sustainable sources of energy;

17.3.12.4 Push forward a global program for agricultural production to achieve maximum sustained yield under conditions which are ecologically sound;

17.3.12.5 Establish conditions for free trade within the Federation of Earth;

17.3.12.6 Call for and find ways to implement a moratorium on nuclear energy projects until all problems are solved concerning safety, disposal of toxic wastes and the dangers of use or diversion of materials for the production of nuclear weapons;

17.3.12.7 Outlaw and find ways to completely terminate the production of nuclear weapons and all weapons of mass destruction;

17.3.12.8 Push forward programs to assure adequate and non-polluted water supplies and clean air supplies for everybody on Earth;

17.3.12.9 Push forward a global program to conserve and re-cycle the resources of Earth.

17.3.12.10 Develop an acceptable program to bring population growth under control, especially by raising standards of living.

17.4   Second Operative Stage of World Government

17.4.1 The second operative stage of World Government shall be implemented when fifty percent or more of the nations of Earth have given either preliminary or final ratification to this World Constitution, provided that fifty percent of the total population of Earth is included either within the ratifying nations or within the ratifying nations together with additional World Electoral and Administrative Districts where people have ratified the World Constitution by direct referendum.

17.4.2 The election and appointment of Members of the World Parliament to the several Houses of the World Parliament shall proceed in the same manner as specified for the first operative stage in Section 3.2, 3.3, 3.4 and 3.5 of Article 17.

17.4.3 The terms of office of the Members of the World Parliament elected or appointed for the first operative stage of World Government, shall be extended into the second operative stage unless they have already served five year terms, in which case new elections or appointments shall be arranged. The terms of holdover Members of the World Parliament into the second operative stage shall be adjusted to run concurrently with the terms of those who are newly elected at the beginning of the second operative stage.

17.4.4 The World Presidium and the Executive Cabinet shall be re-constituted or reconfirmed, as needed, at the beginning of the second operative stage of World Government.

17.4.5 The World Parliament and the World Executive shall continue to develop the organs, departments, agencies and activities which are already underway from the first operative stage of World Government, with such amendments as deemed necessary; and shall proceed to establish and develop all other organs and major departments and agencies of the World Government to the extent deemed feasible during the second operative stage.

17.4.6 All nations joining the Federation of Earth to compose the second operative stage of World Government, shall immediately transfer all weapons of mass destruction and all other military weapons and equipment to the World Disarmament Agency, which shall immediately immobilize such weapons and equipment and shall proceed forthwith to dismantle, convert to peacetime uses, recycle the materials thereof, or otherwise destroy such weapons and equipment. During the second operative stage, all armed forces and para-military forces of the nations which have joined the Federation of Earth shall be completely disarmed and either disbanded or converted on a voluntary basis into elements of the non-military World Service Corps.

17.4.7 Concurrently with the reduction or elimination of such weapons, equipment and other military expenditures as can be accomplished during the second operative stage of World Government, the member nations of the Federation of Earth shall pay annually to the Treasury of the World Government amounts equal to one-half of the amounts saved from their national military budgets during the last year before joining the Federation and shall continue such payments until the full operative stage of World Government is reached. The World Government shall use fifty percent of the funds thus received to finance the work and projects of the World Economic Development Organization.

17.4.8 Upon formation of the Executive Cabinet for the second operative stage, the Presidium shall issue an invitation to the General Assembly of the United Nations Organization and to each of the specialized agencies of the United Nations, as well as to other useful international agencies, to transfer personnel, facilities, equipment, resources and allegiance to the Federation of Earth and to the World Government thereof. The agencies and functions of the United Nations Organization and of its specialized agencies and of other international agencies which may be thus transferred, shall be reconstituted as needed and integrated into the several organs, departments, offices and agencies of the World Government.

17.4.9 Near the beginning of the second operative stage, the Presidium in consultation with the Executive cabinet, shall formulate and put forward a proposed program for solving the most urgent world problems currently confronting the people of Earth.

17.4.10 The World Parliament shall proceed with legislation necessary for implementing a complete program for solving the current urgent world problems.

17.4.11 The World Parliament and the World Executive working together shall develop through the several organs, departments and agencies of the World Government whatever means shall seem appropriate and feasible to implement legislation for solving world problems; and in particular shall take certain decisive actions for the welfare of all people on Earth, including but not limited to the following:

17.4.11.1 Declaring all oceans, seas and canals having supra-national character (but not including inland seas traditionally belonging to particular nations) from twenty kilometers offshore, and all the seabeds thereof, to be under the ownership of the Federation of Earth as the common heritage of humanity, and subject to the control and management of the World Government.

17.4.11.2 Declare the polar caps and surrounding polar areas, including the continent of Antarctica but not areas which are traditionally a part of particular nations, to be world territory owned by the Federation of Earth as the common heritage of humanity, and subject to control and management by the World Government.

17.4.11.3 Outlaw the possession, stockpiling, sale and use of all nuclear weapons, all weapons of mass destruction, and all other military weapons and equipment.

17.4.11.4 Establish an ever-normal granary and food supply system for the people of Earth.

17.4.11.5 Develop and carry forward insofar as feasible all actions defined under Sec. 3.10, and 3.12 of the First Operative Stage.

17.5 Full Operative Stage of World Government

17.5.1 The full operative stage of World Government shall be implemented when this World Constitution is given either preliminary or final ratification by meeting either condition (17.5.1.1) or (17.5.1.2):

17.5.1.1 Ratification by eighty percent or more of the nations of Earth comprising at least ninety percent of the population of Earth; or

17.5.1.2 Ratification which includes ninety percent of Earth's total population, either within ratifying nations or within ratifying nations together with additional World Electoral and Administrative Districts where ratification by direct referendum has been accomplished, as provided in Article 17, Section 1.

17.5.2 When the full operative stage of World Government is reached, the following conditions shall be implemented:

17.5.2.1 Elections for Members of the House of Peoples shall be conducted in all World Electoral and Administrative Districts where elections have not already taken place; and Members of the House of Nations shall be elected or appointed by the national legislatures or national governments in all nations where this has not already been accomplished.

17.5.2.2 The terms of office for Members of the House of Peoples and of the House of Nations serving during the second operative stage, shall be continued into the full operative stage, except for those who have already served five years, in which case elections shall be held or appointments made as required.

17.5.2.3 The terms of office for all holdover Members of the House of Peoples and of the House of Nations who have served less than five years, shall be adjusted to run concurrently with those Members of the World Parliament whose terms are beginning with the full operative stage.

17.5.2.4 The second 100 Members of the House of Counselors shall be elected according to the procedure specified in Section 5 of Article 5. The terms of office for holdover Members of the House of Counselors shall run five more years after the beginning of the full operative stage, while those beginning their terms with the full operative stage shall serve ten years.

17.5.2.5 The Presidium and the Executive Cabinet shall be reconstituted in accordance with the provisions of Article 6.

17.5.2.6 All organs of the World Government shall be made fully operative, and shall be fully developed for the effective administration and implementation of world legislation, world law and the provisions of this World Constitution.

17.5.2.7 All nations which have not already done so shall immediately transfer all military weapons and equipment to the World Disarmament Agency, which shall immediately immobilize all such weapons and shall proceed forthwith to dismantle, convert to peaceful usage, recycle the materials thereof, or otherwise to destroy such weapons and equipment.

17.5.2.8 All armies and military forces of every kind shall be completely disarmed, and either disbanded or converted and integrated on a voluntary basis into the non-military World Service Corps.

17.5.2.9 All viable agencies of the United Nations Organization and other viable international agencies established among national governments, together with their personnel, facilities and resources, shall be transferred to the World Government and reconstituted and integrated as may be useful into the organs, departments, offices, institutes, commissions, bureaus and agencies of the World Government.

17.5.2.10 The World Parliament and the World Executive shall continue to develop the activities and projects which are already underway from the second operative stage of World Government, with such amendments as deemed necessary; and shall proceed with a complete and full scale program to solve world problems and serve the welfare of all people on Earth, in accordance with the provisions of this World Constitution.

17.6 Costs of Ratification

The work and costs of private Citizens of Earth for the achievement of a ratified Constitution for the Federation of Earth, are recognized as legitimate costs for the establishment of constitutional world government by which present and future generations will benefit, and shall be repaid double the original amount by the World Financial Administration of the World Government when it becomes operational after 25 countries have ratified this Constitution for the Federation of Earth. Repayment specifically includes contributions to the World Government Funding Corporation and other costs and expenses recognized by standards and procedures to be established by the World Financial Administration.

Article 18 - Amendments

18.1 Following completion of the first operative stage of World Government, amendments to this World Constitution may be proposed for consideration in two ways:

18.1.1 By a simple majority vote of any House of the World Parliament.

18.1.2 By petitions signed by a total of 200,000 persons eligible to vote in world elections from a total of at least twenty World Electoral and Administrative Districts where the World Constitution has received final ratification.

18.2 Passage of any amendment proposed by a House of the World Parliament shall require an absolute two-thirds majority vote of each of the three Houses of the World Parliament voting separately.

18.3 An amendment proposed by popular petition shall first require a simple majority vote of the House of Peoples, which shall be obliged to take a vote upon the proposed amendment. Passage of the amendment shall then require an absolute two-thirds majority vote of each of the three Houses of the World Parliament voting separately.

18.4 Periodically, but no later than ten years after first convening the World Parliament for the First Operative Stage of World Government, and every 20 years thereafter, the Members of the World Parliament shall meet in special session comprising a Constitutional Convention to conduct a review of this World Constitution to consider and propose possible amendments, which shall then require action as specified in Clause 2 of Article 18 for passage.

18.5 If the First Operative Stage of World Government is not reached by the year 1995, then the Provisional World Parliament, as provided under Article 19, may convene another session of the World Constituent Assembly to review the Constitution for the Federation of Earth and consider possible amendments according to procedure established by the Provisional World Parliament.

18.6   Except by following the amendment procedures specified herein, no part of this World Constitution may be set aside, suspended or subverted, neither for emergencies nor caprice nor convenience.

Article 19 – Provisional World Government

19.1   **Actions to be Taken by the World Constituent Assembly**
Upon adoption of the World Constitution by the World Constituent Assembly, the Assembly and such continuing agency or agencies as it shall designate shall do the following, without being limited thereto:

19.1.1   Issue a Call to all Nations, communities and people of Earth to ratify this World Constitution for World Government.

19.1.2   Establish the following preparatory commissions:

19.1.2.1   Ratification Commission.

19.1.2.2   World Elections Commission.

19.1.2.3   World Development Commission.

19.1.2.4   World Disarmament Commission.

19.1.2.5   World Problems Commission.

19.1.2.6   Nominating Commission.

19.1.2.7   Finance Commission.

19.1.2.8   Peace Research and Education Commission.

19.1.2.9   Special commissions on each of several of the most urgent world problems.

19.1.2.10 Such other commissions as may be deemed desirable in order to proceed with the Provisional World Government.

19.1.3   Convene Sessions of a Provisional World Parliament when feasible under the following conditions:

19.1.3.1   Seek the commitment of 500 or more delegates to attend, representing people in 20 countries from five continents, and having credentials defined by Article 19, Section 3;

19.1.3.2   The minimum funds necessary to organize the sessions of the Provisional World Parliament are either on hand or firmly pledged.

19.1.3.3   Suitable locations are confirmed at least nine months in advance, unless emergency conditions justify shorter advance notice.

19.2   **Work of the Preparatory Commissions**

19.2.1   The Ratification Commission shall carry out a worldwide campaign for the ratification of the World Constitution, both to obtain preliminary ratification by national governments, including national legislatures, and to obtain final ratification by people, including communities. The ratification commission shall continue its work until the full operative stage of World Government is reached.

19.2.2 The World Elections Commission shall prepare a provisional global map of World Electoral and Administrative Districts and Regions which may be revised during the first or second operative stage of World Government, and shall prepare and proceed with plans to obtain the election of Members of the World Parliament to the House of Emerging World Law 225 Peoples and to the House of Counselors. The World Elections Commission shall in due course be converted into the World Boundaries and Elections Administration.

19.2.3 After six months, in those countries where national governments have not responded favorable to the ratification call, the Ratification Commission and the World Elections Commission may proceed jointly to accomplish both the ratification of the World Constitution by direct popular referendum and concurrently the election of Members of the World Parliament.

19.2.4 The Ratification Commission may also submit the World Constitution for ratification by universities and colleges throughout the world.

19.2.5 The World Development Commission shall prepare plans for the creation of a World Economic Development Organization to serve all nations and people ratifying the World Constitution, and in particular less developed countries, to begin functioning when the Provisional World Government is established.

19.2.6 The World Disarmament Commission shall prepare plans for the organization of a World Disarmament Agency, to begin functioning when the Provisional World Government is established.

19.2.7 The World Problems Commission shall prepare an agenda of urgent world problems, with documentation, for possible action by the Provisional World Parliament and Provisional World Government.

19.2.8 The Nominating Commission shall prepare, in advance of convening the Provisional World Parliament, a list of nominees to compose the Presidium and the Executive Cabinet for the Provisional World Government.

19.2.9 The Finance Commission shall work on ways and means for financing the Provisional World Government.

19.2.10 The several commissions on particular world problems shall work on the preparation of proposed world legislation and action on each problem, to present to the Provisional World Parliament when it convenes.

19.3   Composition of the Provisional World Parliament

19.3.1   The Provisional World Parliament shall be composed of the following members:

19.3.1.1 All those who were accredited as delegates to the 1977 and 1991 Sessions of the World Constituent Assembly, as well as to any previous Session of the Provisional World Parliament, and who re-confirm their support for the Constitution for the Federation of Earth, as amended.

19.3.1.2 Persons who obtain the required number of signatures on election petitions, or who are designated by Non-Governmental Organizations which adopt approved resolutions for this purpose, or who are otherwise accredited according to terms specified in Calls which may be issued to convene particular sessions of the Provisional World Parliament.

19.3.1.3 Members of the World Parliament to the House of Peoples who are elected from World Electoral and Administrative Districts up to the time of convening the Provisional World Parliament. Members of the World Parliament elected to the House of Peoples may continue to be added to the Provisional World Parliament until the first operative stage of World Government is reached.

19.3.1.4 Members of the World Parliament to the House of Nations who are elected by national legislatures or appointed by national governments up to the time of convening the Provisional World Parliament. Members of the World Parliament to the House of Nations may continue to be added to the Provisional World Parliament until the first operative stage of World Government is reached.

19.3.1.5 Those universities and colleges which have ratified the World Constitution may nominate persons to serve as Members of the World Parliament to the House of Counselors. The House of Peoples and House of Nations together may then elect from such nominees up to fifty Members of the World Parliament to serve in the House of Counselors of the Provisional World Government.

19.3.2   Members of the Provisional World Parliament in categories (1) and (2) as defined above, shall serve only until the first operative stage of World Government is declared, but may be duly elected to continue as Members of the World Parliament during the first operative stage.

19.4   Formation of the Provisional World Executive

19.4.1   As soon as the Provisional World Parliament next convenes, it will elect a new Presidium for the Provisional World Parliament and Provisional World Government from among the nominees submitted by the Nominating Commission.

19.4.2   Members of the Provisional World Presidium shall serve terms of three years, and may be re-elected by the Provisional World Parliament, but in any case shall serve only until the Presidium is elected under the First Operative Stage of World Government.

19.4.3   The Presidium may make additional nominations for the Executive Cabinet.

19.4.4   The Provisional World Parliament shall then elect the members of the Executive Cabinet.

19.4.5   The Presidium shall then assign ministerial posts among the members of the Executive Cabinet and of the Presidium.

19.4.6   When steps (1) through (4) of section 19.4. are completed, the Provisional World Government shall be declared in operation to serve the welfare of humanity.

19.5   First Actions of the Provisional World Government

19.5.1   The Presidium, in consultation with the Executive Cabinet, the commissions on particular world problems and the World Parliament, shall define a program for action on urgent world problems.

19.5.2   The Provisional World Parliament shall go to work on the agenda of world problems, and shall take any and all actions it considers appropriate and feasible, in accordance with the provisions of this World Constitution.

19.5.3   Implementation of and compliance with the legislation enacted by the Provisional World Parliament shall be sought on a voluntary basis in return for the benefits to be realized, while strength of the Provisional World Government is being increased by the progressive ratification of the World Constitution.

19.5.4   Insofar as considered appropriate and feasible, the Provisional World Parliament and Provisional World Executive may undertake some of the actions specified under Section 3.12.of Article 17 for the first operative stage of World Government.

19.5.5   The World Economic Development Organization and the World Disarmament Agency shall be established, for correlated actions.

19.5.6 The World Parliament and the Executive Cabinet of the Provisional World Government shall proceed with the organization of other organs and agencies of the World Government on a provisional basis, insofar as considered desirable and feasible, in particular those specified under Section 3.10. of Article 17.

19.5.7 The several preparatory commissions on urgent world problems may be reconstituted as Administrative Departments of the Provisional World Government.

19.5.8 In all of its work and activities, the Provisional World Government shall function in accordance with the provisions of this Constitution for the Federation of Earth.

Part Four

Original Signatories to the
Earth Constitution

"We have been here over forty years, a longer period than the children of Israel wandered through the wilderness, coming to this Capitol pleading for this recognition of the principle that the Government derives its just powers from the consent of the governed. Mr. Chairman, we ask that you report our resolution favorably if you can but unfavorably if you must; that you report one way or the other, so that the Senate may have the chance to consider it."

Anna Howard Shaw (1847–1919), U.S. minister, suffragist, and speaker, April 19, 1910, before a hearing of the United States Senate Judiciary Committee.

It has been now more than fifty years since Mary Georgia Lloyd and her colleagues called to convene a World Constituent Assembly to draft and adopt a non-military *Constitution for the Federation of Earth*. Since the first session of World Constituent Assembly in 1968, over forty years have passed. Since the initial signing in 1977, signaling the readiness of the *Earth Constitution* for adoption, more than thirty years have transpired. Nearly twenty years have come and gone since the last review and signing of the *Constitution*. In terms of the human need for self-government at a global level, very little has changed qualitatively since 1991. We strongly believe that the *Earth Constitution* is adequate as it is for the global legal renaissance of emerging world law.

In the quote above, Anna Howard Shaw pled with the United States Senate Judiciary Committee on this matter of self-government, which was timely for that period.

Now we, those citizens of the world who have participated in the creation of the *Earth Constitution*, and those who have thereafter come across this marvelous document, urge the rest of the citizens and civilians of the world to seriously consider the value of the *Constitution*'s rapid adoption, so that there is the elevation of self-government to the planetary level.

On the following pages are the signatures of persons from every walk of life who attended the second and fourth sessions of the World Constituent Assembly, where there were official signing ceremonies, together with a list of persons on the last page who had wanted to attend and who agreed to support the *Earth Constitution*. Since the time of the official ceremonies, thousands more people have signed their support for the document.

Our immediate goal is to get both the joint ratification of a large number of national governments (about 25, perhaps) and also the measured direct ratification by the people of the world adequate to initiate the first operative stage as defined in the *Earth Constitution*.

The Constitution for the Federation of Earth was originally ratified at the second session of the World Constituent Assembly held at Innsbruck, Austria in June, 1977; and was amended and ratified at the fourth session of the World Constituent Assembly held at Troia, Portugal in May 1991. The Amended Constitution is being personally ratified by outstanding personalities throughout the world as the campaign for ratification by the people and governments of the world continues. Signatures of participants in the World Constituent Assemblies are on following pages.

Original Signatories

Participants in the World Constituent Assembly, 16 to 29 of June, 1977, have affixed their signatures to the draft of the CONSTITUTION FOR THE FEDERATION OF EARTH herewith:

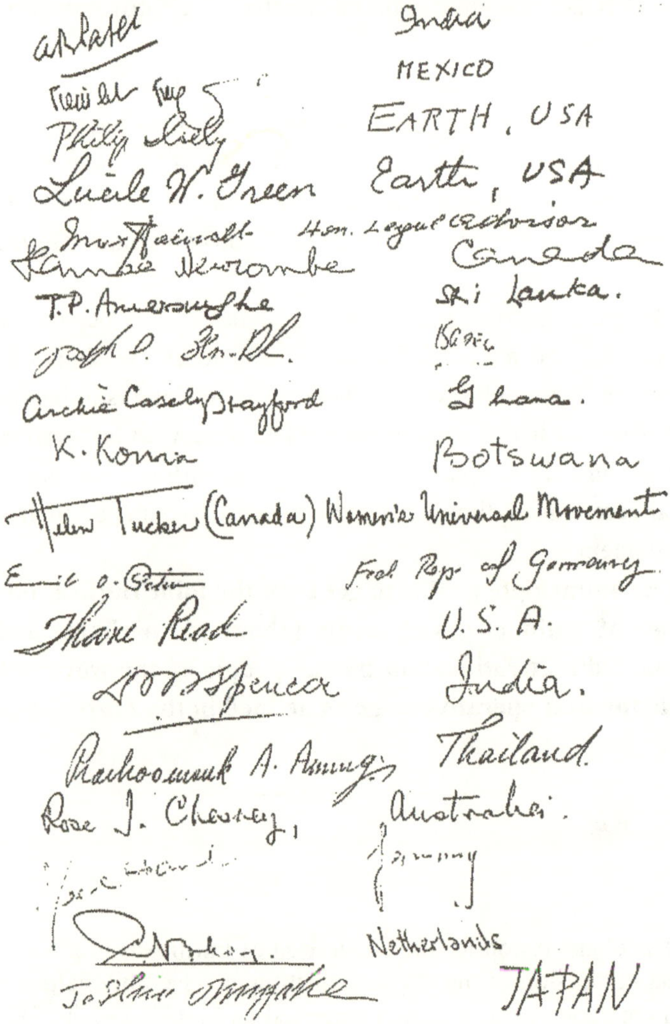

[handwritten signatures with country/affiliation notations:]

India

MEXICO

EARTH, USA

Lucile W. Green — Earth, USA

Hon. Legal Advisor

Canada

T.P. Amerasinghe — Sri Lanka.

Korea

Archie Casely Hayford — Ghana.

K. Koma — Botswana

Helen Tucker (Canada) — Women's Universal Movement

Emil O. Peter — Fed. Rep. of Germany

Thane Read — U.S.A.

Spencer — India.

Rachoomuck A. Amnuay — Thailand.

Rose J. Chaney — Australia.

Germany

Netherlands

JAPAN

210

Original Signatories

Name	Country
ANDREA von SCHNOY	GERMANY
Edith Gaswich	Germany
Gisela Gintzel	Germany
Klaus Thakur-Schlichtmann	Germany
Ann Miscle	
Gerald Mische	World, U.S.A
	U.S.A.
D. Ludwig C. bau	W. Germany
Dr. Fred Karl Scheile	U.S.A.
Max Jaeger	Germany
Olga Jaeger	Germany
Beatrice Meyers	U.S.A.
Elisabeth Klaenbauer	INNSBRUCK
Theo Fenelis	Switzerland
Dr. Helen K Billings	USA
Magister Kirsti Balthasar	Finland, live in Mexico.
Robert Rosamond	United Peoples Federation of Earth
Valerie Hagenhuber	Austria
Herbert Grödler	

211

Original Signatories

Name	Country
Louis R. Gomberg	U. S. A
P. C. Malhotra	India
Hildegard Heuer	Schweiz
PURAN SINGH AZAD	(INDIA)
Dr. Miss. Geeta Shah	INDIA.
Maria Treli	Schweiz
Kurt Kreutz	Innsbruck
Bonnie Allen	U. S. A
Rustom M. Bharucha	India.
Allen Bryant	USA
Jeanne C. Burrows	UniA. World
Leo J. Murray sa	(Pax Christi USA)
Simon R. Tladi	Botswana
Mrs. Renée Dangoor	United Kingdom
Mr. J. Lelaka	Botswana
Reggie Gorman	Australia
Donald L. Selman	Australia
Thomas Erha	AUSTRIA

Original Signatories

Name	Country
Dr. Hildegard Durfee	U.S.A.
Kira Lynne Allen	
Samar Basu	India.
Robert W. Kaminski	Earth USA, Wilm Del
John Thyra	Holland
Yogi Shantiswaroop.	India - for one world
Carmel Kussman	U.S.A.
Mortimer Lifaly	U.S.A.
Hermann Weys	Austria
Kim Haroldi	Canada
Ana Marin	P.R.
Naim Dangoor	U.K.
	(Sri Lanka)
	Bangalore - India
Bernadette F. Trattner.	
Craig Orr White, Ph.D.	Ohio, U.S.A
Everett Refer	Wis. U.S.A.
Mildred P. Parmelee.	U.S.A.
Dr (Mrs) Kamoo Patel	Pondichery (India)
Margaret Gadge	United Kingdom.

213

Original Signatories

Name	Country
Bandula Sri Gunawardhana	Sri Lanka
Margaret Isely	U.S.A.
Maffen Kenya Elisabett	Austria
(signature)	PUERTO RICO
Gregory Alexander	U.S.A.
Edward R. Leader	Puerto Rico
(signature)	India
Dorothy L. Nann Baker	U. S. A.
Carl F. Cattain	Earth!
(signature)	Denmark
Heather Isely	U. S. A.
Foster Paymelee	U. S. A.
Ogoka Justus	Kenya
(signature)	W. Germany
Kemper Isely	U.S.A.
Bernard Shan Mazi	Nigeria
Mitsuo Miyake	JAPAN
(signature)	Netherlands
(signature)	Botswana

Original Signatories

Name	Address
Eggert, Charlotte Luise	Deutschland
Josephine Rahm	Maj. l. WAAC
Martha Zillebrun	USA
Ostenwolli Kurt	Innsbruck Austria
Suzanne Gomberg	San Francisco USA
Holzapfel Heinel	Innsbruck
Holzapfel Amelie	Innsbruck
Leora C. Herold	Mexico "Unity"
Havel Ingeborg	Germany
Schmeding, Hans-Friedrich	Germany
Nary, Ludwig	Germany
B. Molcar	World lite for
Leland P. Stewart	Los Angeles
John Stockwell	San Francisco
Guido Graziani	Rome, Italy
Dorothea Saikari	Hannover, WOMAN

Original Signatories

Name	Country
[signature]	Holla
[signature]	Wien
[signature]	U.S.A.
[signature]	U S A
[signature]	USA
[signature]	stateless
[signature]	Pakistan
[signature]	Italy / México

Por el mundo espiritual
Certan Guru Dr. José M. Ortez

Po la unión en el arte en la pintura (Mejico)
Sa. Elsa *[signature]*
Rev. GAGPA. Maria Carlota Elle Estrada (México)
"Por el mundo Espiritual."
Rev. GagPa *[signature]* (México)
"Por el mundo Espiritual"
W. Resp. Getuls. Adolfo Olivera *[signature]* (México)

Original Signatories

Name	Country
Tiakoga Ruge	Mexico
Stefanie Hollweger	Austria
[illegible]	Austria
Herbert [illegible]	Deutschland (BRD)
Siddhartha I. Patel	Kenya.
Kalaben Patel.	Indian
Umesh A Patel	Great Britain.
Kumud I. Patel	Great Britain.
Ahmad Subanjo [illegible]	Indonesia
[illegible] Setyabudiarti	Indonesia
Sylvia Stiert	New Zealand + USA
Alice Stephens	England.
Elizabeth E. Stewart	United States
[illegible]	Bangladesh
[illegible] Khalsa HARBHAJAN SINGH Yogiji Sikh Dharma Western Hemisphere	USA

Note: This list of initial signers of the CONSTITUTION FOR THE FEDERATION OF EARTH would include several hundred more persons from fifty countries, prevented only by the cost of travel to attend the Assembly at Innsbruck, Austria.

Original Signatories

Prof. Dr. Kalman Abraham, Hungary

Atiku Abubakar, Nigeria

Dr. Ebenezer Ade. Adenekan, Nigeria

Malcolm S. Adiseshiah, India

Abdur Rahim Ahamed, Bangladesh

Shahzada Kabir Ahmed

Mohsin A. Alaini, Yemen

MD. Nural Alam, U.S.A.

MD. Maser Ali, Bangladesh

Dr. Terence P. Amerasinghe, Sri Lanka

Samir Amin, Senegal

Benjamin K. Amonoo, Ghana

George Anca, Romania

Mauricio Andres-Ribeiro, Brazil

Dr. Munawar A. Anees, U.S.A.

Rev. Ebenezer Annan, Ivory Coast

Jose Ayala-Lasso, Ecuador

Ir. Hasan Basri, Indonesia

Samar Basu, India

Tony Benn, United Kingdom

218

Original Signatories

Prof. Mrs. Edvige Bestazzi, Italy

Petter Jakob Bjerve, Norway

Goran von Bonsdorff, Finland

Selma Brackman, U.S.A.

Jean-Marie Breton, Int. Regis. World Citizens

Tomas Bruckman, Germany (East)

Dennis Brutus, South Africa (U.S.A.)

Dr. Mihai Titus Carapancea, Romania

Prof. Henri Cartan, France

Amb. Khub Chand, Indie

Dr. Sripati Chandrasekhar, India

Most Rev. French Chang-Him, Seychelles

Munyaradzi Chiwashira, Zimbabwe

Dr. Pratap Chandra Chunder, India

Prof. Dr. Rodney Daniel, France

Daniel G. De Culla, Spain

Dr. Dimitrios J. Delivanis, Greece

Prof. Dr. Francis Dessart, Belgium

Raymond F. Douw, Germany

Prof. Hans-Peter Duerr, Germany

Kennedy Emekan, Nigeria

M. Necati Munir Ertekun, Cyprus

Douglas Nixon Everingham, Australia

John R. Ewbank, U.S.A.

Original Signatories

Marjorie Ewbank, U.S.A.

Miss Lianmangi Fanai, India

Dr. Mark Farber, U.S.A.

Feng Ping-Chung, China

Prof. Dr. Mihnea Georghiu, Romania

Lucile W. Green, U.S.A.

Dr. Dauli Gupta, India

Kisholoy Gupta, India

Takeshi Haruki, Japan

Dr. Gerhard Herzberg, Canada

Jozsef Holp, Hungary

A. K. Fazlul Hogue, Bangladesh

Chowdhury Anwar Husain, Bangladesh

Margaret Isely, U.S.A. (Earth)

Philip Isely, U.S.A. (Earth)

Ram K. Jiwanmitra, Nepal

Roy E. Johnstone, Jamaica

Mohammed Kamaluddin, Bangladesh

Mohammad Rezaul Karim, Bangladesh

Rev. George Karunakeran, India

Dr. Inamullah Khan, Pakistan

Johnson S. Khan, Pakistan

Roger Kotila, Ph.D., U.S.A.

Original Signatories

David M. Krieger, U.S.A.

Diemuth Kuebart, Germany

Jul Lag, Norway

Ben M. Leito, Netherlands Antilles

Thomas Lim, East Malaysia

Adam Lopatka, Poland

Anwarul Majid, Bangladesh

Dr. M. Sadiq Malik, Pakistan

Guy Marchand, France

Alvin M. Marks, U.S.A.

Bernardshaw Mazi, Nigeria

Dr. Zhores A. Medvedev, U. K. (USSR)

Anna Medvegey, Hungary

R. C. Mehrotra, India

Charles Mercieca, U.S.A.

Lt. Col. Pedro B. Merida, Philippines

Yerucham Meshel, Israel

Sheta Mikayele, Zaire

Original Signatories

Mohamed Ezzedine Mili, Switzerland

Rev. Toshio Miyake, Japan

Shettima Ali Monguno, Nigeria

Swapan Mukherjee, India

Hanna Newcombe, Canada

Brij P. Nigam, India

Josephine Okafor, Nigeria

Johnson Olatunde, Sierre Leone

Rev. Nelson Onono-Onweng, Uganda

Umit Ozturk, Turkey

Yasar Ozturk, Turkey

Linus Pauling, U.S.A.

Fernando Perez Tella, Spain

Emil Otto Peter, Austria

Dr. Alex Quaison-Sackey, Ghana

Soili Raikkonen, Finland

Sudhir Kumar Rangh, India

Thane Read, U.S.A.

Dr. Sayed Qassem Reshtia, Switzerland

Erzebet Rethy, Hungary

Miguel B. Ricardo, Portugal

G. Rivas Mijares, Venezuela

Reinhart Ruge, Mexico

222

Original Signatories

PERSONAL RATIFIERS - page 6

Prof. Sir A. M. Sadek, South Africa

Abdus Salam, Italy

Akbar Ali Saleh, Comoros Islands

Blagovest Sendov, Bulgaria

Indira Shrestha, Nepal

Rabi Charan Shrestha, Nepal

Jon Silkin, United Kingdom

Jozef Simuth, Slovak Republic

Dr. Kewal Singh, India

Blaine Sloan, U.S.A.

Ross Smyth, Canada

Lord Donald Soper, United Kingdom

Scott Jefferson Starquester, U.S.A.

Homi J. H. Taleyarkhan, India

Rev. Yoshiaki Toeda, Japan

Dr. Duja K. Torki, Tunisia

Helen Tucker, Canada

Evelyn Utulu, Nigeria

Mrs. Justina N. Uwechue, Nigeria

Ogieva O. Uwuigbe, Nigeria

Ann Valentin, U.S.A.

Original Signatories

T. Nejat Veziroglu, U.S.A.

Jorgen Laursen Vig, Denmark

George Wald, U.S.A.

Prof. D. A. Walker, United Kingdom

Richard W. Wilbur, U.S.A.

Dr. Sylwester Zawadzki, Poland

Additional Original Ratifiers:

Kenneth B. Clark, U.S.A.

David Daube, U.S.A.

Nzo Ekangaki, Cameroon

ADDITIONAL PERSONAL RATIFIERS -- Signatures on file at the World Office of the W.C.P.A.

PROF. CHIEF J. O. AGBOYE, Nigeria

DR. FRANCIS ALEXIS, Grenada

SIR ABDUL W. M. AMEER, Sri Lanka

HANAN AWWAD, Palestine

HON. LUKASZ BALCER, Poland

CHIEF DR. KOLAWOLE BALOGUN, Nigeria

DR. SABURI O. BIOBAKU, Nigeria

DR. JUR. JAN CARNOGURSKY, Slovakia

DR. GOUIN CEDIEU, Cote D'Ivoire

AMARSINH CHAUDHARY, India

MDM. JUSTICE L. P. CHIBESAKUNDA, Zambia

ASHIS KUMAR DE, India

DR. MOSTAFA EL DESOUKY, Kuwait

DR. ROLF EDBERG, Sweden

DR. BENJAMIN B. FERENCZ, U.S.A.

PROF. VITALII I. GOLDANSKII, Russia

PROF. DR. ZBIGNIEW GERTYCH, Poland

PROF. ERROL E. HARRIS, U.S.A./U.K.

LIC. JUAN HORACIO S., Argentina

SIR DR. AKANU IBIAM, Nigeria

49.

Original Signatories

Part Five

Appendices
1.

DIAGRAM OF WORLD GOVERNMENT IN CONFORMANCE WITH THE CONSTITUTION FOR THE FEDERATION OF EARTH

info@gswp.org

THE PEOPLE OF THE WORLD

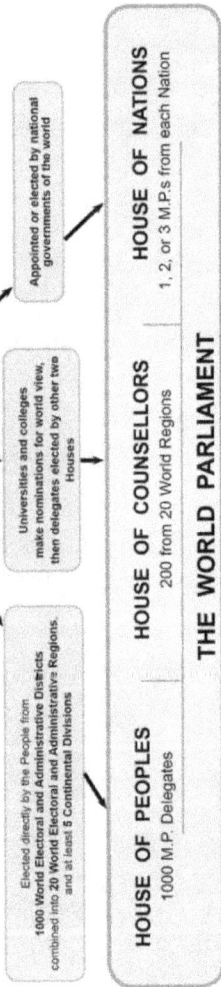

Elected directly by the People from 1000 World Electoral and Administrative Districts combined into 20 World Electoral and Administrative Regions and at least 5 Continental Divisions

Universities and colleges make nominations for world view, then delegates elected by other two Houses

Appointed or elected by national governments of the world

HOUSE OF PEOPLES
1000 M.P. Delegates

HOUSE OF COUNSELLORS
200 from 20 World Regions

HOUSE OF NATIONS
1, 2, or 3 M.P.s from each Nation

THE WORLD PARLIAMENT

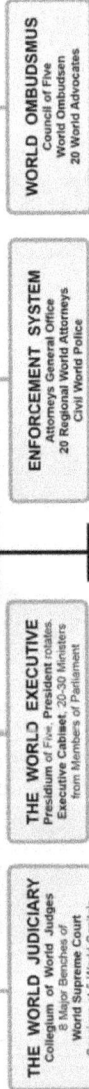

World Legislation requires majority vote by House of Peoples and House of Nations, plus vote by House of Counsellors in case of deadlock.
House of Counsellors nominates candidates for Presidium, World Court Judges, Attorneys General, Ombudsmus, then candidates elected by entire Parliament.

THE WORLD JUDICIARY
Collegium of World Judges
8 Major Benches of
World Supreme Court
Sessions at 5 World Capitals

THE WORLD EXECUTIVE
Presidium of Five. President rotates.
Executive Cabinet, 20-30 Ministers from Members of Parliament

ENFORCEMENT SYSTEM
Attorneys General Office
20 Regional World Attorneys
Civil World Police

WORLD OMBUDSMUS
Council of Five
World Ombudsen
20 World Advocates

THE INTEGRATIVE COMPLEX

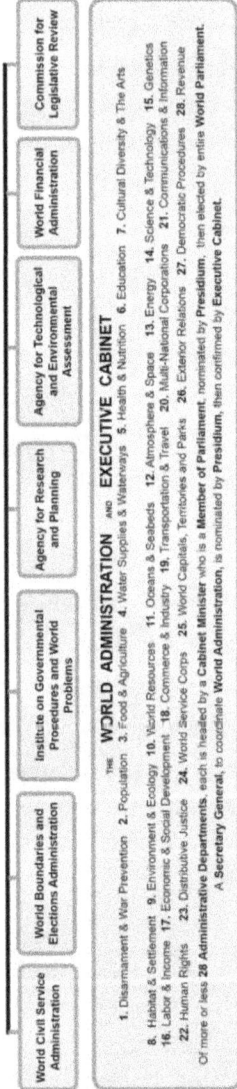

World Civil Service Administration

World Boundaries and Elections Administration

Institute on Governmental Procedures and World Problems

Agency for Research and Planning

Agency for Technological and Environmental Assessment

World Financial Administration

Commission for Legislative Review

THE **WORLD ADMINISTRATION** AND **EXECUTIVE CABINET**

1. Disarmament & War Prevention 2. Population 3. Food & Agriculture 4. Water Supplies & Waterways 5. Health & Nutrition 6. Education 7. Cultural Diversity & The Arts
8. Habitat & Settlement 9. Environment & Ecology 10. World Resources 11. Oceans & Seabeds 12. Atmosphere & Space 13. Energy 14. Science & Technology 15. Genetics
16. Labor & Income 17. Economic & Social Development 18. Commerce & Industry 19. Transportation & Travel 20. Multi-National Corporations 21. Communications & Information
22. Human Rights 23. Distributive Justice 24. World Service Corps 25. World Capitals, Territories and Parks 26. Exterior Relations 27. Democratic Procedures 28. Revenue
Of more or less **26 Administrative Departments**, each is headed by a **Cabinet Minister** who is a **Member of Parliament**, nominated by Presidium, then elected by entire **World Parliament**.
A **Secretary General**, to coordinate World Administration, is nominated by Presidium, then confirmed by **Executive Cabinet**.

2.

A Pledge of Allegiance
to the Federation of Earth

I pledge allegiance to the Constitution for the Federation of Earth,
  and to the Republic of free world citizens for which it stands,

One Earth Federation, protecting by law the rich diversity of the Earth's
  citizens,
One Earth Federation, protecting the precious ecology of our planet.

I pledge allegiance to the World Parliament representing all nations and
  peoples, and to the democratic processes by which it proceeds,

One law for the Earth, with freedom and equality for all,
  One standard of justice, with a bill of rights protecting each.

I pledge allegiance to the future generations protected by the Earth
  Constitution,
And to the unity, integrity, and beauty of humankind,
                    living in harmony on the Earth,

One Earth Federation, conceived in love, truth, and hope,
                    with peace and prosperity for all.

_____

Printed Name   Signature   Date   Country

3.

Resolution for the Creation of a Democratic World Parliament

(sample wording for any municipal, regional or national parliament)

This house, being of the opinion that,

In the present state of world political anarchy, where international agreements and conventions are flouted, and judgments of the World Court are treated as matters of no concern,

In the present state of world militarism, where national governments feel forced to spend vast sums of money on weapons and military defense, while global insecurity continues to increase,

In the present state of world environmental destruction, where ice caps and glaciers are melting, the oceans are rising, and global weather patterns are becoming destructive,

In the present state of world economic inequality, where the wealthy of the world continue to accumulate unimaginable wealth while each year many billions of U.S. dollars are transferred from the poorest regions of the world to the wealthiest regions of the world,

This house calls upon the government of _____, in collaboration with other national governments, to make earnest efforts to convene a World Constituent Assembly, as the first step towards the establishment of a Democratic World Government, with a World Parliament representing all nations and peoples equally, under an enforceable, non-military democratic *Constitution for the Federation of Earth*.

Signature   Title   Date

4.

Executive Summary of main provisions of the CONSTITUTION FOR THE FEDERATION OF EARTH

1. Broad functions of Earth Federation are the following: 1.1. to prevent war; 1.2. to protect universal human rights; 1.3. to end poverty; 1.4. to regulate international processes; 1.5. to protect the environment and ecological fabric of life, that is, the biosphere; and 1.6. to devise solutions to world problems beyond the capacity of national governments.

2. Basic structure of Earth Federation is the following: 2.1. People and nations organize as a universal federation, to include all people, all nations, and all oceans, seas and lands of Earth, including atmosphere and space. 2.2. Earth Federation is non-military and democratic, with ultimate sovereignty of the people of Earth. 2.3. Powers of Earth Federation apply to problems that transcend national boundaries. 2.4. For world elections and administration, Earth is united into 1000 World Districts total, within +/-10% limits equal in population, of 20 World Regions, combining to 10 Magna-Regions in 5 Continental Divisions.

3. Organs of the Earth Federation are the following: 3.1. The World Parliament; 3.2. The World Executive; 3.3. The World Administration; 3.4. The Integrative Complex; 3.5. The World Judiciary; 3.6. The Enforcement System; and 3.7. The World Ombudsmus.

4. This *Earth Constitution* grants Earth Federation the jurisdiction and powers necessary to ensure the effective broad functions of the Earth Federation. Earth Federation must have no military power, but may use world legislation, administration, education, finance, civil police enforcement system, world court system, ombudsmus public defense and other regulatory powers to ensure effective enforcement of world law.

5. World Parliament composes of three legislative houses, to consider, adopt, amend and repeal World Legislation.
People of Earth directly elect **House of Peoples**, with one delegate from each of 1000 World Electoral and Administrative Districts. Term of

office is 5 years, with no re-election limits. Minimum age is 21.

Nations appoint or elect **House of Nations**. Term of office is 5 years, with no re-election limits. Minimum age is 21.

University students and faculty of World Regions nominate regional candidates from anywhere for **House of Counselors**. From nominations, Regional Members of both House of Peoples and House of Nations elect 10 Counselors for Region to total 200, 10 from each of 20 Regions; House of Counselors has nominative, consultative, initiative and referral functions. Term of office is 10 years, with no re-election limits. Minimum age is 25. People of Earth may launch initiatives for world legislation, and may vote on referendums submitted from World Parliament.

6. World Parliament elects and supervises a **World Executive**. House of Counselors nominates and World Parliament elects **Presidium** of an annually rotating president and 4 vice-presidents, all current Members of World Parliament (MPs), and an **Executive Cabinet** of 30 ministers, all MPs. The World Executive must neither veto nor suspend the World Parliament nor the *Earth Constitution*. The World Executive has no military power.

7. The 30 Cabinet Ministers and Vice Presidents head the World Administration, of about 30 ministries. The Presidium nominates and Cabinet elects a Secretary General to coordinate the ministries.

8. Broad functions that naturally duplicate within each ministry integrate in agencies of the Integrative Complex: World Civil Service Administration; World Boundaries and Elections Administration; Institute on Governmental Procedures and World Problems; Agency for Research and Planning; Agency for Technological and Environmental Assessment; World Financial Administration; and Commission for Legislative Review. World Parliament with variable organs of the Earth Federation elect 12-member commissions to head each agency. All agencies except Commission for Legislative Review include a Cabinet Minister or Vice President of the Executive, plus a Senior Administrator from civil service lists.

9. Benches form a **World Judiciary**, including World Supreme Court, Regional World Courts and District World Courts, having mandatory jurisdiction over different kinds of issues: **Human Rights, Criminal Cases, Civil Cases, Constitutional Cases, International Conflicts, Public Cases, Appellate Bench, Advisory Bench**, and **Superior Tribunal** for cases of extra-ordinary public importance. World Judiciary has 5 continental seats. House of Counselors nominates and World Parliament elects a **Collegium of World Judges** of 20 to 60 Members, headed by a **Presiding Council** of 5 members which assigns judges to the several Benches. Judge minimum age is 30. Judge minimum juristic or legal experience is 10 years.

10. The Enforcement System

World Parliament elects an Office of World Attorneys General with 5 **World Attorneys General** and commission of 20 **Regional World Attorneys**, to head non-military Enforcement System. Earth Federation neither retains nor uses weapons of mass destruction. World Attorney minimum age is 30. World Attorney minimum legal experience is 7 years. Term limit is 3 consecutive 5-year terms. World Parliament may remove World Attorneys. World Attorneys appoint a **World Police Supervisor** and **20 Regional World Police Captains**, all removable by Parliament, with 10-year employment limit. World Police apprehend individual suspected lawbreakers. World Parliament regulates World Police, which shall follow due process, and obtain warrants for search & arrests.

11. House of Counselors nominates and World Parliament elects a **World Ombudsmus** Council of 5 World Ombudsen and Commission of 20 Regional World Advocates to protect human rights and ensure proper government functioning. Limits are two 10-year terms. Ombudsan minimum age is 30. Ombudsan minimum legal experience is 5 years.

12. Bill of Rights guarantees inalienable human rights, including all those customarily guaranteed by civil nations: equal rights, equal protection, freedom of expression, association & religion, habeas corpus rights, universal suffrage, property, privacy, & other prohibitions against government intrusions.

13. Directive Principles of 19 sections list additional civil rights and benefits to be guaranteed and implemented over time for all people.

14.1. Earth Federation guarantees the following: full faith and credit to public acts, records, legislation and judicial proceedings of member nations; nations retain jurisdiction over internal affairs; asylum for refuge seekers from nations not in Earth Federation;

14.2. *Earth Constitution* reserves non-delegated powers to Earth Federation member nations and to the people of Earth.

15. World Parliament establishes **five world capitals** in 5 Continental Divisions: 1 Primary Capital and 4 Secondary Capitals. World Parliament establishes **20 World Federal Zones** in 20 World Regions.

16.1. The people of Earth have ownership and Earth Federation has jurisdiction of all oceans from 20 kilometers offshore, the seabeds, vital straits, channels, canals, the Moon and the atmosphere from 1 km. above the general surface of the land.

16.2. Earth Federation shall establish peaceful external relations. The Presidium negotiates external relations and treaties, subject to approval by the World Parliament.

17. *Earth Constitution* implements by stages:

Provisional Earth Federation, before 25 countries or before World Districts including 10% of world population have ratified. **First Operative Stage**, when 25 countries or World Districts including 10% of world population have ratified, or equivalent mix. **Second Operative Stage**, when 50% of countries and World Districts including 50% of world population have ratified, or equivalent mix. **Full Operative Stage**, when 80% of countries, comprising 90% of world population, have ratified.

Nations may give preliminary ratification. Preliminary ratification is subject to final ratification of people at least 18 years of age, by simple majority of votes cast in popular referendum, with at least 25% of electorate casting votes within any respective world district. Viable agencies of the United Nations Organization integrate into the Earth Federation.

18. People may initiate **amendment procedures** to the *Earth Constitution* by 200,000 signatures from each of 20 world districts and submission to vote of World Parliament. Additionally, World Constitutional Convention shall convene not less that every 20 years. Amendments are subject to absolute 2/3 majority vote of 3 Houses of World Parliament voting separately.

19. Provisional World Parliament may adopt world legislation prior to first operative stage, subject to re-confirmation by World Parliament.

5.

The Development of the *Earth Constitution* and Provisional World Parliament: A Brief History

The World Constitution and Parliament Association is dedicated to creating non-military democratic Earth Federation under the *Constitution for the Federation of Earth.* Since 1958, the organization has worked through its worldwide membership to write and ratify the Earth Constitution in four international Constituent Assemblies. Under the authority of Article 19 of the Earth Constitution the WCPA has also sponsored 12 sessions of the Provisional World Parliament to date, building a new world order of freedom, justice, prosperity, and equality within the shell of the old, unjust world order. Below is a summary history of our work.

1958. Agreement to Call a World Constitutional Convention initiated by four persons, circulated worldwide for signatures, requesting both national governments and people of each country to send delegates.

1959-1960. World Committee for a World Constitutional Convention formed. Thousands sign the Agreement, including many prominent leaders. Organizers of this action travel around the world to enlist support.

1961-1962. Definitive Call to the World Constitutional Convention adopted. Many persons sign, including Heads of five national governments.

1963-1964. First Preparatory Congress held Denver, Colorado, USA, with delegates from five continents. Call to the World Constitutional Convention is publicly issued, then circulated for more signers and response.

1965-1966. Second Preparatory Congress held at Milan, Italy. Outline for Debate and Drafting of a World Constitution is formulated, on basis on alternative choices. Plan agreed for a Peoples' World Parliament to meet concurrently.

1967. Decision made at Third Preparatory Congress to begin Convention in 1968, even if no government sends delegates. 300 Peoples Delegates pledged.

1968. First working sessions of World Constitutional Convention and Peoples' World Convention held at Interlaken, Switzerland, and

Wolfach, W. Germany with 200 Peoples Delegates from 27 countries, of five continents. Work begun on drafting the World Constitution.

1969-1971. Strategy for Reclaiming Earth for Humanity is circulated. Emergency Council of World Trustees meets, Santa Barbara, Calif., and issues First Decree for Protection of Life, outlawing nuclear weapons. Directions given to drafting commission.

1972. World Constitution drafting commission of four persons, with a fifth communicating by telephone, works for two months, nearly completing first draft of *Constitution for the Federation of Earth.*

1973-1975. First draft finished, printed in 1974, then circulated worldwide for comment, together with Call to the second session in 1977, now defined as the World Constituent Assembly. Comments on first draft complied.

1976. Drafting Commission meets again. Second draft completed, circulated, 1977. Second Session of World Constituent Assembly held in June, Innsbruck, Austria. Earth Constitution debated paragraph by paragraph, amended, then adopted with 138 original signers from 25 countries of 6 continents. Call for ratification by the nations and peoples of Earth is issued. Constitution is sent to U.N. General Assembly and to all national governments.

1978-1980. *Earth Constitution* is circulated worldwide for debate and ratification. Third session of World Constituent Assembly held January, 1979, Colombo, Sri Lanka; adopts Rationale For a World Constituent Assembly, defining right of people to convene Assembly, draft constitution, and obtain ratification. Appeal issued for national parliaments to ratify.

1981. World Constitution & Parliament Assn. meets at New Delhi, India. Call issued for Provisional World Parliament to convene 1982 under terms of Article 19 of the *Earth Constitution.* Honorary Sponsor list of 150 prominent persons enrolled.

1982. First Session of Provisional World Parliament meets at Brighton, England. Delegates from 25 countries of 6 continents. Five world Legislative Acts are adopted: for World Disarmament Agency, World Economic Development, Ownership of Oceans & Sea beds, Graduate School of World Problems, and World Courts.

1983-1984. First Provisional District World Court organized in Los Angeles; takes up case of outlawing nuclear weapons. Plans for Provisional World Parliament in Sudan and Nigeria thwarted by military coups.

1985. Second Session of Provisional World Parliament held New Delhi, India. Opened by President of India, presided by speaker of Lok Sabha. Three more World Legislative Acts adopted: for Emergency Earth Rescue Administration, World Government Funding, and Commission on Terrorism.

1986. Campaign continued for "provisional" ratification of the *Constitution for the Federation of Earth,* pending review at next World Constituent Assembly.

1987. Third session of Provisional World Parliament held at Hilton Fontainebleau Hotel, Miami Beach, Florida. Three more World Legislative Acts are adopted: for Global Finance System, Environment Protection, and Hydrogen Energy. Provisional World Cabinet begun.

1988-1989. Plan launched for collaboration by many organizations to prepare next session of World Constituent Assembly. 150 organizations join in Preparatory Committee. Two meetings held in New York with U. N. Ambassadors, to explain and solicit help. List of Honorary Sponsors reconfirmed and expanded.

1990. Government of Egypt agrees to host Assembly. Three preparatory meetings held. Call circulated for Governments and People to send delegates.

1991. Location of 4th session World Constituent Assembly abruptly changed due to the 1991 Gulf War. Held at Troia, Portugal, in May. Delegates adopt 59 minor amendments to the *Earth Constitution.* New ratification campaign begun, appealing to both people and governments. Most Honorary Sponsors personally ratify.

1992. Global Ratification & Elections Network organized, including several hundred organizations, to promote ratification of the *Constitution for the Federation of Earth,* then election of delegates to World Parliament. Government heads should also ratify.

1996. The Fourth Session of the Provisional World Parliament held at Barcelona, Spain in September. A number of resolutions passed as well as a "Manifesto" declaring the oceans the property of the people of Earth under the authority of the *Earth Constitution.*

2000. The Fifth Session of the Provisional World Parliament is held on the Island of Malta, November 22nd to 27th. One Omnibus legislative act and a number of resolutions passed, including a resolution strongly supporting the rights of the Palestinian people to their own state.

2003. The Sixth Session of the Provisional World Parliament held in Bangkok, Thailand, March 23rd to 28th. Several important legislative acts passed: a World Peace Act, a World Security Act, a Provisional

Office of World Revenue Act, a Hydrocarbon Resource Act, and a Statute for the World Court on Human Rights. The Commission for Legislative Review is formed. Parliamentary law format commences with the Sixth Session. The Institute on World Problems (IOWP) is formed as a 501C3 non-profit organization in the U.S.

2003. The Seventh Session of the Provisional World Parliament is held at Chennai, India, December 23-29. Several important legislative acts passed: a Criminal Penalty Code, Rules for Procedure and Evidence, a World Bench for Criminal Cases Act, a World Patents Act, a Global Accounting and Auditing Standards Act, and a Preservation of World Government Records Act. The Manifesto of the Earth Federation and the "Pledge of Allegiance to the Earth Constitution" (included in this Appendix) are unanimously ratified by the Parliament.

2004. The Eighth Session of the Provisional World Parliament held at Lucknow, India in August. Several important legislative acts passed, including creation of a World Bench for Juvenile Cases, a Child Rights Act, an Elections Act, and a Water Act. The International Criminal Court in the Hague is empowered by world legislation. A global Education Act is passed as well as a World Economic Equity Act establishing the Earth Currency on an independent and fully democratic basis. A Global People's Assembly is created to activate grass roots participation in the House of Peoples. The "Declaration on the Rights of Peoples" (included in this volume) is unanimously ratified.

2006. The Ninth Session of the Provisional World Parliament held in Tripoli, Libya in April. Eight World Legislative Acts are passed, an enabling act for the World Ombudsmus, the creation of a Department of Conflict Resolution for the Earth Federation, a ban on the production of fissile materials for weapons, a nuclear weapons elimination protocol, a nuclear contamination act prohibiting the use of depleted uranium and other weapons, a quit Guantanamo directive, an agreement on world privileges and immunities (revising the weaker version of the Assembly of States Parties, and a public utilities act. The former "Global Ratification and Elections Network (GREN)" is transformed into the Earth Federation Movement (EFM).

2007. The Tenth Session of the Provisional World Parliament held in Kara, Togo in June. Four world legislative acts are passed: an act prohibiting unauthorized destruction of illegal financial instruments, an act creating a system of divestment from illegal weapons manufacture, an act requiring posting of the world illegal stock law in stock exchanges around the world, and an act providing a guaranteed annual income for all adults within the Earth Federation.

2008. The 50th Anniversary Celebrations of the founding of WCPA hosted by Dr. Phichai Tovivich and the WCPA Chapter of Thailand.

2009. The Eleventh Session of the Provisional World Parliament held in Nainital, India, July 2-8, 2009. Several world legislative acts were passed into provisional world law, including a procedure for the dismantling of nuclear weapons, a law protecting the people of Earth from too much bureaucracy in the world government, an act criminalizing human trafficking for sexual or other purposes, an act abolishing all secret intelligence agencies like the CIA, M5 or Mossad, a bill elaborating the restrictions on the military uses of depleted uranium, and a law protecting the right of civil disobedience for the people of Earth under the Earth Federation (included in this volume). The delegation from Bangladesh presented the parliament with a new translation of the *Constitution* into its 23rd language: Bengali or Bangla.

2010. June 1-11, IOWP officers participate in the General Review Conference of the International Criminal Court in Kampala, Uganda, with proposals to link the court with the *Earth Constitution*. The Twelfth Session of the Parliament held in Kolkata, India, December 27-31, 2010. World Legislative Acts passed for funding the decommissioning of nuclear weapons, abolishing legal corporate personhood, establishing a Collegium of World Judges, establishing a Shipbreaking code, creating global economic prosperity, and amending some earlier acts of the Parliament. Resolutions were passed allowing states, cantons, or Pradesh to join the Earth Federation independently, enumerating citizen and governmental responsibilities under the Earth Federation, and modeling the world peace system created by the *Earth Constitution.*

6.

What You Can Do to Support the Earth Federation Movement

Many of these materials can be downloaded from our websites: www.wcpa.biz, www.worldproblems.net, www.earthfederation.info, www.radford.edu/gmartin

1. Encourage individuals to become members of the World Constitution and Parliament Association (WCPA) and/or the Institute On World Problems (IOWP) by filling out and returning a membership application form. (This is free for persons from developing countries.)

2. Encourage individuals to become personal ratifiers of the *Constitution for the Federation of Earth* by signing the Pledge of Allegiance and sending it to Dr. Glen T. Martin at World Headquarters, 313 Seventh Ave., Radford, VA 24141, USA (gmartin@radford.edu). The pledge is on-line at our web sites. By doing this, individuals are officially recognized as legal World Citizens under the *Constitution*.

3. Establish, develop, and participate in local chapters of WCPA.

   WCPA chapters tend to be advocacy chapters for ratification of the *Earth Constitution*. Organize seminars on behalf of IOWP and WCPA. IOWP promotes courses, study groups, and seminars on world problems and their solution under the *Earth Constitution*. WCPA chapters can do this as well as visit legislators, judges, as well as political and civic leaders on behalf of the *Constitution* and the Earth Federation Movement (EFM).

4. Initiate attention-getting social service projects in your area at which you hand out information concerning the Earth Federation Movement. This can include development of permaculture projects, educational projects, environmental projects, sustainable development projects, etc. Hand out literature for WCPA and the Earth Federation Movement as part of every project.

5. Urge organizations to which you belong to become members of the Earth Federation Movement (EFM). (Membership is free for organizations.) Organizations that are members of EFM affirm ratification of the *Earth Constitution* and make this known in their literature at the same time that they continue to work for their specific organizational goals. They should display an insignia stating "Member – Earth Federation Movement."

6. Establish and develop web sites concerning WCPA and IOWP or linking existing sites to WCPA and IOWP sites. Make postings to Facebook, Twitter, or on-line blogs.

7. Form study groups to study the *Earth Constitution* and use the knowledge gained to educate others. Hold seminars and lectures on world problems and their solution under the *Earth Constitution*.

8. Form local advocacy groups to visit, educate, and urge members of national and regional governments to support the *Earth Constitution*. Cultivate a working relationship with sympathetic members of your parliament to have them attend events for WCPA or introduce resolutions on behalf of the *Constitution*.

9. Write letters and op-eds to local media supporting the Earth Federation Movement and your local work on its behalf. Forward copies of these letters to World Headquarters. Get radio and TV interviews about this work.

10. Get municipal, regional, or national government to debate the resolution above (Appendix #3). Lobby to get the resolution passed.

11. Attend sessions of the Provisional World Parliament as an observer or a delegate. The 11th Session was held July 2-8, 2009 in Nainital, India. The 12th Session was in Kolkata December 27-31, 2010. Have your group raise funds to send one of its members to the Parliament.

12. As a delegate to the Provisional World Parliament volunteer to work for Commissions involved with developing provisional world government. Use the prestige of being a "Delegate to the Provisional World Parliament" to promote this work within your own country.

13. Advertise, work for, and promote (working with World Headquarters) a Founding Ratification Convention for the *Earth Constitution*.

14. Keep World Headquarters appraised of your activities on behalf of the Earth Federation Movement so that these may be announced in on-line newsletters and publications.

15. Support the WCPA and IOWP financially. Make a monthly commitment to IOWP as a tax deductible 501C3 organization. (IOWP Treasurer: Phyllis Turk, MS. CNM. 313 Seventh Ave. Radford, VA 24141, USA, pturkcnm@yahoo.com.) Put a bequest in your will. Raise funds on behalf of the Earth Federation Movement. Get others to do the same. Share the joy of building a real future for humanity and our precious planet Earth.

Bibliography and Works Cited

The web sites of nearly all organizations mentioned in this volume can be found through a Google Search for the organization's name.

Adler, Mortimer J. (1991). *Haves Without Have-nots – Essays for the 21st Century on Democracy and Socialism.* New York: Macmillan.

Allott, Philip (1990). *Eunomia – New Order for a New World.* Oxford: Oxford University Press.

Almand, Eugenia and Martin, Glen T., eds. (2009). *Emerging World Law, Volume One: Key Documents and Decisions of the Global Constituent Assemblies and the Provisional World Parliament, Volume One.* Sun City, AZ: Institute for Economic Democracy Press.

Arendt, Hannah (1958). *The Human Condition.* Chicago: U. of Chicago Press.

Arendt, Hannah (1969). *Crises of the Republic.* Orlando: Harcourt Brace & Co.

Arendt, Hannah (1972). *The Origins of Totalitarianism.* New York: Meridian Books.

Arendt, Hannah (1977). *On Revolution.* New York: Penguin Books.

Arendt, Hannah (1979). *The Recovery of the Public World.* New York: St. Martin's Press.

Arendt, Hannah (2005). *The Promise of Politics.* New York: Schocken Books.

Aurobindo, Sri (1997). *The Human Cycle; The Ideal of Human Unity; War and Self-Determination.* Pondicherry, India: Sri Aurobindo Ashram Press.

Baratta, Joseph P. (2004). *The Politics of World Federation.* Two Volumes. Westport, CT: Greenwood Press.

Barber, Benjamin (1984). *Strong Democracy: Participatory Politics for a New Age.* Berkeley: University of California Press.

Barker, Ernest (1967). *Reflections on Government.* Oxford: Oxford University Press.

Barry, Kathleen (2011). *Unmaking War, Remaking Men: How Empathy Can Reshape Our Politics, Our Soldiers, and Ourselves.* Santa Rosa: Phoenix Rising Press.

Basu, Samar (1999). *The UNO, The World Government and The Ideal of World Union – As envisioned by Sri Aurobindo.* Pondicherry, India: Sri Aurobindo Ashram Press.

Belitsos, Byron with Tetalman, Jerry (2005). *One World Democracy: A Progressive Vision for Enforceable Global Law.* San Rafael, CA: Origin Press.

Biersteker, Thomas J. and Weber, Cynthia, eds. (1996). *State Sovereignty as Social Construct.* Cambridge: Cambridge University Press.

Bidmead, Harold S. (1992). *The Parliament of Man. The Federation of the World.* North Devon, UK: Patton Publications.

Bloch, Ernst (1970). *Philosophy of the Future.* New York: Herder and Herder.

Blum, William (2005). *Rogue State: A Guide to the World's Only Superpower.* Monroe, ME: Common Courage Press.

Borgese, Giusepe A. (1953). *Foundations of the World Republic.* Chicago: University of Chicago Press.

Bibliography

Boswell, Terry and Chase-Dunn, Christopher (2000). *The Spiral of Capitalism and Socialism: Toward Global Democracy*. Boulder, CO: Lynne Rienner Publishers.

Brown, Donald E. (1991). *Human Universals*. New York: McGraw Hill.

Brown, Ellen Hodgson (2007). *Web of Debt: The Shocking Truth about Our Money System*. Baton Rouge, Louisiana: Third Millennium Press.

Caldicott, Helen (1992). *If You Love this Planet*. New York: WW Norton & Company.

Camus, Albert (1980). *Neither Victims Nor Executioners*. New York: Continuum Publishers.

Caufield, Catherine (1996). *Masters of Illusion: The World Bank and the Poverty of Nations*. New York: Henry Holt & Company.

Chomsky, Noam (1996). *What Uncle Sam Really Wants*. Boston: South End Press.

Chossudovsky, Michel (1999). *The Globalization of Poverty: Impacts of IMF and World Bank Reforms*. London: Zed Books.

Committee to Frame a World Constitution (1965). *A Constitution for the World*. Santa Barbara, CA: Center for the Study of Democratic Institutions.

Dahl, Robert A. (1989). *Democracy and Its Critics*. New Haven: Yale University Press.

Daly, Hermann E. (1996). *Beyond Growth: The Economics of Sustainable Development*. Boston: Beacon Press.

Daley, Tad (2010). *Apocalypse Never: Forging the Path to a Nuclear Weapon-Free World*. New Brunswick: Rudgers University Press.

Davis, Garry (1984). *World Government Ready or Not*. Sorrento, ME: Juniper Ledge Publishing Co.

Desai, Meghnad and Redfern, Paul, eds. (1995). *Global Governance: Ethics and Economics of the World Order*. New York: Pinter.

Eagleton, Terry (2011). *Why Marx Was Right*. London: Yale University Press.

Einstein, Albert (1960). *Einstein on Peace*, Otto Nathan and Heinz Norden, eds. New York: Simon and Schuster.

Elkins, Paul (1992). *A New World Order: Grass roots Movements for Global Change*. New York: Routledge.

Engdahl, F. William (2009). *Full Spectrum Dominance: Totalitarian Democracy in the New World Order*. Weisbaden: edition: engdhal.

Falk, Richard A. (1992). *Explorations at the Edge of Time: The Prospects for World Order*. Philadelphia: Temple University Press.

Falk, Richard A. and Johansen, Robert C., eds. (1993). *The Constitutional Framework of World Peace*. Albany, NY: State University of New York Press.

Fromm, Erich (1941). *Escape from Freedom*. New York: Rinehart & Company.

Fromm, Erich (1968). *The Revolution of Hope: Toward a Humanized Technology*. New York: Bantam Books.

Fromm, Erich (1996). *To Have or To Be?* New York: Continuum.

Gandhi, Mahatma (1990). *The Essential Gandhi. An Anthology of His Writings on His Life, Work, and Ideas*. Louis Fischer, ed. New York: Vintage Books.

Germino, Dante (1972). *Modern Western Political Thought: Machiavelli to Marx*. Chicago: Rand McNally & Company.

Bibliography

Glossop, Ronald J. (1994). *Confronting War: An Examination of Humanity's Most Pressing Problem,* Third Edition. Jefferson, NC: McFarland Publishers.

Glossop, Ronald J. (1993). *World Federation? A Critical Analysis of Federal World Government.* Jefferson, NC: McFarland Publishers.

Goener, Sally J., Dyck, Robert G., and Lagerroos, Dorothy (2008). *The New Science of Sustainability: Building a Foundation for Great Change.* Chapel Hill: Triangle Center for Complex Systems.

Goff, Stan (2004). *Full Spectrum Disorder: The Military in the New American Century.* Brooklyn: Soft Skull Press.

Green, Lucile W. (1991). *Journey to a Governed World. Thru 50 Years in the Peace Movement.* Berkeley, CA: The Uniquest Foundation.

Green, T. H., *Principles of Political Obligation*

Habermas, Jürgen (1992). *Autonomy & Solidarity: Interviews with Jürgen Habermas.* New York: Verso Press.

Habermas, Jürgen (1994). *Justification and Application: Remarks on Discourse Ethics.* Cambridge: MIT Press.

Habermas, Jürgen (1998a). *On the Pragmatics of Communication.* Cambridge: MIT Press.

Habermas, Jürgen (1998b). *Between Facts and Norms: Contributions to a Discourse Theory of Law and Democracy.* William Rehg, trans. Cambridge: MIT Press.

Habermas, Jürgen (2001). *The Postnational Constellation: Political Essays.* Cambridge: MIT Press.

Habermas, Jürgen (2003). *The Future of Human Nature.* William Rehig, et. al., trans. Cambridge, MA: Polity Press.

Harris, Errol E. (2008). *Twenty-first Century Democratic Renaissance: From Plato to Neoliberalism to Planetary Democracy.* Sun City, AZ: Institute for Economic Democracy Press.

Harris, Errol E. (2005). *Earth Federation Now! Tomorrow is Too Late.* Sun City, AZ: Institute for Economic Democracy Press.

Harris, Errol E. (2000). *Apocalypse and Paradigm: Science and Everyday Thinking.* Westport, CT: Praeger Publishers.

Harris, Errol E. (1966). *Annihilation and Utopia: The Principles of International Politics.* London: George Allen and Unwin.

Harris, Errol E. and Yunker, James A. (1999). *Toward Genuine Global Governance: Critical Reactions to "Our Global Neighborhood."* Westport, CT: Praeger Publishers.

Hart, H.L.A. (1994). *The Concept of Law.* Oxford: Oxford University Press.

Heater, Derek B. (1996). *World Citizenship and Government: Cosmopolitan Ideas in the History of Western Political Thought.* New York: St. Martin's Press.

Held, David (1995). *Democracy and the Global Order: From the Modern State to Cosmopolitan Governance.* Stanford: Stanford University Press.

Hodge, James and Cooper, Linda (2004). *Disturbing the Peace: The Story of Father Roy Bourgeois and the Movement to Close the School of the Americas.* Maryknoll, NY: Orbis Books.

242

Bibliography

Jaspers, Karl (1953). *The Origin and Goal of History.* New Haven: Yale University Press.

Jaspers, Karl (1957). *Man in the Modern Age.* Edward Gorey, trans. New York: Anchor Books.

Jaspers, Karl (1959). *Truth and Symbol.* Wilde, Kluback and Kimmel, trans. New York: Twayne Publishers.

Jaspers, Karl (1971). *Reason and Anti-Reason in our Time.* Stanley Godman, trans. Hamden, CT: Archon Books.

Johnson, Chalmers (2006). *Nemesis: The Last Days of the American Republic.* New York: Metropolitan Books.

Jonas, Hans (1985). *The Imperative of Responsibility. In Search of an Ethics for the Technological Age.* Chicago: University of Chicago Press.

Kant, Immanuel (1957). *Perpetual Peace.* Louis White Beck, trans. New York: Macmillan.

Kant, Immanuel (1964). *Groundwork of the Metaphysics of Morals.* H.J. Paton, trans. New York: Harper Torchbooks.

Kant, Immanuel (1965). *The Metaphysics of Morals.* John Ladd, trans. New York: The Liberal Arts Press.

Kant, Immanuel (1974). *On the Old Saw: That May be Right in Theory But It Won't Work in Practice.* E.B. Ashton, trans. Philadelphia: U. of Pennsylvania Press.

Klare, Michael T. (2001). *Resource Wars: The New Landscape of Global Conflict.* New York: Metropolitan Books.

Klein, Naomi (2008).*The Shock Doctrine – The Rise of Disaster Capitalism.* New York: Metropolitan Books.

Laszlo, Ervin (2008). *Quantum Shift in the Global Brian: How the New Scientific Reality Can Change Us and Our World.* Rochester, VT: Inner Traditions.

Levinas, Emmanuel (1961). *Totality and Infinity.* Alphonso Lingis, trans. Pittsburg: Duquesne University Press.

Levinas, Emmanuel (2006). *Humanism of the Other.* Nidra Poller, trans. Urbana, IL: U. of Illinois Press.

Lindner, Evelin G. (2006). *Making Enemies: Humiliation and International Conflict.* Westport, CT: Praeger Security International.

Lindner, Evelin G. (2009). *Emotions and Conflict: How Human Rights Can Dignity Emotion and Help Us Wage Good Conflict.* Westport, CT: Praeger Publishers.

Locke, John, *Two Treatises on Government.*

Lovelock, James (1991). *Healing Gaia: Practical Medicine for the Planet.* New York: Harmony Books.

Loriaux, Sylvie (2010). "Global Ethics" in *Ethics: A University Guide.* Richard H. Corrigan and Mary E. Farrell, eds. Gloucester: Progressive Frontiers Press.

Martin, Glen T. (2005a). *Millennium Dawn: The Philosophy of Planetary Crisis and Human Liberation.* Sun City, AZ: Institute for Economic Democracy Press.

Bibliography

Martin, Glen T. (2005b). *World Revolution through World Law: Key Documents of the Emerging Earth Federation.* Sun City, AZ: Institute for Economic Democracy Press.

Martin, Glen T. (2008). *Ascent to Freedom: Practical and Philosophical Foundations of Democratic World Law.* Sun City, AZ: Institute for Economic Democracy Press.

Martin, Glen T. (2010). *Triumph of Civilization: Democracy, Nonviolence, and the Piloting of Spaceship Earth.* Sun City, AZ: Institute for Economic Democracy Press.

Martin, Glen T. (2010). *Constitution for the Federation of Earth: With Historical Introduction, Commentary, and Conclusion.* Sun City, AZ: Institute for Economic Democracy Press.

Marx, Karl (1978). *The Marx-Engels Reader: Second Edition.* Editor: Robert C. Tucker. New York: W.W. Norton & Company.

Meadows, Donella H. (2008). *Thinking in Systems: A Primer.* White River Junction, VT: Chelsea Green Publishing.

Milgram, Stanley (1974). *Obedience to Authority: An Experimental View.* New York: Harper & Row.

Mill, John Stuart (1956). *On Liberty.* New York: The Liberal Arts Press.

Moltmann, Jürgen (1996). *The Coming of God: Christian Eschatology.* Margaret Kohl, trans. Minneapolis: Fortress Press.

Newcombe, Hanna (1983). *Design for a Better World.* Lanham, MD: University Press of America.

Ornstein, Robert (1991). *The Evolution of Consciousness: Of Darwin, Freud, and Cranial Fire.* New York: Prentice Hall.

Palast, Greg (2007). *Armed Madhouse: From Badhdad to New Orleans – Sordid Secrets and Strange Tales of a White House Gone Wild.* NY: Penguin Books.

Parenti, Michael (1995). *Against Empire.* San Francisco: City Lights Books.

Petras, James and Veltmeyer, Henry (2005). *Empire with Imperialism: The Globalizing Dynamics of Neoliberal Capitalism.* London: Zed Books.

Pinker, Steven (1995). *The Language Instinct: How the Mind Creates Language.* New York: Harper Perennial Books.

Pogge, Thomas and Horton Keith (2008). *Global Ethics: Seminal Essays.* St. Paul, MN: Paragon House.

Rapoport, Anatol (1992). *Peace – An Idea Whose Time Has Come.* Ann Arbor: U. of Michigan Press.

Reardon, Betty (2000). "Sexism and the War State" in David P. Barish, ed., *Approaches to Peace: A Reader in Peace Studies.* NY: Oxford U. Press.

Renner, Michael (1996). *Fighting for Survival: Environmental Decline, Social Conflict, and the New Age of Insecurity.* New York: W.W. Norton Company.

Reves, Emery (1945). *The Anatomy of Peace.* New York: Harper & Brothers.

Rich, Bruce (1994). *Mortgaging the Earth: The World Bank, Environmental Impoverishment, and the Crisis of Development.* Boston: Beacon Press.

Righter, Rosemary (1995). *Utopia Lost – The United Nations and World Order.* New York: The Twentieth Century Fund Press.

Rousseau, Jean-Jacques (1947). *The Social Contract and Discourses.* G. D. H.

Cole, trans. New York: E. P. Dutton & CO.

Ruge, Reinhart (2003). *Profiles of Lord Reinhart.* San Marcos, Mexico: Sistemas Tecnicos.

Russell, Bertrand (1962). *Has Man a Future?* New York: Simon and Schuster.

Sanders, Barry (2009). *The Green Zone: The Environmental Crisis of Militarism.* Oakland, CA: AK Press.

Senge, Peter M. (2006). *The Fifth Discipline: The Art and Practice of the Learning Organization.* New York: Doubleday Books.

Sherover, Charles M. (1974). *The Development of the Democratic Idea: Pericles to the Present.* New York: Washington Square Press.

Sherover, Charles M. (1989). *Time, Freedom, and the Common Good: An Essay in Public Philosophy.* Albany: SUNY Press.

Shiva, Vandana (2002). *Water Wars: Privatization, Pollution, and Profit.* Cambridge, MA: South End Press.

Smith, J.W. (2010). *Economic Democracy: A Grand Strategy for World Peace and Prosperity.* Pamplin, VA: Institute for Economic Democracy Press.

Speth, James Gustave (2004) *Red Sky at Dawn – America and the Crisis of the Global Environment.* New Haven: Yale University Press.

Spruyt, Hendrik (1994). *The Sovereign State and Its Competitors.* Princeton: Princeton University Press.

Stapp, Henry (1988). "Quantum Theory and the Physicist's Conception of Nature" in *The World View of Contemporary Physics,* Richard F. Kitchener, ed. Albany: SUNY Press.

Tannsjo, Torbjörn (2008). *Global Democracy: The Case for World Government.* Edinburgh: Edinburgh University Press.

Thoreau, Henry David (n.d.). *Waldon and On the Duty of Civil Disobedience.* New York: Milestone Editions.

Paul Tillich (1987). *The Essential Tillich,* F. Forrester Church, editor, pp. 143-144.

Wacks, Raymond (2006). *Philosophy of Law: A Very Short Introduction.* Oxford: Oxford University Press.

Walker, Barbara, ed. (1993). *Uniting the Peoples and Nations: Readings in World Federalism.* Washington, DC: World Federalist Association.

Weiss, Thomas G. and Gordenker, Leon, eds. (1996). *NGOs, the UN, and Global Governance.* Boulder, CO: Lynne Rienner.

Wilber, Ken (1996). *Eye to Eye: The Quest for a New Paradigm.* Boston: Shambala Publications.

Yunker, James A. (2005). *Rethinking World Government: A New Approach.* Lanham, MD: University Press of America.

Index

Index

247

Index

Index

Index

Index